Mastering
the
Tarot

A guide to advanced
Tarot reading and practice

PAUL FENTON-SMITH

SIMON & SCHUSTER
AUSTRALIA

Dedicated to Alexander,
my favourite Page of Swords.
With thanks to Blas for his inspired teaching
and to Cathy for her help with the
original manuscript

First published in Australia in 2000 by
Simon & Schuster (Australia) Pty Limited
20 Barcoo Street, East Roseville NSW 2069

A Viacom Company
Sydney New York London Toronto Tokyo Singapore

National Library of Australia
Cataloguing-in-Publication Data

  Fenton-Smith, Paul.
  Mastering the Tarot: a guide to advanced Tarot reading and practice.

  ISBN 0 7318 0859 2.

  1. Tarot I. Title.

133.32424

Illustrations from the Rider-Waite Tarot Deck® known also as the Rider Tarot
and the Waite Tarot, reproduced by permission of U.S. Games Systems, Inc.,
Stamford, CT 06902 USA. Copyright © 1971 by U.S. Games Systems, Inc.
Further reproduction prohibited. The Rider-Waite Tarot Deck® is a registered
trademark of U.S. Games Systems, Inc.

Set in Berkeley 11 /14
Design by Vivien Valk
Printed by Griffin Press, Adelaide

10 9 8 7 6 5 4 3

Other titles by Paul Fenton-Smith
Astrology Revealed
Palmistry Revealed
The Tarot Revealed
A Secret Door to the Universe
Finding Your Soulmate

Contents

Introduction • vi

PART ONE
Using Your Reading Style to Specialise • 2
Limitations of the Tarot • 4
Intuitive and Logical Reading • 9
Drawing a Blank • 13
Giving Emergency Readings • 15
Reading For Yourself • 16

PART TWO
The Major Arcana • 20

PART THREE
The Reading Process • 54
The Basic Questions • 56
Yes/No Questions • 58
The One Card Cut • 66
Reversed Cards • 68

PART FOUR
Layouts • 72
Designing Your Own Layout • 78
Sample Readings • 81

PART FIVE

The Four Approaches to Life • 124
The Minor Arcana • 127

PART SIX

Becoming Professional • 188
Stranger than Fiction • 195
The Client's Story • 202
Setting Boundaries • 203
Difficult Clients • 207
Cleansing Your Workplace • 210
Guidelines for Practising Tarot Readers • 213

PART SEVEN

The Court Cards • 216

PART EIGHT

'How Long Will This Take?' (A Final Word) • 246

Index • 250

Introduction

An adept Tarot reader can make it all look deceptively simple. If you stand and watch a reading in an open-air market, it seems like no more than a conversation over a few cards selected at random. An experienced reader can make the whole process seem like a conversation with a trusted friend.

Of course, in reality people may not like to bother their friends with such matters, so they seek out a stranger. Twenty-one years' experience of reading for others has taught me that, as humans, we are often more prepared to trust a complete stranger than those whom we most care about. It makes sense when you consider that a stranger has less to lose by telling you the truth, whereas a friend has associations with you and an emotional investment in your life going a certain way.

Consulting the Tarot (the book of life) for guidance as to the wisest course of action can make the difference between being successful and living with regrets. However, sometimes even when your client asks what appears to be a straightforward question, you can arrive at an answer which is confusing.

Readers of my previous Tarot book, *The Tarot Revealed* (Simon & Schuster Australia, Sydney, 1995) often asked for more information on 'yes/no' questions and on how to interpret the answers to them. As the book was only designed to be an introduction to the Tarot, it did not go into great detail regarding the wording of questions, interpretation of cards in combination, or even questions which are better left unasked. This book deals with these areas and more. Using actual card layouts from readings with consenting clients and students, I've collected a variety of questions and given my interpretations at the time.

As telephone readings become increasingly popular, it is only fair to include mention of specific techniques for telephone readers, as telephone readings differ from giving face-to-face readings. Some readers prefer telephone readings as they can relax through the process and not have to worry about their appearance or their methods being scrutinised. Others find them more difficult than face-to-face readings because they cannot see the expressions of the client to confirm their own accuracy.

In *Mastering the Tarot* you will also find information on successfully setting up a practice, with tips on, for example, handling difficult clients and setting boundaries between yourself and your client. Cleansing and rebalancing techniques are also included in *Mastering the Tarot*, as professional readers need to be aware of psychic hygiene to avoid being psychically or emotionally drained by clients (and the friends they read for).

I hope you find this book a useful tool in streamlining your Tarot readings and improving your working knowledge of the Tarot. It is designed to be a useful daily guide when giving readings, and a guide to career opportunities involving Tarot card readings.

Part One

★ Using Your Reading Style to Specialise ★

Your style as a Tarot reader depends on many different things. It can be determined by, for example, your psychological makeup, your ability to be honest with yourself, and the issues you happen to be dealing with in your life.

Carl is a reader who has vivid memories of his father's alcoholism and his abandonment as a child, and he finds that many clients consult him regarding these issues in their lives. For example, some have problems with alcohol themselves, whereas others are living with an alcoholic. Carl's experience with his father's alcoholism has led to him examining the options available to those who live with alcoholics, and he is therefore in a good position to advise many of his clients of some of the choices available to them.

Another reader, Peter, has lived alone for more than five years and is considering entering another relationship. During the past six months most of his clients have been people who have avoided relationships for a prolonged period, and they often ask him if they are ready to trust another person again.

Another reader, named Michael, was raised by a father who secreted large sums of money away from his wife and children, forcing them to live a life of poverty and deprivation. As a clairvoyant Michael has a reputation for being able to trace hidden money. When a woman consults him regarding an impending divorce, Michael is able to see if her husband has hidden money offshore, and, if so, where it lies.

In his first such reading, the client explained that she was about to be divorced. Michael mentioned that she'd be financially secure as her husband was wealthy. She said that her husband was almost broke and Michael laughed. He knew there was a large sum of money hidden away, and tuned in to the situation clairvoyantly.

'He has five million dollars stashed in two banks in the Dominican Republic,' Michael said as they looked at one another blankly.

'Where's that?' she asked him.

'I'm not sure,' he replied, and disappeared into another room to collect his globe of the world. They found that the Dominican Republic lies near the Bahamas in Central America.

Fourteen months later the client returned to Michael for another reading. Through her lawyer and a private investigator, this woman had located $2.2 million of her husband's hidden money and she wanted to know where he'd moved the rest. Michael directed her to a bank in the Channel Islands and she left smiling. Michael's deprived childhood has made him keen to pursue hidden money so that other families don't suffer as his did.

Another reader, Kim, had to achieve self-discipline before getting the life she desired, and now she attracts clients who lack this quality and shows them how to develop it within themselves. 'Most people I read for want freedom and I have to point out to them that true freedom comes from self-discipline,' she told me one day.

Marie grew up in a family that did not understand her or allow for her individuality, so she had to find friends who were able to accept her for who she is. The majority of her clients are the same. They feel misunderstood, and Marie takes it upon herself to help them to find where they belong in life. She is part-Tarot reader and part-careers counsellor, advising people what is likely to suit them workwise. She is able to identify quickly who her clients are and where they fit in. As a result, Marie is able to guide them towards friendships, hobbies, careers and localities which help them to grow and blossom in their lives.

For myself, I went through a period when almost all of the clients I read for wanted to know how they could be financially secure, and not have to worry about where the money was coming from to pay their bills. I looked at my own life, and there it was. I was living hand to mouth, never sure from where my income would derive, and my clients were reflecting this back to me.

As you gain more experience reading the cards, observe yourself and notice what innate qualities you bring to the reading. I presently have an interest in finding the client's blind spot. This area of blindness allows others to approach them and control them easily without the client noticing.

Children are quick to notice an adult's blind spot, and they use it to their advantage. Notice how a child asks each parent for something they want, especially when afraid they'll be refused. With one parent they might make demands, and sulk to get their way. With another parent they might cajole, as they work slowly around to the point where they hint at what they desire.

My son knows that I never give him chocolate, but his mum sometimes does. He periodically works on me to soften my approach to giving him chocolate.

'Mummy sometimes gives me chocolate. Not always, but sometimes. Sometimes when I'm good,' he'll say to me.

'That's nice, but I won't give you chocolate because I don't like what it does to you,' I'll respond.

He ponders this reply for a moment, realising that I have agreed with him and stated that Mummy and I have different rules around chocolate, and that's okay. He hasn't given up on me, however. He is still seeking a way to motivate me to give him chocolate, although realising that his system with his mother doesn't work with me.

In short, your reading style is likely to depend on your life experiences and what qualities you have acquired. You'll draw to you those who can best hear what you have to say; look carefully at your clients and you'll know what it is you're attempting to learn within yourself, or what you've already mastered in your life. Often clients unconsciously seek you out for your unique approach. Know what your approach is and how it can benefit the client, and you'll build your clientele more quickly.

I prefer accuracy over tactfulness, and so those who seek a warm, cosy chat by the fire don't usually seek me out. They can find me confronting and will probably choose a reader who suits their needs. When clients have exhausted all their known avenues for understanding why they cannot achieve their goals, and they are frustrated and stuck, they usually appreciate my straightforward approach to how they can free themselves from their restrictions. This is why I never felt too competitive about other readers working alongside me at markets. Each reader draws their most suitable clients. In this way, as they feel understood, both the client and the reader are pleased with the outcome.

★ Limitations of the Tarot ★

The Tarot has its limitations, especially if you consider the possibility of human error and confusing layouts. Other things which can cause difficulties are desire, paranoia, denial and poorly worded questions. Also, of course, a good Tarot reader does not override the free will of the client. Professional readers predict the future, detail the past and illuminate the underlying causes of events, but they do not tell the client what they *should* do.

One of the most consistent factors in inaccurate Tarot readings is desire. When a client comes to a reading with excessive desire for a particular outcome, this highly charged longing is likely to affect the cards they choose. This is why as a reader you may experience confusion between what you see in the cards on the table and what you actually feel about the question your client has asked.

When I experience such confusion, I bring it up immediately by saying: 'I'm confused here. The cards tell me this relationship looks fabulous, but I can't shake the feeling there are deep-seated problems which are not being addressed'. I usually then proceed to tell the client what I see in the cards and what I sense myself. This typically leads to a conversation that clarifies the actual issue in the question.

This occurred with Craig. He arrived a few minutes late for his reading and I guessed that he'd slept on a park bench the previous night. He explained that he hadn't slept at all in three nights. His dishevelled appearance, bristly face and harrowed look betrayed him as a man who was deeply troubled.

Before I could explain the shuffling procedure he began sobbing and I noticed that he was shaking. He said: 'She just walked out. We were happily in love and … living together and … and … one day she just walked out the door'. I offered him some tissues and some time to compose himself. The shaking subsided, but he looked momentarily lost. It was as though he didn't know how he had come to be sitting across from me, holding a pack of cards.

Craig had an all-consuming desire and it influenced every card in every layout in the reading. After a chaotic general reading he asked his first question, which was, 'What does the future hold for our relationship?'. After I laid out the cards, I became suspicious of the perfect spread in front of me. The layout detailed happiness, commitment and a peaceful stability resulting from a relationship between two compatible people with common goals. However, Craig had just explained, during the general reading, that Sonia had decided she did not love him, and that she had left without any explanation. He was distraught, and yet beneath his pain I sensed anger.

The cards and the reality were not matching because of Craig's longing to have Sonia back again. Reading for a client in such a state rarely results in an accurate forecast, and you are advised to try to arrange an appointment a week away to give them time to rebalance. (The only reason I had not done this with Craig was that he'd spoken with the receptionist, who had given him a last-minute cancellation.) In short, when a client is in a heightened state of desire, the cards are more likely to reflect their desires than their situation.

Another mental state which can affect the accuracy of a Tarot reading is paranoia. I have a friend who loves to cut my Tarot pack with emotionally loaded questions such as, 'Is my girlfriend faithful to me?'. He has even gone one step further by asking, 'Will she *always* remain faithful to me?'. When he told me that, I asked him, 'Have you always remained faithful to yourself (to his own principles)?'.

He continued with similar questions and I continued to refuse to answer any of them.

'Why won't you answer the questions?' he asked me.

I replied: 'If you want to pick a fight with Camellia then do it honestly. Don't use your own stupidity and insecurity to ruin what could be a healthy relationship'.

I had visions of him sitting complacently about the house, treating Camellia badly while safe in the knowledge that she would always remain faithful to him. The Tarot is designed for better things than this and for better questions than my friend was asking.

Your client being in denial is another reason you may not be understood by them. Elizabeth looked perplexed when I detailed her partner's lack of commitment to her and to their relationship. She seemed to perceive their relationship differently. I probed for more details, and then decided against it as she appeared to be unswerving in her beliefs.

A year later she returned with more questions about when she might marry Robert. I told her that it was unlikely to occur within the next two years (the prediction span of the reading) and once again I detailed his lack of commitment and his dishonesty.

In the relationship layout the Three of Cups appeared reversed (suggesting the influence of a third person in the situation) alongside the Seven of Swords (suggesting dishonesty). Elizabeth seemed surprised at this and I delved deeper. It turned out that Robert was keen on physical fitness and he'd take the dog for a walk for three or four hours every night. He had bought the dog as an excuse for the walks, and in time Elizabeth noticed that the dog never appeared to be tired after they arrived home from their exercise.

One afternoon Elizabeth took a different route home from work and chanced upon Robert, who parked his car on the street and disappeared into a house not far from their own. In the following weeks she kept an eye on the house and often saw Robert's car parked outside it.

One evening she couldn't stand it any more, and strode up to the front door and knocked loudly. A woman answered the door in a dressing-gown. Elizabeth asked for Robert and was shown into the house. Robert seemed agitated when he saw her but after he had rushed Elizabeth out the front door, and they were home again, he insisted that he and the woman were just friends.

Elizabeth still wanted to believe that Robert was committed to the relationship and he was quick to reassure her. However, his nightly walks continued, and after six months Elizabeth asked for a trial separation. Robert reluctantly agreed and promptly moved into his girlfriend's house.

Five weeks later Robert phoned to say that the lease on the house where he was staying had expired and that he and his girlfriend were moving to another side of town. It was then that Elizabeth began to realise her relationship with Robert was over.

Clients sometimes have a great deal invested in a certain outcome and as a result may only hear selectively when you read for them. That is, they can ignore all information contradicting what they believe, and, to be fair, we all do this from time to time. (If you are convinced that you see things for what they are, ask a child to describe to you what they see and perhaps you'll be surprised.)

Poorly worded questions can also result in confusion. The simple question, 'Will my business be successful?' can be broken down for the client into several questions to achieve the most accurate reply:

1.   Will my business be financially successful?
2.   Will my business achieve a turnover of $ . . . per year within two years?
3.   Will I realise my business goals within a year?
4.   Will I consider my business a success in two years' time?
5.   Is it wise for me to pursue this project as a business?
6.   Is my current business plan the most appropriate one at this time?
7.   What can I do to improve this business?
8.   What do I most need to change within myself to improve my business?

9.   How can I increase my personal fulfilment within my business?

10.   What is the most important lesson this business can teach me?

11.   Where is my business leading me?

I was surprised the first time a client arrived with a written list of questions. It irritated me that someone was overtly obtuse enough to admit that they wanted only to know about material and emotional things. I was disheartened that spiritual questions were ignored, along with the desire to know and learn all the lessons behind trials and triumphs. I was being somewhat idealistic, I admit, and I calmed down when I realised that this client was in fact more focused than most. She sought a reading with particular goals in mind and afterwards she knew that her needs had been met.

I now recommend all clients bring a list of questions, so as to avoid the frustration of remembering questions after the reading is over. Sometimes the information contained in a reading is overwhelming to the client, and they are feeling too emotional to know if there are any more important questions to ask. The most significant question has to be asked first, as a less important question is usually influenced by a more important one.

Chelsea asked about the possibility of resuming a recently finished relationship. When I told her this was unlikely to happen, she moved on to a question about her career. The career question only brought up cards relevant to a relationship question. I asked Chelsea if she wanted to ask something else about relationships, perhaps in a more general sense, and she confirmed that she did. I placed the cards on the table back into the pack, and she selected more cards with a relationship question in mind. When we returned to the question about her career, I could give her a detailed answer, as the more important issues had been dealt with.

Sometimes a layout after a specific relationship inquiry contains several cards found in the previous relationship spread. This can happen if the client's question has not been answered to their satisfaction or if another aspect of their relationship needs to be highlighted. Liam's general reading was centred around his love relationship and each of his five questions concerned further relationship issues. In the general reading I explained to Liam that his partner was leaving because he repeatedly abandoned her for his career and his friends.

In answer to his first question I revealed that his partner was unhappy and why. In reply to the second, I pointed out that Liam was unhappy also as he attempted to decide what was more important in his life: friends, work or the relationship. In answer to the third question, I highlighted Liam's behaviour patterns within relationships and how he was repeating his father's patterns. After his fourth question, I quizzed him about his expectations for a love relationship and detailed what I perceived to be his partner's expectations; I then compared the two so that he could see the fundamental differences between them. In reply to his fifth question I explained what Liam was likely to gain from pursuing the relationship and what he'd have to sacrifice to continue it.

After these five questions his final one was, 'What does the future hold for me in relationships?'. This reading, which was on relationships generally, went beyond his current partner and allowed for other possible relationships. The layout detailed another woman (the Queen of Pentacles) who was likely to understand his need to work hard and who might support him in his pursuit of financial independence. Liam did not seem to hear the answer to this question, but I felt that it might be a bonus for him in the months that followed when he replayed the tape of the reading.

Again, please remember that as a Tarot reader you do not tell the client what they *should* do. If you tell the client what they should do, you are effectively removing their chance to learn from their current circumstances. However, the following is a recent example of a client *wanting* me to tell her what she should do.

Amber wished for me to tell her to leave her job as it was not satisfying her. However, I knew that her dissatisfaction with her then workplace was merely a symptom of a deeper problem. She wanted me to take responsibility for her life and felt that paying me a fee enabled her to ask me to do so.

I tried three times to point out to her that she was free to change her job but that the underlying causes would not be resolved by a change of workplace. She did not seem to hear me and I knew at that point she was asking the wrong question. The real issue was to find out what type of career would suit Amber, and what qualities she might have to develop within herself to make the most of such a career.

I laughingly described her as one part accountant and one part adventurer. The accountant part wanted to have a safe and precise sort of job, whereas the adventurer wanted an outdoors experience that might challenge her and offer new frontiers every day. These very different aspects of Amber resulted in her job dissatisfaction. Every time she had a secure, comfortable job she was bored to distraction within two weeks. On the other hand, whenever she had a less predictable position she became insecure and longed for the stability offered in other more conventional careers.

As a reader I had the challenge of finding a way to show her that her opposing needs were making her alternately restless and then insecure. After doing this I had to show her a way to fulfil both of her needs. I described the opposing parts and she laughed with recognition. As I searched for a solution it came to me clearly.

'What about the possibility of working in a secure position and saving up to travel overseas for your adventures each year or two. That way you might have the benefits of both worlds,' I suggested.

'Where would I go?' asked the conservative part of her.

'The wilds of Africa, no less,' I said, and we both laughed.

'But ...'

'Yes. You and three others in a jeep with no roof, out on the plains in search of wildlife. This is no comfort cruise, but a real safari with tents and all of your provisions carried on board.'

She pondered this for a minute and realised that it was possible to meet the needs of both parts of herself. I pointed out that was only one way of doing so, but she seemed happy to pursue the method I had outlined.

★ Intuitive and Logical Reading ★

Sometimes when giving a reading you will find you are speaking fluently and confidently without pausing to glance at the cards on the table and without needing to look to your client for confirmation that what you say is correct. What is happening? You are working intuitively. When intuition (inner teaching or knowing) kicks in, you find yourself describing your client's car, deceased dog, children's school uniforms and where their erstwhile husband or wife hides their second income. However, you must still be careful. You need to know the limits of what you can tell your client, despite what they urge you to tell them.

Intuitive reading occurs when you establish a clear, but invisible, psychic cord of energy between yourself and the client. Through this cord of energy you can retrieve from within the client's own energy field all the information the client seeks. (For more information on psychic chords, see *A Secret Door to the Universe*, Simon & Schuster (Australia) Pty Limited, Sydney, 1999.) This may only occur once in the first 120 readings you give, and after that it may only be an occasional occurrence. In time, when you are comfortable with the reading techniques and you feel in control of the whole process, intuitive readings will occur increasingly as you continually tell your subconscious mind that you seek information about your clients. This is done automatically as you search the cards for more detail.

It depends on what type of reader you are whether you get information in the form of dates, names and times, or images and metaphors. Sometimes I receive images which are metaphors for the client's situation. For example, for a man who feels trapped by his job responsibilities I might see an image of a prisoner watching a clock and awaiting his release.

Occasionally in the course of reading you may find that your intuition tells you one thing while the cards on the table tell you another. If this happens, there is a process which can assist you to be accurate. Take a few moments to examine yourself and how you are feeling. Do you have anything invested in the outcome of the reading? Is what you are presently hearing, seeing or feeling related to a previous reading or to your own life at present?

If your intuition conflicts with the cards on the table, bring that into your relationship with your client. You might say: 'I am somewhat confused here. The cards suggest that your business is successful and that it will remain so, but I feel within myself that there is a problem you need to deal with before you can be successful. Does this make sense to you?'.

In doing this you are starting a conversation with the client, and together you can reach an understanding of what is actually happening regarding their question. (If your intuition *enhances* what you see in the cards, simply read the layout and add your intuitive information to the cards as you progress.) Often the client laughs, and agrees with both the cards and your intuition. They may then give you some background information to aid you in clearly answering their question. Sometimes this information tells you that they are asking two questions at once, and for clarification you'll need to separate the questions and do two different layouts, one after the other.

As you become more experienced you'll learn to look beyond the clients' 'press releases' about themselves to see what is actually occurring in their lives. The client is not necessarily being deliberately secretive, but just wants to continue to pretend that life is fine. It's interesting that although clients want you to be accurate and to read them clearly they are sometimes afraid of what you might see, and part of them may seek to hide from your gaze. I call this the 'hole in the underwear' syndrome. They want you to tell them everything, but not notice the hole in their underwear, their odd socks or their incongruous behaviour.

One recent client wanted me to tell him about the future of a possible relationship, and became irritable when I asked him about the small boy and the older girl I could see in the cards. His present wife and children didn't feature in his plans for this relationship, and yet he was not prepared to leave them. I detailed the people around him who would be hurt by his pursuit of the affair, but he was already overly influenced by his desires. He didn't want to know about any fallout, only about the conquest itself.

Other clients come with tales of woe about their 'beastly' partners, perhaps of how they were driven into the arms of another by the cold-hearted nature of their spouse, and my policy is to ask myself, 'Do I buy this?'. If the answer is yes, I treat them accordingly. If the answer is no, I bring this into my relationship with them. That is, I state aloud that I am having difficulty believing that what they have told me is the whole story.

Sometimes it pays to be subtle, and at other times the client is so self-righteous that you need to be more straightforward. In one case I felt that the client was using me to help convince himself of something, so I said, 'Look I'm having difficulty with this'.

'With what?'

'With what you're saying.'

'Why?'

'In short, I'm not buying it.'

'What?'

'This stuff about how you only cheat on your partner and keep it secret so as not to hurt her.'

Such a comment usually generates a well-rehearsed denial of responsibility, which may be spiced with claims of innocence and punctuated with a few tears, all while they carefully conceal rage at being doubted.

If I still don't believe what I'm hearing I protest again. The second protest is still more direct. If I believe I'm being fed a line of deception I lean forward and establish close eye contact, and say something such as: 'You're telling me all this and I'm not convinced. Others may accept what you are saying but I don't. You wouldn't be attempting to deceive a psychic, would you?'.

If you prefer you can allow the client to deceive themselves, but you may lose their respect in doing so. They may leave feeling that you were not altogether observant. Another reason for voicing your observations is that if you are encouraged to overlook some things you risk overlooking many other, perhaps important, things. It is better to work on the understanding that your clients consult you so that you can tell them what you can see.

One client who had a serious illness consulted me about its emotional and spiritual causes. I saw clairvoyantly that when his desire to be well matched the life he was living, he would have good health once again. He sought help from medical practitioners and natural therapists, and both made a difference to his state of being.

During this process he consulted me four times to check whether his desire for wellbeing was in harmony with his life. Each time I pointed out his subtle incongruence (namely that he was depressed by thoughts of the life ahead of him) and, to his credit, he set about correcting it. With the aid of doctors, natural therapists and a clairvoyant to check his attitude, he reversed his 'terminal' condition. If I had colluded with him in not seeing what he didn't want to see I'd have been no help to him in his quest for good health.

There are several practical steps by which you can improve your intuition, and they all revolve around using it; the more you use your intuition the more it develops. One exercise I do with advanced Tarot students is to have a student act as a client, and think of a question and then select cards for a seven card layout. I place each card in position but I leave them face down on the table. I then give the client the reading, never turning up any of the cards. Essentially I am reading the backs of seven cards and answering the client's question. After the reading I place the cards back into the pack without looking at any of them to see what the client selected. This drives the students observing this exercise crazy with curiosity.

What is the point of this exercise? As the client selects the cards with their question in mind, your intuition (as the reader) is already fathoming the answer to the question they have asked. In essence, you know the answer to the client's question before you start to speak, and the above exercise helps you to get in touch with the part of you that holds that knowledge.

Readers can become engrossed in the logical meaning of the cards, the combinations and the number of reversed cards and overlook the big picture. As a simple exercise, before you start to describe the first layout in each reading make the following statement to yourself, 'The client's issue is ...'. When you feel confident with yourself, you can extend this to, 'The client's life pattern is ...' and 'The current spiritual lesson for this person is ...'.

Practice makes perfect, and intuitive training is as important as learning the card meanings.

Using clairvoyance (clear seeing) is not always exciting, and it's not always easy. Looking into the hearts of men and women means that you often come face to face with great pain and sorrow. Sometimes when I see what some people have survived I am awed by the courage it takes for them to get out of bed and approach another day. When I see the scars some clients carry with them I feel my own worries diminish. Despite tortured childhoods and horrendous events which would cause most of us simply to give up and surrender to madness in order to forget, people find the strength to carry on, and even to love and support others again.

If you seek to look into the hearts and minds of others, be prepared to tread carefully and compassionately. Present what you have to say in the way you'd like to receive the same news. This means you need to know the limits of what you can tell your client, regardless of what they press you to tell them. In some cases you may feel that they are not ready to hear what you have to say and it is correct to use discretion in what you say to them.

Several months ago I read for a woman who wanted to know about her two daughters, one married and one single. She pressed me for more and more information, and without thinking I continued speaking. I told her that her son-in-law was having an affair and that when his wife (her daughter) discovered it, their marriage would end. She was shocked. I had told her too much.

She telephoned me the following day to say that I shouldn't have told her, and I knew she was right. It was my job to know when to deny her the information she sought, by knowing her limits. You cannot take back that kind of information. She has to live with it now, whereas if I had denied her the information, she may have left only feeling that I was holding back or that I did not have much to say that was relevant.

We sometimes seek the answers to our questions without thinking of how we might cope with the knowledge they will give us. It reminds me of an old saying that, 'When the Gods want to punish us, they answer our prayers'. The more you see (clairvoyantly) the more power you have, and with power comes responsibility. If you use this power irresponsibly, you are likely to suffer the consequences of your actions.

★ Drawing a Blank ★

What happens when you lay out seven cards and, taking a look, you see nothing? No card stands out to you, but you feel an intense pressure to say something and to have it confirmed by your client. This can also happen to experienced readers, so it is not simply that you may need to learn the cards more thoroughly.

Going blank in front of a client is usually a combination of internal pressure, a lack of self-confidence and not being centred (if you are scattered in your focus, you are less likely to be an effective reader). However, there is a simple technique to help you manage going blank. It's so straightforward that you'll wonder why it didn't occur to you before you read this.

The steps to centring yourself and preparing to resume a good clear reading are as follows:

1. Say to your client, 'Give me a minute to make this clear'. If your client wants a good reading they'll allow you five or six minutes without complaint.

2. Take a deep breath and release it slowly.

3. State silently to yourself what you are aware of in the present moment. You might say to yourself: 'I am aware of the pressure within me. I am aware of the table and the cards. I am aware of my hands. I am aware of the seat beneath me, supporting me'.

4. Once you have become aware of yourself and your surroundings, focus your awareness on the client as you continue with: 'I am aware of my client. I am aware of their hands. I am aware of their shirt', and so on.

5. When you have done this (all within sixty or ninety seconds) you are ready to focus your attention on the cards. Take a brief glance at each card to see how many Major Arcana cards are in the layout. Notice if any card number is dominant, for example, there are three Fives on the table.

6. Explain the layout to your client so that they have some information and can feel at ease with the procedure. When you consult a doctor about an operation they

usually explain how the procedure works in simple terms, and, although you are not medically trained, you can generally grasp what is about to happen. The other reason for explaining the procedure to a client is that you are beginning a conversation with them and giving them permission to interrupt you with questions if something is unclear. Often your blank spot disappears as you start to converse with your client.

7.   If you're a 'big picture' person you may start by giving a general summary of the layout before you. If you're a 'details' person you may wish to start with one card (usually the 'past' card) and build up a complete picture with words from there.

8.   Once you have an overview or have started detailing a particular card (depending upon your style) you are over the blank spot.

Sometimes the feeling of being blank is a sign that you have not attuned yourself psychically with your client or that they have closed down through fear or distrust. To remedy this, you simply start a conversation with your client to put them at ease; if they have closed down or are psychically blocked it is your job to find out why.

They may just need to know that it's okay to relax, or you may not be their idea of a Tarot reader. For over twenty years clients have been telling me that I look too young to be a reader, and some of them have closed down psychically rather than ask me how long I've been reading the cards. (Although once a woman asked me how long I'd been reading the cards, and I looked at her nervously and stammered that she was my second-ever reading. Then I burst out laughing and told her my reading history.) At first I used to squirm with embarrassment if anyone asked me about my age or experience but these days I'm delighted. Now if a client tells me that I look too young I ask them to save the flirting until after the reading, as they may not like me so much then.

The stereotype of a reader being an older person can work in your favour. I've taught a few women in their seventies who have taken up Tarot reading and been surprised that the public love them. In the client's eyes, that little old lady with the silver hair and tea in a delicate china cup must have been reading for fifty years. People believe that wisdom takes time but of course this is not necessarily so. I've seen many an old fool and I've seen small children who exuded wisdom beyond their age.

In any case, as you converse with your client, putting them at ease, they will open up psychically and you'll find yourself attuning to them more easily.

★ Giving Emergency Readings ★

It is fair to say that the least reliable readings you'll give to clients are those given during a client's emergency. As discussed in 'Limitations of the Tarot' when a client phones for a reading and they are in the eye of an emotional storm, the intensity of their desires and fears can affect the reading. This is the case whether they select the cards or you select them on their behalf, as is done in telephone readings.

In such circumstances it is better to delay the reading, even if only for one day. If the client is determined to have a reading immediately, or you feel something they are asking cannot wait, you can determine the questions which need to be answered at once and then hang up. You can then complete a short reading alone, without the client's fears and desires clouding the answer. When you have asked the cards the relevant question, you can phone the client back with your response.

An example of the above occurred with a friend named Lauren, who telephoned me late one night to say that she wanted news about her fifteen-year-old daughter. They lived in the country, and young Shannon had been out to a school dance and was going to a friend's house to sleep over. Lauren had told the girl to phone her as soon as she was safely home for the night and the call had not come. Lauren had telephoned several police stations, to be told that the nearest one open was seven hours' drive away. She had called Shannon on her mobile phone but it was switched off. Starting to panic, she rang me for news.

I established the basic questions and told Lauren I'd call back in ten minutes. I then sat and quietened my mind before asking the cards two simple questions.

1.   Is Shannon safe at present?
2.   Will Lauren hear from Shannon before dawn?

When I had the answers to each question ('yes' in both cases) I telephoned Lauren to tell her. She was relieved but not completely so, as she actually wanted to hear from Shannon herself. Fifteen minutes later she called back to say that Shannon had rung and things were okay. Like any typical teenager, Shannon had been swept up in the excitement of the night and forgotten to telephone her mother.

When telephoning the client back with an answer you have to ensure that they don't talk you into answering a few more questions. When you are giving them the answer, keeping it short and to the point, which I did in the above situation, helps them.

Conducting an actual reading a few days later, when the storm has subsided, or alone after the client has detailed the basic questions, helps to maintain accuracy. You're not helping your reputation by giving an immediate reading which later proves to be wrong.

However, you're not afforded the luxury of delaying a reading if you're a telephone Tarot reader. With telephone readings, clients call the moment problems arise and sometimes hang up if you try to reason with them about how strong emotions affect the accuracy of readings.

A friend who is a telephone Tarot reader told me about one of her first readings. The woman calling explained that her husband had left with his mistress and told her he wasn't returning. He had called into the house to collect some personal belongings and they argued. As he departed he threatened that if she contacted a lawyer to initiate divorce proceedings, he'd return and shoot her dead. As he owned a gun, she took his threat seriously.

Her first question was, 'Will my husband shoot me dead?'.

My friend was reeling when she heard this.

(Later she wondered why the woman didn't apply for a restraining order against her husband.

'Do restraining orders actually prevent unbalanced husbands from shooting their estranged wives?' I asked her.

'No, I guess not,' she replied.)

As a reader, my friend felt that she had to answer the question, as to refuse to have done so might have left the woman believing that she was refusing to deliver the bad news. What the telephone reader can do is lead the caller toward a more constructive line of questioning, for example:

1. What can I do to ensure a positive outcome in this situation?
2. Is it wise to initiate divorce proceedings at this time?
3. Is my husband serious about his threat to shoot me?
4. Is it wise for me to lay low for a period of time until my husband calms down?
5. Is it wise to apply for a restraining order against my husband?
6. What is the lesson for me in this situation?

★ Reading for Yourself ★

In a recent advanced Tarot reading course I asked for a show of hands from the students about whether they agreed that reading for yourself was not good practice because you cannot be objective; all the hands went up. I then asked for a show of hands by those who had read for themselves in the previous four weeks, and again all the hands went up. Readers know that it's not right to read for themselves but they continue to do so for a variety of reasons. Some feel it is a chance to get good practice with the cards. However, this is not usually the case, as when reading for yourself you can take short cuts and ignore card meanings, and even get yourself into a panic.

You may allow yourself to develop sloppy habits and see what you want to see. I believe that few readers could tell you all the cards which appeared in a seven-card spread five minutes after a reading they have given themselves, because they only saw in it what they wanted to see. It's a bit like falling in love: we see what we want to see and our hearts skip a beat; we hear what we want to hear and we walk on air. I believe that readings require clarity, and we all know that falling in love sometimes prohibits us from seeing the obvious.

When you read for others to gain experience and you forget a card meaning, it's likely you'll return to your books afterward and review the forgotten card's significance. Chances are you'll never forget that card meaning again during a reading. When you read for yourself and you forget a card meaning, it is easy to add extra cards until you come to a card you know well, but you have not improved your knowledge of the cards at all. You have merely become a lazy, haphazard reader and there are enough of those in practice already.

Also, readers frequently panic when reading for themselves. They ask loaded questions and then wonder why they become hysterical when their worst fears are confirmed. A reader might ask herself, 'Will Barry ever love someone more than me?', and collapse when the answer is 'yes'. She doesn't consider that Barry's first love is his twelve-year-old dog named Bozo or perhaps his old mum.

So, when answers are given to loaded questions, the person asking sometimes wishes they could retract the question and return to the innocence they did not value previously. Another loaded question is, 'When will I die?'. I have heard many arguments as to why the person asking that question might benefit from knowing the answer, but as a person who knows the age I will be when I die I can tell you that it doesn't always sit easily with me. You cannot forget that knowledge easily, and it doesn't benefit you, no matter what you think.

'Will my mother die in the next two years?' is also the type of question that causes anguish. Once you have panicked yourself it is almost too late to sit down and take some sound advice. And yet, that's the time the reader makes a call to me. I answer, to hear a polite voice with an urgent undertone, which occasionally breaks into thinly veiled hysteria.

It's time for me to sound reassuring and calm, and eventually reproachful that the reader should break such an obvious rule. Soon afterwards I offer to send a 'slap-a-gram' around to their front door. This is someone who knocks loudly, and when the door is answered, slaps the host firmly across the face, before politely asking for their signature to confirm that they've delivered the slap. When you're reeling from being soundly slapped, your worries subside somewhat; do you really care when you're going to die if your face is glowing with a fresh palm print?

In case there is any doubt about what I'm telling you in this chapter, let me spell it out for you: *don't read for yourself*. If you cannot see generally what is wrong with your life or your circumstances, reading for yourself will not help.

I like to teach groups and at the start of each training I am forthright with the students. I tell them: 'Make friends with some or all of the other students. Why? Because if you like someone here you may have free readings for life. You know how and when they were trained, and you have time to observe their reading style. After this course is completed you can read for their friends and they can read for yours. That's the real practice you need, because reading for strangers stretches you, and in being stretched to your limits you improve'.

They usually laugh nervously and I can immediately spot the Wands types because they nod to themselves at my straightforward approach. Wands people like it straight up. ('No bullshit, no regrets and no prisoners', as a Queen of Wands once put it to me.)

Part Two

★ The Major Arcana ★

The Major Arcana is a series of twenty-two cards numbered from zero to twenty-one, and they depict the spiritual lessons of life in twenty-two separate lessons or steps.

Each astrological sign has a particular lesson to master and these lessons are part of the Major Arcana. These cards highlight the underlying lessons in the challenges presented to you by your career, relationships, health and family. By being aware of the lesson contained within a challenge, you can actively seek to master the lesson and resolve the issues around it. If, for example, you selected the reversed Emperor card after asking why you were not promoted in your career, this would signify the need for you to develop more practical discipline. If you then set out to improve your sense of discipline, you may increase your chances of career success.

When more than half the cards in a spread are Major Arcana cards, it is worth asking the client to add an extra card to each of the Major Arcana cards. This helps to avoid the reading being overly slanted towards the spiritual, which can make it difficult for the client to fathom.

Having five Major Arcana cards in a seven card spread makes for a deeply spiritual reading which few clients may understand. By adding extra cards you can reveal to the client the underlying thoughts, beliefs and lessons in their everyday lives.

When a Major Arcana card appears reversed you return to the lesson of the previous card, just as you do with the Minor Arcana. The only exception is The Fool, as it has no previous card.

In advanced Tarot courses I usually ask the students which Major Arcana represents them at that time, and then we select from only the Major Arcana cards to see if they were accurate. This can be extended to which Major Arcana card represents you financially, emotionally, spiritually, in relationships and in your career. By deciding which card represent each area before you select any, you are forced to think about yourself, your life and the card meanings.

Simply slide the Major Arcana cards in a line face downward onto a table and ask yourself which card you feel represents you at this point in your life. After deciding on a card, select from the pack before you and view the card. If you select a different card from the one you had in mind, try to notice five things in this card which you had not previously seen, before putting it back into the pack. This helps you to understand the card better.

The Fool

The Fool represents that time in life when you know something is possible, despite all the logical reasons for it to be otherwise. There is something positive to be said for the kind of innocence suggested by the Fool: it enables us to tackle goals and challenges we probably would not consider with the wisdom of hindsight. Others may caution you against your intended actions, but when the Fool is upright, you know within yourself that opportunities await you.

As such, it is clear that with the innocence and faith of the Fool we gain valuable life experience we otherwise may not. For example, it is innocence and blind faith that prompt people to pursue new relationships after previous unsuccessful ones. Also, in simple terms, the Fool is how the average person may perceive the wise man or woman, who doesn't follow convention and can be considered eccentric. It is interesting that one French word for eccentric is 'originale' or '*original*' (and unconventional); the Fool is an original.

For me, a physical demonstration of what the Fool represents occurred in 1986. I was working as a reader in a health centre that was spread over four floors of a city building. I was on the basement level along with the centre's bookshop. The building was separated from a large park by four lanes of moving traffic and another two lanes of parked cars.

The flow of traffic was constant, but one day at around 3 pm I decided that it was possible for me to run upstairs and out into the street, crossing it without stopping or looking for traffic, and safely reach the park. I leapt up out of my chair and bolted up the stairs. Without glancing at the traffic I tore across the street and into the park, collapsing with laughter and excitement as I turned to look. I had made it through a momentary break in the traffic flow.

I wouldn't attempt anything like this again, but at that moment, I was convinced that it was possible. The Fool represents a window of opportunity which you can see but which may not be visible to others. Trusting your instincts is essential if you want to develop your intuition.

Reversed

The Fool reversed represents a need to follow convention, to take advice even when you know it does not apply to you at that particular time. Your client may be seeking to conform when life suggests they should live in the moment, in their own way. Alternatively, it can suggest they are trying to live in the moment in spite of responsibilities that would have them do otherwise. The Fool reversed may indicate they are living out their adulthood as a child. Perhaps they have found someone to look after them or an organisation that supports them, and they have no desire to open the pack on their rod to examine the tools of the Magician. However, these tools may start to deteriorate if they are not used for a long period of time.

The Magician

In everyday terms the Magician represents a time for your client to be effective in realising their plans in the physical world. This may result in them changing their job or starting a new business, or simply remaining aware of their opportunities in life. It is time for them to choose their path and then to concentrate their efforts in pursuit of goals.

It is said that good luck is where planning meets opportunity, and this partly describes the Magician. Outwardly, the Magician is confident, capable and successful; inwardly he plans, rehearses his moves and awaits his opportunity. When the opportune moment arrives he moves resolutely towards achieving his aims.

We are all Magicians at various times in our lives: for example, when we first stood up, mastered a musical instrument or graduated from school. Just watching a child learning to read is watching the Magician in action. A whole new world opens up to them; many parents will have experienced driving around with a child in the back seat reading signs and shop names aloud.

Pursuing study or applying yourself to your career, or any other project, is usually a successful enterprise when the Magician appears in the answer position in a layout. This card represents your client being effective, due to being grounded in reality and yet simultaneously aware of life's spiritual dimension.

Reversed

The Magician reversed often indicates a lack of success due to being out of touch with reality. Confusion, impatience and the lack of a clear plan can be indicated. The timing of your client's plan or project may be wrong, or they may be pushing something which is not going to succeed, so the Magician reversed suggests they should take some time to reassess the situation. It is time for them to return to the lesson of the Fool, to be freed of the current situation in order to see it more clearly.

It can also suggest an unbalanced and wilful person whose desires and goals keep changing. Wilfulness is no substitute for pursuing the right opportunity at the right time with steady application, but the Magician reversed cannot be shown a better way. An example of the Magician reversed is the small child who seeks to control their parents with tears and tantrums.

If it appears in answer to a relationship query the Magician reversed may represent a partner who can be possessive, domineering and unreliable. They sometimes manifest as several personalities in one person, and I often tell a client to name the different parts or personalities so that they know who they are dealing with at any given time.

The High Priestess

Reflection is essential, if only to establish our goals and to ask ourselves what might fulfil us. The High Priestess depicts this act of reflecting upon our purpose, either through meditation or simply by spending time alone in quiet surroundings. Holidays were originally holy days, times set aside to reflect. However, with the hectic pace of life today, holidays are often spent maximising precious time; reflection, if it takes place at all, is often squeezed into a short meditation each working day.

In this card the scroll in the hands of the High Priestess represents the inner knowledge we have about our true purpose. Our spiritual being remembers this true purpose, which is our destiny. Our conscious minds forget it, in the struggle to achieve goals in the physical world. The moon at the High Priestess's feet symbolises our remembering our true purpose at night, when we go to sleep. Slipping into dreams, we reacquaint ourselves with those things which have lasting spiritual value for us. Upon awakening, we endeavour to carry some of that spiritual purpose into our daily lives.

The veil behind the High Priestess limits her view of the pool of water, encouraging her to focus on the physical world. Her natural intuition and spiritual nature make the veiled world behind her more attractive than the harsh realities of life before her.

This card represents the lesson for Pisces, which is to remember your true purpose and yet make your way in the material world. This can be a difficult balancing act. However, sometimes artists carry their memories of spiritual life into the physical world, transferring spiritual energy into their sculpture, paintings or music.

Reversed

The High Priestess reversed represents a time when your client happily walks away from a period spent in reflection, in order to pursue things offered in the physical world. They are, in effect, returning to the Magician to focus their energies on achieving a tangible purpose. Sometimes the High Priestess reversed suggests that it is time for them to seek out those who can help them put their plans into action.

After withdrawing to glimpse their purpose, your client needs to return to life to live it. The message of the reversed card is to keep your eyes open for opportunities while remembering your purpose as glimpsed in the upright card.

The Empress

In simple terms the Empress represents living life to the full in an uncomplicated way. This can mean something as straightforward as taking pleasure in a sunny afternoon; the Empress seeks all kinds of reasons to feel content with life.

The Empress typically brings joy to those around her. Years ago a receptionist who worked at a healing centre in which I had my practice demonstrated Empress behaviour. Jessica loved people, and she often brought homemade biscuits, scones and cakes for the clients to eat as they awaited their practitioner.

I'd step into the waiting room to greet my next client and find them with a face full of chocolate cake or settling down to some scones and tea, and see Jessica looking pleased with herself.

'You know, I'm very lucky these days,' she said to me.

'Oh yes? How's that?'

'I love to bake and my husband can only eat so much, but a few months ago I discovered a house full of university students living next door, and now when I bake I pop over. They're always happy to help out with eating what I make.'

I had to stop myself from laughing, as I envisioned a group of hungry students with their noses out the window saying, 'Another ten minutes and she'll be over, so put on some coffee, will you?'.

In a general or relationship layout it can suggest pregnancy or a woman who is at home with lots of children. If she has two children of her own, you'll find seven or eight other local children using her home as a base or a playground. They'll often be well fed and looked after in her care.

In a career layout the Empress card can suggest that your client is working from home, or partly from home, as the Empress represents domestic harmony and stability. The Empress 'makes a house into a home' with unmistakable touches such as fresh flowers or herbs from the garden, indoor plants and warm colours in fabrics and paintings.

Recently, in a question about a career project, a client asked me, 'What is my role in this project?'. In the answer, the Empress indicated that his role was to support others, helping them to feel good about the project and themselves so that they could work together as a team. The Empress represents teamwork, harmony and shared rewards.

Reversed

The Empress reversed can suggest domestic instability. It can also indicate your client is not feeding their senses, but retreating into their own thoughts. When development is blocked or retarded, it is time for your client to return to their plans, to see if the path to their goal needs to be altered in some way. This means returning to the High Priestess to review the goal.

In a career spread it may mean that your client is using their home as a base for work and that this is disrupting the usual home feeling. In a relationship layout the Empress reversed can signify reluctance to pursue a relationship to its next natural stage. It shows the need to return to the lesson of the High Priestess to reflect upon their relationship purpose.

Also, when cut off from their own senses your client may need to return to the High Priestess in order to feed themselves through spiritual means, such as meditation.

The Emperor

True freedom is the result of self-discipline. The Emperor represents the disciplined man, whose success in the material world is the direct result of his self-discipline and determination. His battles are all outward ones, meaning his conflicts are visible to the eye.

The orange backdrop in the card and the Emperor's red clothing highlight his passion and enthusiasm for life and the challenges it offers. His world is black and white. He believes in what he can see and touch, and if you ask for his opinion you'd better be prepared to hear it.

Although the Emperor is not an emotional or romantic man, he is reliable and practical, and an antidote to the King of Wands reversed, who leaves a job half-finished, or the King of Swords reversed, who doesn't start it because he's too busy talking about it. The Emperor enlists the help of others and gets on with the job.

In romantic relationships this man doesn't send flowers or write poetry. His way of showing his partner that he cares is to keep her front gate oiled and car running properly, and to change all her light bulbs soon after they cease to work. He is usually a material provider.

The appearance of the Emperor in answer to a specific question can suggest success due to self discipline. Through working longer hours and remaining focused on the job at hand, your client can achieve a position of power whereby they can make real impact.

Reversed

There are two possibilities when the Emperor is reversed. The first is that it represents a man who has been disciplined and is now mellowing, realising that structures exist only to give us freedom to live. The second possibility is that this man is undisciplined, and when faced with a hard decision, shrinks away from it. The Emperor reversed is argumentative but when pressed backs down. He is, in effect, 'all bark and no bite'.

In romantic relationships this man is undisciplined, shrinking from decisions and looking for a strong woman to make them for him. This card can represent a mother–son relationship between marriage partners. Although the man makes a show of running things it is always the woman who makes the real decisions.

As an answer to a question, the Emperor reversed can suggest a return to the Empress to fill a need for sensual fulfilment or to receive physical nurturing they may have missed out on earlier in life. When reversed, this man is likely to seek more than one partner at a time. Perhaps a relationship with a nurturing, sensual woman could feed him and enable him to mature into the upright Emperor.

The Emperor reversed can also suggest a lack of success due to insufficient self-discipline. This refers to the person who feels that the world owes them a living and who seeks a partner who'll provide it for them.

The Hierophant

The Hierophant represents the teacher, institute or organisation that favours a traditional approach. The Hierophant's task is to preserve knowledge and to pass it on intact to those who want to benefit from past insights.

The Hierophant (or Pope or High Priest) is an authority figure, shown on the card by his sitting above the disciples; he is a role model for them. The disciples surrender their free will to their teacher in order to benefit from his experience. However, in reality he cannot teach them by enforcing his will on them; they can only choose to learn from him. That is, he can make the information more or less palatable, but he cannot teach them unless they are willing to learn. It is only our willingness to learn and to challenge what we believe to be true that deepens our understanding of life and spirituality.

The disciple on the left has the passion to learn, shown by the red roses on his tunic, whereas the disciple on the right displays purity of motive in the form of the white lilies. The ancients used the cross as a symbol depicting humankind's lesson of compassion, shown by the horizontal bar being at the height of the human heart. Having passion, purity of motive and compassion leads us to an understanding of life which has previously been hidden from us.

We all have role models in different areas of our lives. A clear example of this is that when I conduct Tarot courses I give demonstration readings in front of the class, using a volunteer. The students observe the reading and so I become a role model for them when they read for others. Having a role model is essential until we are familiar enough with a subject to experiment with it or explore it on our own. Once we are able to do this we may choose a different path to our teachers, even rebelling against them in order to establish our own sense of identity. (This action is shown in the Hierophant reversed.)

Reversed

The Hierophant reversed represents the search for new ideas and possibilities, including possible new paths to tread in search of spiritual wholeness. This is the opposite of the upright Hierophant, which represents the belief that the current path is the only one. A certain path may seem the only one for you at a particular time, but it can be argued that we will each tread many paths in our search for the truth.

Many different perspectives are required to gain a deeper understanding of anything in life. Consider an apple: a big, juicy green apple may trigger hunger in one person, and allergies in another; to a dietician it might be a source of vitamins and iron; to a worm it might be home; to a dog it may seem to be a funnily shaped ball. They are all perspectives and they are all correct, yet each of these represents only one aspect of the apple. To the apple tree, an apple is a chance to reproduce itself, for the seeds contain generations of apple trees.

Therefore, the pursuit of new ideas represented by the Hierophant reversed is necessary to increase awareness. This, in turn, helps with achieving spiritual wholeness. The Hierophant reversed offers an opportunity to take responsibility for your spiritual direction by presenting many paths beyond the familiar one you currently pursue.

In a relationship layout the Hierophant reversed suggests an unconventional relationship. Perhaps gender roles are reversed, as in the case of Kenneth and Marian. The Hierophant reversed appeared in Kenneth's relationship layout, and he explained that he stayed at home and raised the children and Marian had the high-powered career. As an artist it suited Kenneth to stay at home, while Marian was very successful in her chosen field.

The Lovers

Many readers don't look beyond the depiction in this card of a couple, to see its deeper significance. The Lovers card represents the combining of masculine and feminine energies in order to move forward in your life. It signifies the need to take into account both your physical and your spiritual needs when making a decision. 'Am I ready to move forward in my life or is it better to stay where I am?' is the dilemma represented by the Lovers card. When the Lovers card appears upright, your client is ready to move forward.

In this card, physical needs are represented by the tree of knowledge behind the woman and spiritual needs are shown by the tree of life behind the man. Although the man in this card looks to the woman for comfort and fulfilment, she looks up to the angel for hers, recognising that lasting fulfilment can only come from within. The cloud stretching between them suggests that their spirits are already intertwined despite their physical distance.

The masculine part of us continuously pushes us forward toward possible challenges and achievements, whereas the feminine part appreciates the stillness in which we can explore feelings, hopes and our deeper needs. Put into the context of everyday life, the Lovers represents a time when your client decides whether to buy a house, marry a particular person, take a trip overseas or relocate to another town.

Ten years ago I decided to move within Sydney, away from the eastern suburbs to the north shore of the city. I was nervous about this prospect, as the north shore seemed to be light years away from the night-life I had enjoyed and the people I mixed with. One afternoon, before I had even looked for somewhere to live, I sat down and took a close look at the reasons behind the decision: I no longer took pleasure in the inner-city night-life and my friends lived all over Sydney, not only in the eastern suburbs; I also wanted a garden again. Therefore, I looked around and found a suitable home on the north shore.

However, it took me another six months to know for certain that I had made the right decision. This was when I visited a friend in the eastern suburbs one weekend and had to park three streets away from his house. His back garden consisted of a slab of concrete and two deckchairs. 'You should have come an hour ago, the sun was right on these chairs then,' he said, as I sat in the shade listening to four different stereos from neighbouring houses. When I had decided to move I had listened to my instincts, and had made the correct decision.

Reversed

The Lovers reversed suggests that your client is not ready to move on from their current circumstances. This is because they have more to learn where they are or because this is not the right time for them to move forward.

In 1980 I moved from my home town to Sydney. The move was prompted mostly by a friend who had been badgering me to make it for two years. I left town on a complete high, feeling that my life had never been so good. However, I walked into four hard years when I could not seem to find where I fitted in and yet could not return home. I learned to like Sydney, but I started off badly because I left my home town too soon.

Another example of the reversed Lovers card occurred when my students recently badgered me to conduct a palmistry course. I had not planned to teach one until later but because of their enthusiasm I decided to schedule one for the middle of that year. The course filled up before my assistant had time even to telephone the list of people who had requested course brochures.

When I reached the maximum number of students for the room I would be using for the class, I asked the cards if it would be wise to hold it at a larger venue. The Lovers reversed appeared in the answer, suggesting that it was not wise for me to move forward to a new venue at this point. However, applications for the course continued to arrive, and I hired a larger venue.

I thought about the card reading when four students had to cancel for various reasons. New applications covered those who had cancelled, leaving me with a full course and two additional students. However, the cost of a larger venue was the course fees of three extra students, so, in effect, the Lovers card was accurate.

In a relationship question the Lovers reversed can suggest a desire for romance but not for a deeper relationship. Its appearance can sometimes indicate the desire for change for its own sake or to get away from an unpleasant feeling or situation. The Lovers card reversed suggests it is advisable to return to the Hierophant in order to enjoy the stability offered there.

The Chariot

The Chariot is a many-layered card, depicting the struggle between thoughts and desires. It represents a time when we keep control over ourselves and our lives through exercising mental discipline, but deep down may be crying out to be supported.

In this card the blue-faced moons on the shoulders of the man in the chariot betray his softness despite his being in a situation where he is in charge. Many other aspects of this card also show the partnering of the masculine and the feminine: the black and the white sphinxes, the armour and the blue moons, the land and the water, and the city behind the chariot and the country before it.

In some respects the Chariot represents the qualities of the Magician combined with emotion. That is, the Magician can see things in black and white, and stays in control, but it is not so easy to do this when you are affected by your own feelings. An example of this conflict between the head and the heart came up with Lloyd.

Over the six years he was married to Karen he had become more and more immersed in his job, until Karen felt that she was alone in the marriage. Karen had an affair and Lloyd found out. They went through a bitter separation (during which Lloyd displayed anger to cover his pain). In his struggle during their marriage to be what he thought Karen wanted him to be, strong and controlled, he had concealed his emotional side, ignoring his feelings. After some negotiating with Karen he discovered that it was his soft, gentle nature which had attracted her to him in the first place.

The lesson of the Chariot card is that your client must use their mind to make a decision, but also take their feelings into account when making it. This may not appear to be a difficult challenge, but ask any Cancerian, with their propensity to feel their emotions so powerfully, how difficult it can be.

Reversed

The Chariot reversed represents becoming completely absorbed by your emotions and losing sight of any clarity of thought you once possessed. This can mean having explosive outbursts or becoming overwhelmed with grief for times past, leading your client back to the Lovers.

The Chariot reversed can describe the powerful businessperson who arrives home, closes the front door and goes to pieces, overwhelmed by life and its demands. For such a person there is no harm in returning to the Lovers, if someone special in their life can give them the love and support they need to heal before moving forward into life once again.

The Chariot reversed appearing as the answer to a question can suggest your client is overreacting to something or choosing unwisely. Perhaps they have too much responsibility or are becoming overwhelmed by life at this time. It implies this could be the right moment for them to retreat from life to a safe place or pattern of behaviour. For example, if walking along the side of a river in the late afternoon has brought them peace in the past, this may be an appropriate anchor to reaffirm feelings of inner peace.

Strength

The Strength card represents a time of having inner strength, of displaying courage despite doubts. Courage isn't only saving someone from a burning building (although this is a physical example of strength and courage). There are many forms of courage represented by the Strength card.

Courage is required in order to get up in the morning when your child has lost their fight with cancer. Courage is facing all those friends and fellow parents who are silently terrified and relieved that it was your child and not theirs. It takes real courage to get up in the morning when life holds no promise for you, and to feed yourself when you'd rather be dead and let your child have a few more years on the earth. Sometimes we find great reserves of courage to keep on living until a reason to do so returns to us.

Sometimes courage is telling a close friend who is leaving that you'll miss them, and that they have made a difference to your life. When I was young the family spent what seemed like every Sunday at the house in which two of my aunts lived. They were generous hosts, giving up half of almost every weekend to our family of ten. Some years ago I learned that one of my aunts was dying in hospital. I was unable to visit her, so I sat down and wrote her a letter, telling her that she had made a difference to my life and that I was thankful to have known her. Although I was young and wild at the time of writing the letter, I instinctively knew that it was one of those rare opportunities to speak my kindest thoughts aloud to someone who deserved to hear them. I knew, too, that this opportunity would soon pass, and I didn't want to live with that regret.

At times, by forging ahead and setting new frontiers in our chosen career we may use our courage to inspire those around us to become more than they are. If the Strength card appears in an answer position, it suggests success resulting from inner strength.

Reversed

Strength reversed can represent a time of fear or erosion of confidence. Perhaps your client is overreacting to a situation as a result of anxiety, and seeking to control those around them. When the card appears reversed, it is time for your client to return to the Chariot to tackle the opposing forces within them. Perhaps they are battling their own inner demons, and require the separation of the mind and emotions in order to see themselves clearly.

The lion depicted in this card represents passion, and passion is certainly not a bad thing in itself. It is where that passion is directed that makes it good or bad. However, whatever their passions are directed towards, the reversed card suggests that your client is controlled by their passions at present.

Strength reversed appearing in an answer can indicate a lack of success resulting from insufficient inner strength or confidence. When lacking confidence in our ability to succeed, we sometimes fail to put our best efforts into the challenge at hand.

The Hermit

When the Hermit card appears in a layout, it is time for your client to sit and reflect, in order to see why they are where they are in their life. Time spent alone in reflection is a very important part of gaining an understanding of past actions.

The Hermit card represents winter, in the sense that while others are achieving goals in the material world, the Hermit himself is alone and reflecting. However, when inner growth is taken into account, the Hermit represents a time of understanding, reconciliation with oneself, and a time to crystallise one's path.

It is surprising how many people resist spending time alone to reflect in case what they see within themselves disturbs them. There can come a point in your life where if you were to stop and reflect, you'd risk realising the enormous number of things you needed to change in order to become fulfilled. With twenty-four hour live entertainment and television, you never have to feel alone, despite the fact that more of us are actually alone than ever before in history (I refer, of course, to being alone in the world with no one to share your hopes).

However, refusal to spend time in reflection can result in repeating undesirable actions and receiving unwanted results. Knowing where you have come from, where you are now and where you are going in life are powerful things. Being aware of them allows you to be centred in the present, and all power in life lies in the present. You cannot change the past or anticipate all future possibilities and problems. You can, however, make changes in the present which allow you to perceive the past differently and to narrow your possible future directions in life.

So, although the Hermit does not reveal action and movement, it is a card about using your strength to resolve inner conflicts. In reality, the more you reflect, the more you realise how little you know about the universe; the more you reflect, the less action is required to realise your goals because careful planning can reduce unnecessary efforts in their pursuit.

The Hermit can suggest a period of counselling will assist your client to make sense of their past. Alternately they may choose to keep a diary of thoughts and feelings or to spend time away from others, reflecting.

Reversed

The Hermit reversed can suggest your client has started to reflect on life and become overwhelmed by it, or by the actions they have taken and the results of those actions. The Hermit reversed calls your client back to the Strength card to enable them to ascertain those parts of their life over which they have some control and to remind them that they have the courage to confront those things about their life which are not working.

It requires real courage to look within yourself and admit who you are, both your light and your shadow. However, when you have owned up to those parts of yourself which were previously hidden away in the shadows, you are free to accept others more fully. When you are calm within yourself, you can choose to reflect again, tackling your feelings of insignificance or regret one at a time.

The Hermit reversed can suggest that your client is keeping busy with work or practical things in order to avoid dealing with emotional issues. It can describe a job which takes up the evenings and weekends, depriving them of valuable reflection time.

WHEEL ₒ FORTUNE.

The Wheel of Fortune

The Wheel of Fortune card represents the wheel of life, which is in constant motion. As it turns upwards, things in your life appear to improve. As it turns downwards, things appear to finish, fall away from you or lose their momentum.

The four animals depicted on the card (the eagle for Water, the winged lion for Fire, the winged bull for Earth and the angel for Air) represent the lessons learned in the four suits of the Minor Arcana. If a person has diligently learnt these lessons they will be able to see the changes in their life for what they are: revolutions of the wheel of life.

In life there are seasons for pain, loss, joy, renewal and growth. In fact, if you were to chart your past years you'd probably find that each year had a time for each emotional season. We don't rage against God when the leaves start to fall from the trees in autumn because we understand that winter is coming, and after winter, spring will follow. Soon summer will be with us again, and each season is necessary.

If you were to liken your emotional life to the seasons, starting a new relationship could be considered spring. The blossoming of that relationship could be summer, and the reassertion of boundaries and a partial return to behaviour patterns formed before the commencement of the relationship could be autumn. The close of the relationship, or a time when one or both partners becomes immersed in their own issues, could be winter.

An example of the existence of these 'seasons' occurred recently with a clairvoyant named Ben, who complained to me about his client load. As a psychic he felt that he ought to know why his business was quieter than usual, despite his increasing advertising budget. I asked him to tell me when it was last very busy for months at a time. He said it had been two years since things were that busy.

'And before that? When were you very busy before two years ago?'

'Oh, about five years ago.'

'Could it be that you are in your career winter and that you have to slow down?'

He pondered this for a moment and let out a long sigh. Charting the pattern in his mind showed him that he was indeed in a career winter but it also reassured him that summer was on its way.

Knowing your personal seasons can make you more successful in your endeavours, as you don't waste your time planting seeds or starting new projects in winter. Ben could have saved himself the extra money he spent on advertising by realising he was in a personal winter time, and so advertising wouldn't make much difference. In this card, the sphinx above the wheel guards the secret of personal seasons and, as we have seen, those who understand this secret make better use of their time and energy.

When the Wheel of Fortune appears in a layout it is time for your client to realise what is happening in the greater scheme of things because this perspective is likely to give them peace of mind. If they remain focused on their own lives and resist comparison with others, they will be aware that circumstances are improving. They may be overtaking those around them at this time. However, in the bigger scheme of things such comparisons are inappropriate.

Reversed

The Wheel of Fortune reversed represents a downturn in circumstances. However, of course, when you reach the lowest point on the wheel there is only one direction for you: upwards. The reversed card suggests that your client needs to return to the Hermit in order to reflect upon the patterns in their life.

When the Wheel of Fortune reversed appears, opportunities are decreasing. It depicts a business which is shrinking or a relationship which is losing its appeal for your client. Remind them that the wheel is continually turning, so in time new opportunities will arise.

Winter approaches to give you the opportunity to reflect, and is the perfect time to look within yourself to make sense of your actions in the previous spring and summer. An appreciation of the big picture is essential to reach the World card (suggesting permanent success), as later, in the Major Arcana, they'll be required to surrender various beliefs and possessions, and without an understanding of the big picture, they'll probably struggle against their own progress. It is worth their remembering that if they are entering a personal winter, summer can only be two seasons away.

Justice

The Justice card represents the awareness that your decisions and actions have consequences; that your circumstances are usually the result of these. If your client keeps this in mind, they are less likely to blame others for their circumstances when they are unhappy, and they are more able to change the course of their life through deciding to do so.

In this card, Justice herself is cloaked in red; she can take action but considers the consequences of this. The one white shoe reminds us of spiritual consequences (white being used throughout the Tarot to signify spiritual purity) and her blue sword represents mental clarity. The purple cloth draped behind her signifies compassion, and the grey pillars, also behind her, represent the constraints of the physical world. With all of the above, and taking into account restraints, she is able to arrive at the most appropriate conclusion.

In everyday terms the Justice card can be about deciding, for example, 'Yes, I do want my marriage to work' and taking all the necessary steps toward the desired goal. These steps may include your client resolving past issues with their partner, carefully considering the role they want within their relationship in the future, and taking responsibility for their part in any current problems they face in the relationship.

Reversed

If Justice appears reversed in a client's layout, they may be feeling that life has been unfair to them and have a need to lay blame for their circumstances elsewhere. They need to be reminded that life is not always fair, it is just life. They may also be comparing themselves with others, but life is not a race to achieve, and even if it were, we each have different starting points. Also, you can never truly know what another person is experiencing, even in their successful moments. Unresolved arguments and ongoing litigation, too, are indicated by Justice reversed.

An example of the kind of situation that could be suggested by the reversed card happened last year and concerned my neighbours. My next-door neighbour complained to me one day that his rear neighbour's dog was driving him mad by barking incessantly. I suggested that he have a word with the neighbour, but he just shook his head. Later that day I phoned a dog-training business that advertised they could humanely silence annoying dogs using simple training techniques.

The company sent me out a brochure, which I took over to my neighbour. He shook his head again, saying that the rear neighbour probably would not want to spend $240 training the dog. I suggested they each pay $120, and that it would be worth it for my neighbour's peace of mind. He took the brochure but he didn't seem to take in what I had said. (I didn't mind; I can't hear the dog from my house.) My neighbour seemed to me to be more intent on maintaining his rage than resolving the problem. He felt that the situation was unfair whereas I felt that it was unfinished.

Before your client becomes bogged down in thoughts of who is responsible for their life at a particular time, they perhaps need to return to the lesson of the Wheel of Fortune. Then they may realise that spring will eventually arrive and with it opportunities for growth.

The Hanged Man

The Hanged Man is about those moments when life has 'tied us up': when we feel restricted, unable to change our circumstances or to choose a better path for ourselves. However, our spirit is still free to come and go in its search for understanding. When the Hanged Man appears in a layout, your task is to gently but firmly remind your client that they must look within for fulfilment.

Meditation may reward them at this time. When life weighs heavily upon us and we feel alone as we face our burdens, it can reconnect us to our higher source of energy and grant us a glimpse of the big picture again. This can release us from the struggle, even if only momentarily. A profound meditation can allow us to realise that we are truly stronger than the test at hand. This kind of reminder is essential if we are to maintain faith in our eventual success in the face of life's challenges.

If people habitually go within themselves to glimpse their spiritual path, the Hanged Man becomes a welcome stop on the path of spiritual development. It offers a communion with light which is much prized by those who know its value, as at the end of the path most of us seek inner peace and stillness.

The wise man or woman remains aware that their journey through life is only temporary, and does not become overly attached to worldly things, to people (becoming overly attached to people can be a recipe for disappointment) or to outcomes. The Hanged Man is thankful that life reminds him about his true purpose here on earth: to perfect himself in readiness for the time he no longer has a physical body. With the appearance of the Devil card he will again be seduced by the material world, but before this he is blissful that outer restrictions have forced him back to spiritual considerations and to his path homeward.

Reversed

The Hanged Man reversed indicates a loss of faith by your client in their ability to surmount life's obstacles. They may be refusing or forgetting to go within for spiritual nourishment or pitting themselves against life with a weakened spirit. When the Hanged Man appears reversed, the person is in great need of a reminder that the spirit is greater than the flesh, and that in some place and time the obstacles they presently face are already resolved.

'The darkest hour is just before the dawn' is a saying that most truly applies here. The inner peace we find through meditation may not change our physical circumstances, but it can restore our faith in our ability to do so when the right moment arrives. If we become detached from the outer worldly appearance of success and the worldly appearance of failure, when we encounter obstacles in our path, we do not have to compare ourselves with those who presently appear to be succeeding.

When the Hanged Man appears reversed in a layout, your client needs a reminder that this difficult time, too, will pass. Struggle at this point is futile, so ask your client to find inner peace and acceptance of life's circumstances. It is time for them to return to the lesson of the upright Justice card to take responsibility for their part in being where they are presently.

Death

The Death card is all about clearing away the old to make room for the new. Small deaths come to us all, many times in an average life, almost as if to prepare us to cope with the final death. In grieving and releasing the losses we experience, we are free to return to life again.

Imagine if death called for you and took you away, only to return to you after a year, to tell you that it was a mistake? You're suddenly free to return to life with your rejuvenated physical body, but many aspects of your life have 'closed up': you have no job, no home and all your belongings may have been sold or dispersed among your friends and family. You may want very much to return to the life you didn't even know you cherished, but it is likely to be gone.

If you scale down this scenario, it occurs many times throughout a single life. A relationship finishes, and no matter how much you stare into your ex-partner's eyes, there is no longer any place for you in their heart. You resign from your job and all you can actually take with you are the memories of what you achieved in your former position. Bearing this in mind, it seems sensible to live without regrets as much as you can.

When the Death card appears, signifying sweeping changes, your client needs to release these things gracefully, and allow the changes to take their regrets also. Only then can they truly see the long-term vision offered by the Temperance card, which follows Death. It is not death or change that shapes us, but how we deal with the changes Death brings. The lesson here is to surrender to the changes life presents.

Reversed

Death reversed indicates your client needs faith that life will provide opportunities for new things to replace the old ones. It shows your client is holding on to past people, situations or behaviour patterns as they fade from their life.

If we refuse to release what death seeks to take from us, or to grieve, we cannot return to life with as many energetic parts of ourselves present as before. In the darkest hours, when we have gone beyond tears and sit numb and alone in the world, it pays to have even the tiniest grain of faith that in the greater scheme of things death only takes from us what we no longer need for our growth. Withered leaves have to fall so that new shoots can appear in spring.

Temperance

The Temperance card offers a glimpse of a person's longer-term purpose. Temperance is an awareness that there is a path for both the spiritual and the human parts of you. (This is a card for the sign of Sagittarius, and those born under this sign particularly need to have a purpose.) In everyday terms this card can suggest learning. This can be through taking a course, or through travelling and exploring life in all its dimensions.

The auric energy depicted around the head of the figure in this card represents understanding attained, while the path behind the figure leads to the sun, symbolising purpose. Although the path beckons, the figure is content to stand still, finding peace through balancing the cups (Water, for emotions). Also shown on the card are the orange triangle (Fire, for enthusiasm), the white square (Earth, for practical application of understanding) and the third eye chakra (Air, for understanding).

When appearing as an answer to a question the Temperance card can suggest success through keeping a balanced approach. With a career question, it can indicate careers involving travel and teaching. In simple terms Temperance is a card that signifies acting moderately as a result of keeping the bigger picture in mind. Your client is aware of the desired consequences of their actions and they regulate their actions accordingly.

Reversed

Temperance reversed suggests a person who is acting without any long-term vision. 'You only live once' is the prevailing attitude of such a person, who then often has to live with the consequences of their actions. Temperance reversed indicates a time of hasty action.

An example of someone who acted without thinking about the long-term was Holly, who ate whatever she wanted and often stated, 'Well, I'll have to die of something'. However, it wasn't the dying itself that caused her to suffer, so much as living for seventeen years with severe diabetes. If it were as simple as keeling over one day and dying immediately, we'd all live like there was no tomorrow. Those of us who observe others' lives, however, realise that often our old age is spent according to the decisions we made in our younger years.

An example of hasty action shown by Temperance reversed might be a man who leaves his fourth wife for his secretary, unaware that he is repeating a pattern of behaviour. If he contemplated his actions he may realise that paying child support for children in four past relationships may not have been what he had planned for himself.

When the Temperance card appears reversed, it is time for the client to return to the lesson of the Death card, to release those things which prevent them from seeing the big picture clearly. Clearing the path to make way for their destiny is the purpose here. Speedy action is not required, as the Death card will gradually remove those things which are no longer useful in their life. All they need is faith that life will leave them what they need to survive.

THE DEVIL .

The Devil

The Devil card represents being seduced by the material world. Often as we strive to possess things and people, we lose sight of our true purpose: to learn through experiencing new things. Overly regimented routine and then stagnation and mediocrity can result when we stifle our thirst for knowledge. The Devil card is about learning how fulfilment cannot coexist with the responsibilities which stem from too much ownership and seeking to control your own world.

With each new possession we acquire comes a period of excitement which soon passes as the thing itself loses its novelty. If we pursue the ownership of more and more things, our time soon becomes taken up with procuring objects and then with maintaining those things we own. Therefore, in time we become possessed by that which we seek to own. It is essential we learn that possessing things cannot bring us fulfilment; ironically, the best way to learn this is to possess things.

In this card there are two figures in front of the Devil. They have placed golden chains around their necks, and they find a level of security in their bondage. In effect they are saying, 'Better the devil you know than the devil you don't', in an attempt to quieten their spiritual hunger. The scenario represented is that the figures soon tire of life, and they long to fall asleep at night so that their spirits can leave their physical bodies and the limiting beliefs held by the conscious mind. Memories of the Death card and the losses they have experienced motivate them to stay where they are. They have forgotten that the spirit cannot be destroyed and that all they risk losing are their limiting beliefs.

When it appears in a layout the Devil card can describe the act of regarding with suspicion anything which seems new or different. This suspicion is preventing your client from trying anything they don't already know, and this perpetuates their current situation.

Point out your client's options carefully and calmly, and be prepared to hear every reason why each option you suggest won't work. You almost have to offer an option which is new but looks familiar, or closely resembles an approach they have tried. Vigilance is necessary, however, to avoid becoming as stuck as your client through only seeing limited choices.

Reversed

The Devil reversed suggests that your client is ready to hear their alternatives and to change. After realising that there are alternatives to their current path they can become aware that change requires them to surrender to what life has in store for them. Therefore, control gives way to acceptance of a force greater than them.

The Tower

The Tower is a reminder that attachment often brings disappointment. It represents a sudden change, separating your client from a person or thing to which they have become attached (whereas with the Death card the change is gradual).

When the Tower appears in a spread, change is approaching your client too quickly for them to avoid it. A person for whom the Tower appears could fall from a ladder and die on the way to hospital or win an enormous sum of money and have their life take on a new direction immediately. (I laughingly tell students that the enormous-sum-of-money type of change is clearly demonstrated in Einstein's theory of relatives, which states, 'The number of relatives one acquires after becoming suddenly wealthy is directly proportionate to the amount of wealth suddenly acquired'. Of course, the opposite is also true, as demonstrated in Bernie Einstein's theory that, 'The number of relatives one loses is directly proportionate to the amount of debt one suddenly admits to acquiring'.)

The Tower represents rapid change, often unexpected and usually out of the person's control. Your client needs to remember that the change is leading to the Star (see below) and to fulfilment.

Reversed

The Tower reversed indicates your client was warned ahead of impending change, and has avoided it, remaining where they were in life. (Their actions are reminiscent of the Devil card, as they cling to those things which give them security.) It can be a warning of change in the form of ill health that results in medical tests, but that will be resolved by the 'all clear'. If the warning is ignored, however, the change will approach again, from another angle.

William survived the horrors of World War II as a prisoner of war in Europe for three years. Afterwards he developed the habit of hoarding everything he saw. Egg cartons, newspapers and old bottles were carefully stored away by him for over twenty years, and his house was cluttered to the ceiling. One morning as William was cooking breakfast, a stack of egg cartons stored above the stove caught fire and his house was soon ablaze. He managed to control the fire but didn't change his habit of hoarding.

Soon William's health deteriorated and he was moved into a serviced retirement home to which he could not take anything but his clothes and a few personal items. Within two days of his departure, the entire contents of his house had been cleaned out and transferred to a garbage tip. William's habit of hoarding, which he did not abandon even after a clear warning of change, caused him to be heartbroken over losing his things. The lesson is to return to the upright Devil to realise that those things we possess can possess us in return.

THE STAR .

The Star

The Star represents a time when your client is feeling centred in their life, and does not require exterior structures and routines to give them a sense of security or purpose. This is a card for the sign of Aquarius, and part of the lesson for Aquarians is to release themselves physically from structure and routines which bind, and to make the most of the mind and the imagination. In simple terms the card can represent a holiday, or a period of mental and emotional freedom resulting in fresh ideas and creative projects. Therefore, it can represent a time of recreation or re-creation. It is a card of hopefulness, creativity and faith in life's possibilities.

The figure in this card is fascinated by the pool of water (representing the subconscious mind) and the source of creativity it represents. She is pouring water from two jugs, one onto land and the other into the pool. This represents taking ideas from the imagination and making them tangible in the physical world: the jug being poured onto land shows ideas being made real; the jug being poured back into the pool represents the way ideas often stimulate other ideas.

There are also eight stars, each with eight points. Some see this as representing the eight main chakras (seven in the body and one above the head) aligned to allow the natural flow of creative and spiritual energy into the physical world. This increases the relevance of creativity to this card.

If the Star appears in the answer to a question it can suggest that success will result from a positive attitude and creative solutions to problems. While your client may have tried to cling to possessions in the Devil, now they realise how free they can become without the physical and mental constraints resulting from ownership.

Reversed

The Star reversed suggests that your client lacks faith in life, in themselves or in a viable solution appearing to present problems. They may feel unable to see a viable alternative to the path they presently tread. It is time for them to return to the lesson of the Tower in order to be jolted into wakefulness; sometimes it is only through shock that we awaken to life's potential.

In simple terms, the reversed Star suggests a need for your client to have a holiday (however, this may not rejuvenate them, as they may think about work or daily problems instead of resting), or a rest from life's demands. Returning to the lesson of the Tower is an opportunity to reconnect with life and their spiritual purpose in a real way. Sometimes a sudden shock or loss (the Tower) can awaken us to what is important in life. The Star reversed shows the need for such a shock.

The Moon

In everyday terms the Moon can symbolise a time of preferring to retreat from life into dreams rather than facing life squarely and dealing with situations in a practical manner. Another meaning of the Moon card is that your client is having compelling dreams at night that may be offering them insight into their life and their current spiritual journey through life.

In this card the face in the moon has its eyes closed, suggesting that she is going within herself to seek answers to life's questions. The towers beneath stand far apart, further suggesting isolation, both from the earth (because of their height) and from one another. The dog and the wolf howl (the creatures represent the demands of the conscious mind, of people around and of life itself). The sounds the animals make only drive her further into her dreams and memories.

The pool represents the subconscious mind. The path which calls to her is one taken in dreams at night, through astral travel to other places and dimensions. Although these other places visited in dreams are a welcome escape from the pressures of life, they cannot replace the learning offered in the physical world. If a person remains in the Moon energy they can become unreachable and isolated from their physical body and from others, as depicted by the two towers. In these circumstances their imagination is liable to move from creative to becoming delusional.

When the Moon appears in a layout it is necessary to look closely at what is happening beneath the surface. (Many things can be hidden by moonlight that are clearly visible in the light of day.) Looking beyond exteriors was exactly what I needed to do with Donna. I read for her three times over a thirty-month period, and each time I questioned her about her relationship with her partner, Tom. The Moon card appeared in each relationship layout and I suggested that there were some problems with Tom she needed to face.

Donna denied that any problems existed, and told me that she and Tom were very happy together. I did not push the point, as I believe that people will hear what I have to say when they are ready to hear it and not before. However, the fact that she returned to see me three times suggested that she wanted me to remind her of what she refused to see; that she wanted me to be her eyes and to see those things she could no longer recognise with her own eyes and heart.

During her fourth visit she collapsed into tears, admitting that she had strong reasons to suspect Tom was having an affair. Although it was for the best that she do so, I felt I had been somewhat unfair in insisting that Donna see what I could about Tom, especially when I realised how much she had invested in the dream of their life together. I was gentle with her, as I knew that the coming weeks and months would not be so kind. Facing the truth after a period of self-deception is always painful. Nonetheless, using the picture on the card as an analogy, making peace with the creatures by and in the pool of water is the only way to re-enter the pool comfortably and to replenish your soul with its contents.

As mentioned, another meaning of the Moon card is that powerful dreams at night may be offering your client insight into their life and spiritual journey. This occurred recently with a client who asked me how she could find an answer to her ongoing problems with her young child. He had a very short attention span, and became frustrated and aggressive easily.

I explained that she would find the solutions in her night-time dreams and urged her to start a dream journal. Ten months later she phoned to say that she had been keeping a dream diary and that it resulted in her dreaming about a mineral deficiency in her boy. After seeking tests with several medical and alternative practitioners who confirmed what she had dreamed, she was able to give the boy a mineral supplement which resolved his problems.

Reversed

The Moon reversed can suggest there is less deception in your client's life than previously, both in terms of self-deception and deception of them by others. It is time for your client to return to the Star to restore their faith in life and renew their connection with their spiritual energy source.

Those issues which have caused fear resulting in isolation can be faced squarely now, as the Moon reversed represents a need for your client to face life honestly and not hide from fears created by imagined outcomes. The Star symbolises that from the darkness of night, stars appear to give them hope and perspective. Measuring problems against the backdrop of the night sky is often enough to remind a person of their own insignificance in the greater scheme of things.

The Sun

The Sun represents a time of joy in life's possibilities, and the kind of exuberance children exhibit openly. This is not specifically a card for victory, but rather for the pleasure which comes from knowing that life is good, when it is good. (It is easy to know that life was good when difficulties arise; few of us know at the time when life is perfect.)

However, children often live in the moment and, as a result, they are 'available' for happiness when life offers them sunshine and things for which to be joyous. In the Sun card the orange banner attached to the pole in the child's left hand represents the passion and enthusiasm which were tempered through love in the Strength card. (That is, the lion in the Strength card has become a banner in the sun; the passion and enthusiasm represented by the colour orange feature in both cards.)

Believing in life's possibilities and sharing your energy joyously requires a reliable source of passion and enthusiasm. As mentioned, children usually innately have this enthusiasm, and as long as adults retain their connection to their spiritual side they can access this energy easily.

The Sun is the second card representing the sign of Leo, and so it represents the joy and enthusiasm which Leo people can bring to situations. In a career layout it can signify a career in the public eye, such as acting or singing.

Reversed

The Sun reversed can indicate the existence of a situation from which your client is unable to derive joy or fulfilment. It also represents the dark side of Leo, the sign represented by this card, as it suggests the existence of unhealthy competitiveness.

I witnessed an example of one kind of situation suggested by the Sun reversed some years ago in an introductory Tarot class. A student named Michael had exuded energy and enthusiasm when he arrived on the first day of the course, his extroverted nature suggesting that he was a Knight of Wands. However, his behaviour soon changed, revealing he had the nature of a competitive and spoilt child. He complained that he was unable to ask questions in class, and that the other students were talking over him and excluding him. I could see that this was not the case, but that he had regressed into being a small child demanding all the attention in a room containing fifteen people.

During a demonstration reading it came to light that Michael had been an actor but had abandoned his career abruptly after a bad review almost ten years previously. A pattern emerged of his discarding any activity that did not deliver success early on. As the course continued Michael realised that learning the Tarot was not going to be as easy as he'd first imagined, so he started to look for reasons not to participate. It seemed to me that he was searching for a way to be asked to leave the course, or to storm out and blame us all for his inability to continue, in order to avoid facing the reality that he might only ever be a mediocre reader unless he tried harder.

This epitomises the sort of circumstances represented by the Sun reversed. Fearing imperfection, Michael sought a face-saving way of leaving the class because he was unable to say, 'I don't like this' or 'This is too hard for me right now'. If he had devoted the energy he spent on his classroom tantrums to studying, he would have made an excellent reader. Instead his competitive instinct made enemies of all those students who might have supported him in his endeavour to master the Tarot.

The Sun reversed suggests a need to return to the lesson of the upright Moon, to face yourself and your fears honestly. Michael needed to return to the Moon in order to face his fears that he might not have been very good at reading the Tarot. In looking at these fears squarely, he might very well have decided that they were unfounded, or simply part of a negative learning pattern from the past. Returning to the Moon card allows people such as Michael to cry and to dissolve the anger which has built up. After the tears, they can clearly see what troubles them for what it is. When the fears eventually subside and the Sun returns, they can be happy in the moment once again.

In a career layout the reversed Sun represents competition, often indicating your client's involvement with a career in sales. The reversed Sun can also suggest that your client feels pressured to achieve or perform.

Judgement

In simple terms, the Judgement card represents a time when your client needs to listen to their inner voice and consider the repercussions of their actions. Sometimes the card simply indicates they have a clarity of judgement. Good judgement stems from self-knowledge and is often the basis for lasting success. Sometimes short-term sacrifices are necessary to achieve long-term fulfilment.

On the card the red cross on the flag depicts the meeting of linear time (or time as we know it) and universal time. It suggests that success has been earned; the figures have exercised good judgement and the time is now right for them to reap the harvest of their seeds planted when learning the lesson of the High Priestess.

An example of clarity of judgement and its long-term rewards occurred with Helen, who decided on a career in natural therapies. She studied for six years and despite offers to travel overseas with her friends, Helen kept her eye on her goal. At the age of twenty-six she started her own business; now, at thirty-five, she has a thriving business and takes an overseas holiday for one month every year.

It can be difficult sometimes to appreciate the accomplishments and possessions of someone who is achieving more than you and still value your own way of life. However, having clear judgement involves realising that your path is for you and another's path is for them, and realising what is right for you spiritually in the long term.

Reversed

Judgement reversed suggests your client lacks clear vision of the consequences of their actions. 'Act in haste; repent at leisure' is the saying which encapsulates this card. It can also describe the emptiness which accompanies a lack of awareness of spiritual purpose. Your client may be seeking short-term fulfilment through material goals without any thought of their deeper, spiritual needs.

Bob had a business employing fifteen people. Over the previous eleven years he had built up this company carefully and steadily. He was comfortable with his efforts and he derived a good income from the business. Over a long lunch at his golf club one afternoon, Bob was introduced to Reece, a high-flier who had accumulated an enormous amount of wealth in under five years. Bob was envious of Reece's lifestyle, and Reece offered Bob a piece of the action. Bob's greed was triggered, and soon Reece was filling his head with thoughts of a bigger house, a large yacht and a holiday home in the south of France. What Reece didn't mention was that with increased returns comes increased risk.

Despite having arrived at the club satisfied with himself and his life, Bob left the restaurant with a burning hunger for more than he had; Reece had passed on some of his own innate hunger to Bob. Bob secured the finance necessary to invest in Reece's new deal, and fourteen months later the receivers were called in to dismantle Bob's existing business. Reece's deal had gone sour.

How did all this happen? It happened because Bob didn't stop to use his own judgement. He was afraid that he'd miss out on a chance to be seriously wealthy, and he was 'uncentred' in his decision-making because of Reece's hunger and his own ambitions. After losing his business, the result of all his hard work, Bob realised that cutting corners often doesn't work.

The World

In general terms the World card suggests long-term success resulting from inner balance and harmony. As an answer to specific questions it represents very positive outcomes. In simple terms the World card can represent travel around the world. It can also suggest the existence of a partner from another part of the world, or someone your client will meet while overseas.

The figure on the card depicts success as an ongoing process of having the right mental outlook. She carries her wands lightly for she is aware that success is a state of mind. She achieves the results she desires with minimum effort, because she understands when opportunities will best serve her.

The World appeared as the answer to Edward's question about a film he had directed and entered in a film festival competition. He asked if it would win a prize and I explained that it would do better than he imagined. The film won a top prize, secured him a deal with a studio for two more films, and he was given a budget of five times the amount he'd spent on the original film for each of his subsequent films.

In a spiritual direction layout, the World refers to a balance between the four elements of Fire, Water , Air and Earth, leading to harmony within. Keeping these four elements balanced requires effort and concentration. However, it is worthwhile, because while success can sometimes be a disappointing destination, keeping the elements within balanced gives success a purpose beyond a destination.

Reversed

The World reversed is still a positive card, suggesting that your client has climbed the highest mountain visible, only to arrive at the summit to see that it obscured an even taller mountain. That is, each challenge is being mastered and is then followed by an even greater challenge.

If your client seeks more lasting success they need to return to the Judgement card in order to make an appropriate decision as to which mountain to climb next. If all the mountains are, so to speak, layered in mist, your client cannot see with their eyes which mountain is the tallest. They need to see the mountains with their inner vision, or intuition.

The World reversed can also suggest that your client has travelled from another part of the world to be where they are now, and that soon they will return to their place of origin. It represents the completion of the journey around the world. However, the general description of the card reversed is that although your client has been successful, there are even greater challenges ahead of them, which promise still greater success.

Part Three

★ The Reading Process ★

The obvious difference between an experienced reader and a novice is how they lead the client through the reading process. The experienced reader inspires the client's confidence by their seamless format, starting with a greeting and ending with a wave goodbye.

Although every reader has their own unique style, there are some basic steps which can be followed to make the reading process a smooth event for both you and your client. The following steps are intended to illustrate a full face-to-face personal reading; bear in mind that short market readings and telephone readings require different sets of rules (see below):

1. **Introduction:** Introduce yourself and show the client to their seat. Some light conversation at this point can help them to feel at ease. Ask the client if they've had a Tarot reading before, and briefly detail what you will be doing throughout the reading; for example, that you will give them a general reading, which will be followed by their questions. Telling the client what to expect allows them to plan their approach and therefore get more from the reading.

2. **Instructions:** Show the client how to cut the pack, reversing some cards, and ask them to shuffle it. Have them place the cards one at a time into three piles on the table. They will end up with two piles of twenty-six cards and one pile of twenty-seven cards, provided you include the blank card. Combine the three piles into one, and slide the cards across the table in front of your client.

3. **Selection:** Have the client select the appropriate number of cards for the layout you have in mind, using their non-writing hand and with their eyes closed. Count aloud as the client selects each card, and place the given cards in order on the table.

4. **Silence:** Tell the client that they can open their eyes and that you need a minute to make the layout clear. Spend some time silently observing the cards in front of you. Only a nervous beginner starts talking as soon as the layout is on the table.

5. **Explanation:** Tell the client in detail what you see from the cards before you, and at the end of each layout ask, 'Is this clear to you or would you like me to make something clearer?'. This gives the client a chance to clarify any part of the reading which is confusing to them and prevents them from coming to the end of the reading feeling puzzled.

6. **Questions:** Follow the general reading with several question layouts and a twelve-month layout or a Karma reading (revealing where the client's strengths and weaknesses lie and showing what they can do to become spiritually balanced).

7. **Reminder:** Preface the client's last question with a reminder that it is their final question before the close of the reading. If they have several questions, help them to select which one they'll ask.

8. **Last question/layout:** Complete the last layout, and finish the reading on a positive note, summarising the theme of the reading.

9. **Tape/farewell:** Give the client a tape of the reading and a business card (with the tape), and after you receive your fee escort them out. Recommend they replay the tape in the coming week and again in six months.

10. **Cleanse:** Cleanse yourself by gently brushing over your body with your hands and shaking off any residual psychic energy and/or wash your hands between clients. If you have finished for the day, cleanse the reading room and yourself. In a readers' row (that is, one of a row of readers at a psychic fair or a fete, etc.) you may need to leave the hall or the room in order to cleanse, and time constraints may only allow for cleansing every four or five clients.

A market reading is usually only 20–30 minutes, so you have time for a general reading and one or two questions. You start with a quick hello and move straight into Step 2. You have less time to pause and reflect as in Step 4. Steps 9 and 10 are also unnecessary.

In a telephone reading you cut the cards, reverse, and, after asking the caller's name, shuffle the pack on behalf of the client while thinking of it. You select the cards while mentally asking, 'What does the future hold for —', or the client's specific question. Laying the cards out as you would for a face-to-face client, you continue with Steps 5, 6, 7, and 8.

★ The Basic Questions ★

Most clients seek a reading because they want answers to life's fundamental questions. These questions may cover personal relationships, career, finances, family and health, and your task as a reader is to determine exactly what question your client is asking in each category. To help you with this, each category is listed below, and possible questions within each category are also listed.

These are by no means the only questions within each category, but they are a useful reference.

Personal relationships

1. What does the future hold for me in personal relationships generally?
2. What does the future hold for mine and my partner's relationship specifically?
3. What can I do to improve our relationship?
4. Is it wise for me to pursue this relationship?
5. Is it wise for me to pursue a relationship with [another party]?
6. What is the lesson for me in my current relationship?

Career

1. What does the future hold for me in my career generally?
2. What does the future hold for me in my current career?
3. Is it wise for me to continue in this particular career ?
4. Will I still be in this job in [x number of] months?
5. Am I suited to a career in [alternative occupation]?
6. What is the lesson for me in my current career?

Finances

1. What does the future hold for me financially?
2. What can I do to ensure financial success for myself?
3. What am I currently doing to prevent myself from becoming financially secure?
4. Is it wise for me to sell my shares in [x number of] months?
5. Is it wise for me to invest in [suggested investment]?
6. What behaviour patterns do I need to change to ensure financial stability for myself?

Family

1. What does the future hold for my mother/father [etc.]?
2. What does the future hold for my brother's/sister's [etc.] business?
3. Is it wise for my mother/father [etc.] to purchase the house at [address]?
4. What does the future hold for my mother's/father's [etc.] health?
5. What can my family teach me this year?

Health

1. What does the future hold for my health?
2. What does my physical health currently reveal about my attitudes to life?
3. Is it wise to have an operation?
4. Is there a viable alternative to an operation at this stage?
5. Will osteopathy/chiropractic/massage/Reiki/meditation/yoga [etc.] resolve my current spinal problems?
6. How can I maintain and improve my physical health?

   (Please note: Unless you are medically trained, or trained in an alternative health field, ensure that you recommend your client seeks confirmation by a qualified medical or alternative health practitioner of all that you have said to them about their health.)

Spirituality

1. What is my current spiritual lesson?
2. What are my current spiritual strengths?
3. What do I need to learn in order to fulfil my life's purpose?
4. What do I need to resolve from my past in order to pursue my life's purpose?
5. How can I confirm that I am on my own path spiritually?
6. How can I contact and communicate with my higher, or spiritually evolved, self?

Travel

1. What does the future hold for me regarding travel?
2. Will I travel overseas in the next twenty-four months?
3. Is it wise/safe for me to travel to [location] this year as planned?
4. Will I have enough money to travel to [location] as planned this year?
5. Will I be able to earn an income as I travel?
6. What will I learn from this travelling?
7. What is my lesson in my forthcoming travelling to [location]?

Children

1.   What does the future hold for my child [the child's name]?
2.   Is it wise to encourage my child in the study of music?
3.   What is the underlying cause of my child's nail-biting/bed-wetting/ nightmares/inability to learn [etc.]?
4.   What do I need to concentrate on developing in my child?
5.   What can I do to help my child to be happy?
6.   What is my child here to teach me spiritually?

★ Yes/No Questions ★

Wording a question so that it can be answered 'yes' or 'no' is useful if you want to eliminate several alternatives in order to focus on the most suitable path for your client. An example of this might be if your client asks about financial investment and they have five alternatives. The alternatives are:

1.   Investing in shares
2.   Purchasing a house
3.   Starting a business
4.   Buying a share of a friend's business
5.   Placing the funds in a cash management fund.

Faced with the above list of options the obvious choice is to eliminate some of them by asking yes/no questions. The questions might be worded this way.

• Is it wise for me to invest this money in [the particular shares]?
• Will an investment in . . . be worthwhile?

Determining the answers takes skill, and this develops with experience. (Hopefully you will develop this skill before someone approaches you regarding the investment of their life savings.) For a clear 'yes' answer, both the *answer* card (the fourth card in a seven-card spread) and the *outcome* card (the seventh card in a seven-card spread) need to be upright and in agreement with one another. A sample layout follows.

Q 1: Is it wise for me to invest in shares this year?

Interpretation:

Please note this is only one interpretation of the cards shown, and that another reader may see additional things in this layout and still be right. Adding your own intuition to the logical meanings can also increase the amount of information given to the client.

Card 1: The past

The Six of Wands suggests that there has been financial success in the past.

Perhaps the client has invested in shares previously and this investment has paid off handsomely.

Card 2:   The present
The Ten of Pentacles describes a situation where the client is cashed up, possibly with solid investment opportunities around them.

Card 3:   The near future
The Death card suggests that change is coming, if not in the share market, then in the companies in which the client hopes to invest. It can also suggest that the client will undergo a transformation in the coming months, and their needs may be different then.

Card 5:   The energy surrounding the question
The Knight of Wands describes an almost cavalier attitude to investment at this point, and an eagerness to move ahead with financial plans. The client may have confidence in the share market at this time, and an enthusiasm about being a part of it.

Card 6:   The client's attitude to investment in the share market
The Four of Pentacles suggests that the client is keen to hold on to their money, and may prefer a more solid investment. This card may detail the client's need to invest in blue chip companies with sound business management and solid track records.

Card 7:   The outcome
The Ten of Cups reversed suggests that an investment in shares at this point could leave the client feeling excluded from groups of people who are important to them. This could refer to fellow investors or to those from the client's own peer group. The fact that this card is reversed suggests it is unwise for the client to invest in shares at this point.

Card 4:   The answer
The upright Hierophant card suggests that the client may feel the need to invest where others are investing, or have an inner need to conform to what is expected of them. Being an upright Five, the Hierophant suggests that this approach is narrow-minded, and that there may be other more suitable approaches to investment at this time.

If your client then asks their second question, you would lay out another seven cards.

Q 2: Is it wise for me to purchase a house this year?

Interpretation:

This is a basic interpretation done before any additional cards were added.

Card 1:   **The past**

The Two of Cups suggests that there may have been a house purchased with another person in the past. This arrangement worked well as they were equal partners, and both felt fulfilled by the arrangement.

Card 2:   **The present**

The Emperor in the present and the King of Swords in the surrounding energy position suggest people from the legal profession giving advice. Perhaps these are advisers around your client, counselling them about their current financial affairs.

The Emperor can indicate a disciplined man who is an advisor, or your client, if they fit the Emperor's description.

If not describing a person, the Emperor card suggests that your client needs to be disciplined, practical and unemotional in their approach to buying a house, to prevent decisions being made on purely emotional grounds.

Card 3:   **The near future**

The blank card highlights the fact that life has plans for your client which are bigger than those they have for themselves.

Other opportunities which may not presently be visible will appear to your client in the next few months, perhaps making the house option redundant.

Card 5:   **Surrounding energies**

The King of Swords can describe a legal or professional person currently advising your client.

It can also highlight the need for clarity of thought when weighing up the purchase of a house.

Card 6:   **The client's attitude**

The client or someone close to the client (a woman) may be cautious. Perhaps they have vivid memories of previous difficulties involved in owning property and view purchasing a house negatively.

The fears are greater than the hopes with this Queen reversed, and there is a possibility that the client has unresolved issues about owning or living in a previous house.

Card 7:   **The outcome**

The Page of Swords reversed can suggest a child is involved. If so, it is a talkative, mentally curious child.

If the card represents an aspect of the client, it can be describing a state of hesitation, when they have many options but cannot make a decision.

Unrealistic plans are also suggested by this reversed Page, such as an intention of your client to view houses they simply cannot afford.

Card 4:   **The answer**

The Five of Cups describes grief and loss, which related to the question can mean several things. It can describe the loss of a relationship which resulted in the division of property, and that provided the client with the money to invest in a house in the first place.

It could signify that the client will feel alone if they purchase a house at this point. This aloneness may be the result of restricted finances, having to move to a neighbourhood far away from where they previously lived. The river in this card separating the figure from the castle gives the impression that the client wants to live where they cannot.

The answer is no, it is not wise to purchase a house this year.

If at this point your client wants to know about romantic relationships, they can ask about them. This is likely, because you have mentioned it in relation to their changes in lifestyle and having money to invest due to a recent divorce. They can return to investment questions afterwards.

Sometimes a client will attempt to ask a question within a question, such as 'Would it be wise to invest in a flat instead of a house?' or 'Is it wise to leave real estate investments alone until next year?'. These questions cannot be readily answered by examining the above layout, as it was centred around another specific question.

As the reader it is your task to explain that they can ask those questions as separate layouts or leave them in order to pursue more important questions. Often the client is not prepared to ask these incidental questions as separate layouts. Sometimes they are trying to ask fifteen questions during a one-hour session despite being advised that they will have time for up to six questions.

It is better to be firm with your client so that they don't invest thousands of dollars in purchasing a flat on the strength of a passing comment you made as you gathered cards up from a previous question.

Q 3. What does the future hold for me in romantic relationships?

Interpretation:

Please note that extra cards are usually added to any layout which ends with the Death card, so as to leave the reading on a positive note. Although the Death card is a positive and necessary card, clients often fear it and it can leave them with feelings of dread.

Card 1:   The past

The Nine of Wands describes a state of caution or nervousness regarding relationships, often due to past experiences. The client may not have wanted to be in a love relationship or to start a new one during the past two years, due to earlier hurts.

Card 2:   The present

Temperance suggests that emotions have settled now, leaving the client with a clear view of relationship possibilities. Their attitude is positive and their life is balanced at present.

Card 3:   The near future

The Page of Wands can suggest an enthusiastic approach to starting a new relationship. It can also indicate an enthusiastic child or young person being around the client in the coming months.

Added card:

A card has been added for clarity: the Queen of Wands. This can describe the client (if female) or the partner of a male client. This woman is passionate, enthusiastic and forthright. She could be a Sagittarian, as the Temperance card is also a card for the sign of Sagittarius. The Queen of Wands is often a fire sign (Aries, Leo or Sagittarius) or generally someone of a passionate temperament.

If the client is male the card can mean the start of a relationship or a new stage of relationship with an independent woman. In a layout for a female, it can describe her starting afresh with confidence and inner strength.

Card 5:   Surrounding energies

The Hierophant describes some pressure from others to have a particular type of relationship, as it shows the need to conform to expected patterns in relationships. In simple terms, this can signify the pressure from others (peers, friends or family) to select a partner from the same cultural background and a person who shares a similar view of life.

Card 6:   Attitude

The Ace of Cups describes the client's attitude as one of hopefulness, confidence and clarity; they view relationships as spiritually and emotionally uplifting experiences offering fulfilment. The client is therefore hopeful of starting or being in a fulfilling relationship.

Card 7:   The Outcome

The Death card in the outcome position describes the need to shed old relationships or relationship patterns to make way for a new and more fulfilling type of relationship. The client must release these before the new partner can approach them.

Added cards:

Two cards were added: the Five of Pentacles reversed and the Page of Pentacles.

The Five of Pentacles reversed describes walking away from past relationships without regret. It is a card for releasing what you know you don't need in life; in this case, a particular person or type of relationship.

The Page of Pentacles describes the start of a relationship where the client feels young again or new to the particular type of relationship. It can also suggest a child is involved in the situation; this child is serious, conservative and realistic.

Card 4:   The Answer

The Lovers reversed concerns the decision whether to stay with a particular person, or type of person, or to move forward to a new person, or type of relationship. The fact it is reversed suggests that the client is likely to remain with the current partner or type of partner at this point.

Added card:

The Queen of Cups was added here, suggesting in a man's layout that there will be a Queen of Cups woman around him. The Lovers reversed suggests remaining with the existing person or in the existing situation, rather than pursuing someone new. In a woman's layout the Queen of Cups can mean a decision about how she wants to approach relationships.

★ The One Card Cut ★

The One Card Cut is the simplest method for gleaning information from the cards, and can operate as an exception to the reading-for-yourself rule. (Ordinarily, of course, I recommend that you don't read for yourself; however, this recommendation is rarely heeded so, if you *must* read for yourself, simple One Card Cuts are acceptable.) Simple, practical yes/no questions are suitable for the One Card Cuts; it is not the most accurate of readings as only one card is used to give the whole answer. It is not recommended as a reading method for complicated or important questions. Therefore, simple questions such as 'Should I arrange an appointment with my hairdresser for next Wednesday?' are suitable for it but not 'Will we be at war with [name of country] in the next three months?'.

The steps are as follows:

1.   Briefly shuffle the pack, reversing the cards three or four times during the shuffling process.
2.   Place the pack face downward on the table and close your eyes.
3.   While thinking of the question, cut the pack with your non-writing hand, turning the cards in your hand over to reveal the face of the card cut. Remember to turn

the cut cards over as one unit, sideways to ensure the card remains as it was (upright or reversed) when it was cut.

4.   Study the card before you and relate it to the question you asked.

5.   If this card doesn't make sense to you, slide it onto the table to reveal the card immediately beneath it. These two cards combine to answer your question.

(Resist the temptation to slide fifteen cards from the top of the cut pack one by one until you arrive at a card which is perfectly suitable for your desired outcome.)

Don't be tempted to cut the cards for every minor decision you have throughout the course of the average day:

Should I book a cab ahead of time?

Should I ring Marianne before dinner tonight?

Is it wise to cancel the newspaper?

Two cuts for a decision between cereal or toast for breakfast is bordering upon addiction. It begs the final question, 'Is it wise for me to stop asking pointless questions?'.

However, there are times when a series of One Card Cuts may prove worthwhile, as in the case of Emily, who was about to set up practice as a professional reader, having done 120 readings and successfully completed her written and practical examinations. Emily wanted to know where best to advertise her services to maximise her returns. (There is an old adage in advertising which states, 'Half of all advertising money is wasted, but which half?'.)

Emily spent a week looking through magazines and newspapers, and seeking out noticeboards, before preparing a list of possible places in which to advertise. Her list contained six possible advertising avenues when she sat down to cut the cards. She cleared her mind and asked, 'Is it wise for me to advertise in … this month?' for each of the six avenues.

The cards gave a clear 'yes' to two of the six avenues, but said 'no' to a free local newspaper which she had felt sure was a worthwhile place in which to advertise. She went ahead and advertised in the two places to which the cards had said yes, and kept an eye on the newspaper which had received a clear no, to see why the cards had declined it.

At the end of the month she was satisfied that the cards had been accurate, as it had rained heavily on three of the four delivery days for that weekly newspaper that month. As wet newspapers don't get read, Emily knew that to have advertised in it would have been a waste of money.

Emily's question to the cards had been precise, limiting the advertising period to one month, as her budget was limited; she had laid the groundwork, researching the advertising possibilities before sitting down to cut the cards. This is an example of the powerful combination of logic, intuition and practical application. Logic and intuition make good partners.

If you prepare for your card cut with some groundwork, you can get a clearer answer by asking a more precise question. The clearest questions receive the clearest answers. If Emily had asked generally if it were wise to advertise in the local weekly newspaper, she might have wasted three out of the first four weeks of advertising money.

If your client has an important question they need a full reading, not a One Card Cut. If you are a reader and you need a full reading, you of course need to find another reader. That in itself can be a challenge, as the moment you find a good reader you can be assured that she has booked a removalist for the next weekend because she's moving 1000 km away without any intention of returning. Readers can be like circus folk, always moving on.

I have a friend who, when she wants a reading and doesn't have a regular reader, phones me to ask when I'm conducting my next examinations. Students have to give a reading with a tape to a stranger as a part of their practical exams, and she receives a free reading and is able to assess the reader. If she likes the reader then she becomes their first regular client. I've seen her make bookings with readers for full private readings before she's left the exams. When the particular reader moves away or retires, she phones me again and repeats the whole procedure.

★ Reversed Cards ★

To allow for all the shades of grey in life, it is essential to include reversed cards in readings. Reading only with upright cards suggests that you want to tell your client only *some* of those things they need to know in order to make their important decisions. Taken to its natural conclusion, if you are only prepared to read upright cards, why not remove any of those cards which might make the client uncomfortable, such as Death, the Tower, the Devil, the Three of Swords and the Ten of Swords? That's only one step away from reading with playing cards, and leaving all the spiritual lessons of the Major Arcana out of the equation. When a card appears reversed, it suggests that the client has not learned the upright meaning of the previous card, and that they need to return to the previous card to master the lesson contained therein.

Reading with reversed cards is essential if you want to give answers to yes/no questions, as it gives a more accurate answer (reversed cards in the answer [fourth card] position or the outcome [seventh card] position usually give a 'no' answer). When you consider the importance of some questions clients are likely to ask you, there is a great deal of pressure to be right. For example, they may inquire: 'Is it wise to purchase this house?'; 'Will my son be sentenced to jail time at the end of his trial?'; 'If I stay on at work, will the company be able to afford to pay my superannuation when I retire in four years?'; 'Is it better to leave work now while the company can still afford to pay me my entitlements?'.

Students often complain that remembering reversed card meanings is difficult. However, there is a simple method that requires you only to remember the upright meanings and enables you to interpret reversed cards easily: just remember that the client has to return to the previous card to learn its lesson.

If the Seven of Wands appears reversed as the answer to a question about starting a new business, it means that the client needs to return to the Six of Wands to enjoy a period of stability resulting from clearly focusing on their goals before they are ready to tackle anything more at this stage. The Seven reversed shows a man struggling with overwhelming obstacles; by returning to the Six he simplifies his approach to achieving his goals, and triumphs.

If Temperance appears reversed as the answer to a relationship question, it suggests that the client is unable to see the long-term effects of their actions and decisions, and that they need to return to the upright Death (the previous) card. By surrendering to the change signified by Death, unnecessary people and things will be removed, clearing the path for them to see clearly the long-term effects of their actions.

An Ace of Wands reversed indicates that the client is unable to start new projects because they have too many things weighing them down. An Ace of Swords reversed implies confused thinking that delays planning. When the Fool reversed appears in a layout it suggests hasty, or simply foolish, action. It can also show the client is afraid to trust himself or herself and relies upon others for advice. However, the Aces reversed and the Fool reversed have no obvious cards preceding them to which the client can return.

When an Ace appears reversed the client should return to the Ten of the same suit. In returning to the Ten of Wands they can see what is weighing them down and so recognise the need to delegate some of their responsibilities before they can start a new project. When the Ace of Swords appears reversed the client needs to return to the Ten of Swords, as the many swords it depicts represent the beliefs about life that hinder the client thinking clearly. When the Fool appears reversed, the client must return to the upright World card so that they may know their place in the world and in the universe; this can help them to know which choices and actions are appropriate.

Kings reversed can return to the upright Knights of the same suit, and Queens reversed can return to the upright Pages of their suit. More often than not, the reversed Court cards reflect the person's negative qualities (for example, immaturity) being uppermost. This is shown by the reversed Pages being either very young children physically or still very young emotionally.

If you are confused about the meaning of a reversed card, ask the client to add another to the card in question, as this can sometimes clarify things. Sometimes you need to engage the client in conversation to establish what is going on, so that you can apply the correct meaning to the reversed card in question.

It's a gross simplification to suggest that all reversed cards have negative meanings. Aside from the Devil and all the Fives (which are *more* positive reversed), most reversed cards, as discussed, simply mean that your client has not yet mastered a particular lesson. Your task as a reader is to point out to them what they need to do in order to master it. If they have learnt all their lessons they are unlikely to consult you in the first place.

A metaphor for the reversed cards and the lessons contained within them is repeating a year at school. If you do not successfully complete Grade Five you have the opportunity to repeat the year in order to master the course content. The reversed cards take this one step further: if you are not coping with Grade Five, you have the opportunity to return to Grade Four to reacquaint yourself with the lessons you have successfully completed. This may give you the confidence to approach Grade Five afresh so that you can master its lessons.

On a lighter note, I telephoned a Queen of Wands friend recently and asked her how she was feeling.

'Reversed. That's how I'm feeling. Bloody reversed,' she answered, and we both laughed. I guess we all have 'reversed' days.

Part Four

★ Layouts ★

There are countless layouts used for determining the past, the present and the future. Below are several simple ones. Complicated layouts are unnecessary, unless you seek to impress or to confuse your client. Your task as a reader is to clarify the client's life, and simple, straightforward layouts can assist you with this.

The Seven Card Layout

This is a simple layout which can be used for general readings or for specific questions.

Method:

1. The client shuffles the pack, inverting (reversing) the cards occasionally.
2. You ask the client which hand they write with so as to ensure they select the cards with their non-writing hand.
3. You slide the cards out into a line, from which the client selects seven cards at random. This selection is done with their non-writing hand and with their eyes closed. If it is a general reading the client does not think of anything in particular. If it is to be a question layout, then the client concentrates upon an agreed question as cards are selected. You need to know the question they are asking.
4. You place the cards on the table in the order they are selected.

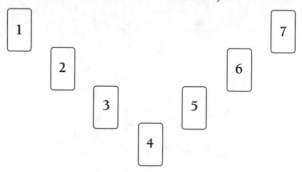

You then interpret the cards according to the positions listed below.

1. **The past:** Up to twenty-four months ago.
2. **The present:** Four weeks either side of today.
3. **The near future:** Usually up to three months into the future.
4. **The client/answer:** This represents the client at present and what is occurring in their life. In a question layout this card represents the answer to the question, and then it is read last, despite being the fourth card.

5. **Surrounding energies:** This shows the people or circumstances surrounding the client or relevant to the question at present.
6. **Attitude:** The client's hopes and fears are shown in this position. If it is a question layout, the hopes and fear surrounding the question are shown here.
7. **Outcome:** The outcome of present circumstances up to twenty-four months from now is shown here. If it is a question layout, then the outcome of the question is shown here.

The Action and Consequences Layout

This layout is designed for a client who wants to know what has caused or contributed to their present circumstances, and what they can do to effect a particular outcome. Five cards are selected, as the client thinks of a statement such as 'My current job' or 'My relationship with Jon'.

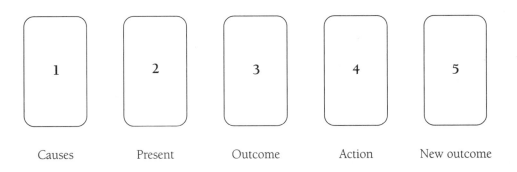

| 1 | 2 | 3 | 4 | 5 |
| Causes | Present | Outcome | Action | New outcome |

1. The cause of the current circumstances. This card can represent the issue causing your beliefs, which in turn have led you to your present circumstances.
2. The present circumstances. The job or relationship with which the client is presently concerned.
3. The outcome of the present circumstances.
4. Action to take for an alternate desired outcome.
5. The new outcome resulting from the action taken in card number 4.

This layout is designed to give the client some control over their destiny by showing them the consequences of their actions before the actions are taken. By examining some of the causes of their current circumstances, the client hopefully can put the given situation into perspective before deciding upon a course of action.

The Horoscope Layout

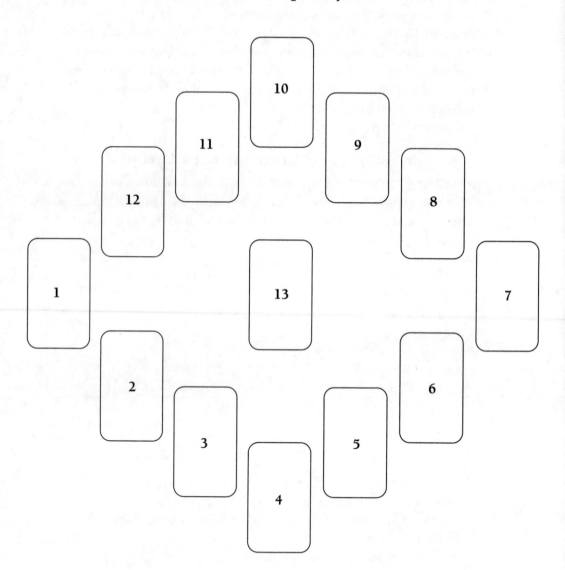

The cards are detailed below.

1. **Persona:** How the client presents themselves to the world generally.
2. **Values:** What the client values, or needs to value, both within themselves and materially.
3. **Communication:** This card shows the client's ability to communicate with those in their immediate environment at home (with neighbours, siblings and relatives) and at work. Short trips are also shown here.
4. **Home environment:** The client's home or home feeling.
5. **Creativity:** The creative energies available to the client, and opportunities for self-expression and financial speculation. Children are also shown in this position.
6. **Health, work and service:** This is not about career, but about the client's day-to-day working environment. Physical and mental health and wellbeing are also shown in this position.
7. **Relationships:** Partnerships and relationships; what friends can teach you.
8. **Transformation:** Legacies, taxes, inner transformation and regeneration are all shown here.
9. **Higher learning:** Philosophy, longer journeys, and adult learning and education.
10. **Career:** The client's position in the world and worldly achievements.
11. **Friends:** Types of friendships preferred, and hopes and wishes are shown.
12. **Secrets:** Hidden fears and worries are shown here, along with sacrifices for spiritual advancement.
13. **The year ahead in general terms.**

The Three Generations Layout

The Three Generations Layout is useful when a client wants to glimpse the bigger picture, as it enables them to see what patterns of behaviour and beliefs have been passed down through three generations of their family.

As the reader you need to ask how many children the client has, because they will be selecting two cards for each person involved in this layout.

The card positions represent:

Father	**Mother**
Client	**Client's partner**
Son	**Daughter**

Two cards are selected for each of the above and they are positioned as below.

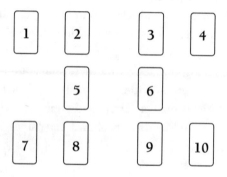

1. The father's negative traits.
2. The father's positive traits.
3. The mother's negative traits.
4. The mother's positive traits.
5. The client's nature.
6. The nature of the client's partner.
7. The son's learned negative traits.
8. The son's learned positive traits.
9. The daughter's learned negative traits.
10. The daughter's learned positive traits.

If you wish, you can add a card to each of the children to see what might balance their learned negative traits.

Cards in combination

Meaning	Cards which can confirm this interpretation
Death	Death, The Tower, blank card, Judgement, Ten, Six, Four or Three of Swords. You need at least four of any of these cards to suggest a physical death.
Karmic situations/lessons	Justice, Judgement or the Star
Legalities forthcoming	Justice, King of Swords, Five of Swords
Meditation	Four of Cups and Swords, the High Priestess or the Hanged Man
Money	Earned: Six of Pentacles, Eight or Nine of Pentacles Being spent: Ace, Four or Six of Pentacles, all reversed Lack of: Ace, Two, Nine or Ten of Pentacles, all reversed, Five of Pentacles upright Borrowed: Six and Ten of Pentacles Saved: Ace and Four of Pentacles
Moving house	Knight of Wands, Four or Three of Wands
Pregnancy	The Empress, Nine of Pentacles with any of the four Pages in the future position
Relationship commitment	Six of Wands, Eight of Pentacles, Four of Wands, Ten of Cups Marriage: Three of Cups (the celebration), the Empress (domestic stability)
Study	Three or Eight of Pentacles, Ace of Swords, Temperance Psychic/spiritual study: the High Priestess Study of law: Justice Religious/philosophic studies: the Hierophant Self-exploration: the Hermit Study to benefit your client's career, or practical plans: the Devil
Travel	Temperance, the Knight, Ace, Three or Eight of Wands, Six of Swords By air: Page of Swords, Eight of Wands By road/rail: the Chariot with the Eight or Three of Wands Overseas: Eight of Wands, Six of Swords
Vivid dreams	The Moon, Nine of Swords

★ Designing Your Own Layout ★

Designing a layout to suit your needs is a relatively simple process. When you have identified what information you want from a layout, you can then decide how many cards are necessary to give it to you. Devising a layout to suit your's and the client's needs can be both practical and rewarding.

An example of this might be the following. James is planning to travel to England to speak at a convention and to sign copies of his latest book. He may choose to ask four or five questions about the proposed trip using the Seven Card Layout, or I could devise a layout expressly about the issues involved.

So, what questions does James have about the planned trip to England?

1.   Will it be financially successful?
2.   Is it wise to visit England at the time currently planned?
3.   Will I feel content with the outcome upon my return home?
4.   What obstacles await me in the pursuit of my plans?
5.   What is the underlying spiritual lesson for me in attending this convention?

Instead of asking five individual questions I can design the layout to answer them all. James shuffles the pack and selects five cards. Their positions are as follows.

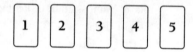

1.   The financial aspects of the planned trip.
2.   Whether it is wise to visit at the currently intended time.
3.   How James will feel about the trip and the talk upon his return home.
4.   The obstacles (if any) James can expect in this trip.
5.   The underlying spiritual lesson in visiting England to deliver a talk at the convention.

It is essential that the reader determines how many cards will be selected and what each position means before the client selects any cards. It's hardly an effective reading if you decide after the cards have been selected that the best ones are about the client's relationship and the worst ones are about their career.

One reader I know works in a shop where she gives fifteen-minute readings which have to be clear and concise. She has designed a layout which answers the three basic concerns her clients have: relationship, career and financial issues. With these three issues in mind you may choose to design a layout such as the one below.

The Three Issues Layout

The client shuffles the cards, cutting the pack and inverting the cards three or four times. The reader then fans the cards across the table into a gentle arc, allowing the client to select six cards with their non-writing hand. When the client has selected the six cards, the reader then asks for another three cards, placing them in the order shown below.

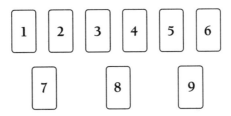

The positions are as follows:

1. Current relationship circumstances.
2. Future relationship circumstances.
7. The underlying lesson for the client in relationships at present.
3. Current career circumstances.
4. Future career circumstances.
8. The underlying lesson for the client in career at present.
5. Current financial circumstances.
6. Future financial circumstances.
9. The underlying lesson for the client regarding present finances.

This layout is designed for readings limited by time constraints. In full one-hour readings this kind of layout is unnecessary as each area is explored in greater depth.

The Seven-Year Cycle Layout

For those seeking a glimpse of the bigger picture, the Seven-Year Cycle Layout is useful for a partial, or even a whole, life reading. It is most useful when the client needs to know what period of their life is adversely affecting them presently. This layout can also be used with specific questions in mind, such as 'Which period of my life has most affected my attitudes to money?'; or 'From which period of my life do I have the most unresolved issues?'; or 'From which period of my life does my fear of horses stem?'.

A word of caution: this reading is best done when the client is feeling positive. If they are feeling sensitive and the cards are negative (particularly the future seven-year period), such a reading may linger in the client's mind for many years. Resist the temptation to read the remainder of the client's life, as you're likely to end up with the Death card, the Tower or the blank card. Of course, we are all going to die eventually, but knowing the age at which this will take place is not helpful to your clients, and, indeed, it may panic them. If your client is consulting you from the intensive care unit of the local hospital, avoid this layout or prepare for uncontrolled sobbing.

Method:
The client selects one card for each seven-year period of their life. That means one card for each seven-year period up to their present age and for, at most, seven years ahead.

So, Bradley sits down for a reading and he is thirty-six years of age. He will select six cards, taking him up to forty-two years of age.

Card 1:	0–7 years
Card 2:	7–14 years
Card 3:	14–21 years
Card 4:	21–28 years
Card 5:	28–35 years
Card 6:	35–42 years

Bradley essentially wants to know which period of his life is affecting him most at present. The cards selected are listed below:

Bradley selected two cards for position 2, thinking that he had only one card in his hand. I included the extra card for the sake of clarity.

Interpretation:

1. **0–7 years:** Temperance reversed
    This period was chaotic, and Bradley was unable to glimpse where he was heading as he grew to adulthood. Perhaps his home life contained a great deal of upheaval or he moved houses often in that first seven years.

2. **7–14 years**: the Knight of Wands; the Hermit reversed
   Filled with enthusiasm, Bradley was active but unable to reflect upon his past actions in order to learn from them. The influence of a Sagittarian person is possible, as both the Temperance and the Knight of Wands are cards for the sign of Sagittarius. The Hermit reversed suggests that he had started reflecting on his past actions when alone.

3. **14–21 years**: the Emperor reversed
   Bradley exhibited poor discipline and may have lacked adult male role models. He may have been somewhat reckless in these years.

4. **21–28 years**: the Hanged Man reversed
   This was a difficult period for Bradley, as he needed to stop and reflect upon his past actions and decisions about life, but he is likely to have struggled against this. The Hanged Man reversed suggests that Bradley was restless, but powerless to change his life until he recognised the need to clear away some of his emotional baggage in order to know his true purpose.

5. **28–35 years**: the Seven of Swords
   Through this period Bradley was hiding from life and attempting to control his destiny through using his mind. He was adaptable but did not reveal himself emotionally to those close to him.

6. **35–42 years**: the King of Cups
   Bradley is maturing into the King of Cups, and he is emotionally available, self-disciplined and is likely to choose a creative and/or emotionally rewarding career. The chaos of the early years is behind him now, and ahead lie opportunities with which he is emotionally equipped to deal.

Before I completed the reading I pointed out to Bradley the possible influence of people of three different astrological signs. These were Sagittarius (Temperance and the Knight of Wands), Virgo (the Hermit) and Aries (the Emperor). He confirmed that he has a sister who is a Sagittarian and his parents were a Virgo and an Aries.

★ Sample Readings ★

Claire sat down with a specific career question, expecting to have her hopes confirmed. When I tell a client something they haven't expected, it is my task to suggest questions which can help them toward the information they seek.

Claire asked if she would be offered an interstate job by a company who had interviewed her the previous day. The question was, 'Will I be offered this position?'.

Will I be offered this position?

Past: Seven of Pentacles

'It appears that you have become satisfied with your career efforts, and been thinking about adding to your skills to improve your career prospects.'

Present: Two of Pentacles

'It's likely you'll have two or more choices of career path, so examine your options carefully. You're also weighing up the costs involved in relocating for this job.'

Near Future: Eight of Swords

'You may feel restricted if you wait for this position, and if you accept it you may feel limited in what you can achieve in the job.'

Surrounding energy: Eight of Pentacles reversed

'The reversed Eight of Pentacles suggests you are no longer committed to your current job, or that the company who have interviewed you are not committed to hiring you. '
(At this point the reader can request another card to determine the card meaning.)

Additional card: Six of Pentacles reversed

'You are likely to be leaving your job soon (within four weeks), so keep your eyes open for opportunities.'

Attitude (hopes and fears): King of Cups

'Is there a man interstate that you're interested in?'

'Yes. My ex-partner moved there seven months ago and we've been in touch on the phone quite a bit lately. I'm not sure how things will go with Ferdi. Does it say what the future holds there?'

'No, that's another question, which we'll come to after this.'

Outcome: The Chariot reversed

'The reversed Chariot card suggests that you won't be offered this position as expected.'

Answer: Page of Pentacles reversed

'The reversed Page suggests that you won't be working in the position, and with the reversed Chariot as the outcome, it may take some time before you give up hope of being offered it. (The Chariot is a reversed number Seven, suggesting not to hold on too long.)

'In short, I don't see you being offered this position. Now I'd like you to select another two cards, please.'

(These are placed either side of the Two of Pentacles in the present position to highlight the two alternatives.)

Additional card 1: Ten of Pentacles

'This suggests an offer from a large company or organisation. Is the company in question a large organisation?'

'No, it's only about fifteen people, I guess.'

Additional card 2: The Wheel of Fortune

'The upright Wheel of Fortune suggests improvements in career circumstances and opportunities, so although you won't be offered the job in question, other opportunities are around you within the next four weeks. This is confirmed by the reversed Six of Pentacles, which can represent the act of leaving a job.'

After this layout it was my task as a reader to narrow the focus of Claire's attention to other possible job opportunities and to the man who had appeared in her first question.

'Would you like to ask me about Ferdi, about your career generally, about another specific job or career direction, or about something else entirely?'

'I'd like to look at the future with Ferdi, especially if I'm not going to be offered this position interstate.'

'There are several possible questions I can see, so I'll give you the choice. As I see it, you can ask:

1. What does the future hold for our relationship?
2. Is it wise to pursue a relationship with Ferdi?
3. What does the future hold for me in love relationships generally?

'This last question is a general one and not limited to Ferdi. Do any of these questions appeal to you, or do you have a different and more suitable question?'

'Oh, I want to ask them all.'

'You can; asking them one at a time. Which question is your most important one?'

'What does the future hold for us and is it wise to pursue one with him?'

'That's actually two questions in one. Let's take each question one by one.' (It is important to know the question your client is asking so as to avoid ambiguous ones. It also helps you to avoid being asked two or three questions at once.)

She paused for a moment to decide which question to ask and then spoke.

'What does the future hold for Ferdi and me?'

'Sure. Then, as you think of that question, I'd like you to select another seven cards with your non-writing hand and with your eyes closed.'

(I shuffled the cards briefly, having placed those from the previous question back into the pack.)

What does the future hold for Ferdi and me in the relationship?

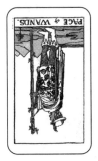

Past: Ace of Wands

'There was an enthusiastic start to this relationship or to a new stage of the relationship in the past. You may have travelled together, as the Wands Ace describes physical movement and action.'

Present: Eight of Cups

'You're considering walking away from this opportunity as you feel you've outgrown it.

This isn't a disaster but a realisation that you have other opportunities which may help you to grow more than this relationship presently does.'

Near future: Page of Wands reversed

'There are likely to be delays in starting a new stage of this relationship or in resuming your love relationship with Ferdi.'

Surrounding energy: Ten of Wands reversed

'The reversed Ten suggests one of you is weighed down with work responsibilities and may be consumed by career obligations. This may hinder attempts to pursue the relationship.'

Attitude (hopes and fears): Blank

'The blank card in this position suggests that you don't know what you want in a relationship with Ferdi, but you hope it will be good. It's the hope you'll find a relationship you never knew you always wanted.'

Outcome: Hierophant reversed

'The reversed Hierophant represents a need to open yourself to opportunities, as it is a reversed Five. This can mean that you can pursue an unusual type of relationship with Ferdi or that life will provide you with suitable relationship opportunities if you remain open minded.'

Answer: Eight of Pentacles reversed

'Your commitment to this relationship is likely to wane over the next two years, and it's unlikely you'll remain as interested in Ferdi as you are presently. The result is that you'll most likely pursue different directions.

   'Does this make sense to you?'

   'Yes. But if it's not Ferdi, then who is for me?'

'Well, you can ask a general relationship question and see what comes up.'

   'Okay, let's do that.'

What does the future hold for me in relationships?

Past: Judgement reversed

'There has been a period of emptiness surrounding love relationships. You may have felt others could not reach you emotionally or that they did not offer you anything worth pursuing.'

Present: The World
'Opportunities for a successful love relationship are around you presently so make sure you keep your eyes open.'

Near Future: Knight of Cups
'There is likely to be a soft-hearted, romantic man around you in the next three months who is offering a relationship.'
  'Can you tell me more about that, please?'
'Yes, if you can select one more card with your eyes closed, please.'

Additional card: Three of Pentacles
'Are you currently studying or planning to attend a course in the next three months?'
  'Yes, I have a course booked for next month. It's just two weekends, though.'
'Well, I see that this man is linked with study or learning in some way. This Three also suggests that you are able to learn from the opportunity presented and to build a solid platform for that or for subsequent love relationships. It shows you doing the groundwork necessary for a stable long-term relationship.'

Surrounding energy: Three of Cups
'The Three of Cups confirms there are several opportunities around you presently. In a relationship layout this card is a bit like standing at a bus stop: not a bus for hours and then two or three in five minutes. Can you add a card to that one?'
  'Sure.'

Additional Card: Eight of Cups
'The Eight confirms your new opportunities may help you release your past and present partners as you realise that those around you cannot give you what you need emotionally.'

Attitude: Knight of Swords reversed
'Is there a man on your mind who is quick-minded, impatient and sometimes unpredictable?'
  'From the past or the present?'
'Either. It's just that your attitude surrounds a man who is impatient and unpredictable. Perhaps you're hoping for an exciting man but fear such a man may prove unreliable. If it is a particular man you have in mind, he might be an Air sign; that is, a Gemini, Libran or Aquarian.'

Outcome: Queen of Pentacles

'The next eighteen to twenty-four months find you settled, focused on your career, content and fulfilled in your life You seem to have a quiet confidence and a serenity resulting from a stable home and work life. At that stage relationships are likely to become a smaller part of your life only as you pursue career and other goals.'

Answer: Justice

'The Justice card suggests that you are taking responsibility for your relationships and your life generally and that you are likely to be pleased with the results of your decisions and your actions. This is a card for the sign of Libra, along with the Queen of Pentacles and the Knight of Swords. Is there a Libran man around you presently?'

'Not that I know of.'

'Could you add another card to the answer, please?'

Additional card: King of Swords

'This King is clear minded, often a professional man, and someone who enjoys a good conversation. He could be a Gemini, Libran or Aquarian but his nature is more clearly shown than his astrological sign. Having said that, there are now four possible cards for the sign of Libra, so keep an eye out for Libran men.

'To summarise, it appears there are two men coming into your life. The first is romantic, and he arrives within three months. The second man is more emotionally mature than the first and probably older.

'You have free will in all things predicted so you can take either, both or neither of the men I've described.

'It's interesting that Ferdi, who appeared as the King of Cups in your first question, has not appeared in this layout. Does this make sense to you?'

'Yes, it does.'

'Now, shall we return to your career questions?'

'Yes. If I'm not moving interstate for that job, what's coming up?'

'As you select seven cards I'd like you to think of the question, "What does the future hold for me in my career?"'.

What does the future hold for me in my career?

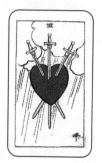

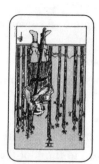

Past: Three of Swords

'There was a strong disappointment in the past with career. What happened?'
'I was retrenched from my job after six years, without notice. It was such a shock.'

Present: King of Swords

'I see a professional man around you in your work. He is intellectual, organised and clear minded. Can you relate to this description?'

'My boss. He's a project manager and he heads up teams of twenty to thirty people. He's pretty organised. Why's he coming up?'

'It's likely he's a positive influence in your work environment at present.'

'Yes, that sounds about right.'

New Future: Nine of Cups

'There's a great sense of personal fulfilment related to career in the next three months. You're able to derive great joy and a sense of accomplishment from your work in the coming months.'

Surrounding energy: Nine of Pentacles

'This suggests you have a successful career, resulting from careful planning and long-term commitment. It describes a comfortable lifestyle but the need to share it with a close partner. In short, your work life is fine at present, so you can focus on other things.'

Attitude: Death

'You hope to change job and perhaps career. This card suggests you hope to conclude a chapter in your working life and move on to other things in your career. I see it as hoping for the death of your current career or type of career because the card is upright.'

Outcome: Three of Wands

'You're likely to move forward with career plans, perhaps travelling with your work. Career opportunities may take you to new cities as this Three can include travel.'

Answer: Nine of Wands reversed

'It appears you're afraid of committing yourself to any one career long term. When you review your past career you tend to focus on the frustrations and ignore the achievements. Try to keep a balanced viewpoint when looking at your past, and if you've been working too hard for too long, it may be time for a long holiday overseas. The reversed Nine reverts back to the Eight of Wands, which suggests you need one of those glorious, memorable summers of fun, friends, love and travel before you consider long-term career commitments.

'To sum up, the three Nines tell me you're finishing a chapter in your career; the Death card tells me you're happy to let the old chapter go in favour of new opportunities. Does this make sense to you?'

'Yes.'

'Would you like me to make anything clearer to you?'

'Just the answer section.'

'Sure. Please close your eyes and select one more card for me. (This card is placed beside the answer card or card number four.)'

Additional card: Four of Cups

'This highlights your need to go within to find what connects you to life. In doing so, you can find what fulfils you in your career. After the period of fun, it's likely you'll need to release those things around you from which you derive fulfilment, and find contentment within. Can you add another card for me, please?'

Additional card: Three of Cups

'After the period of reflection you will once again be presented with career opportunities, probably more than you need, but it's good to have choice. Now both the answer and the outcome are number Three cards, suggesting growth in career.

'In summing up I now notice that there are three Nines and three Threes in this layout. When a number appears three or more times in a layout it has greater significance. The Nines refer to a career chapter concluding and the Threes describe growth and progression in career. With the Three of Swords in the past position, the hard part is behind you where your career is concerned.'

Claire consulted me with a list of questions, but it was up to me, the reader, to guide her as to the appropriate order for them. As her former partner Ferdi appeared in a question regarding a career move, he was obviously an important influence.

Before tackling a general career layout I directed Claire to ask about a possible relationship with Ferdi. If things had looked good regarding a relationship with Ferdi, I'd have directed Claire to ask different questions, such as whether there would be a different job offer in Ferdi's city or whether Ferdi would return to be with her.

As it was, one question eliminated Ferdi from the equation and Claire was then directed to ask about relationships before returning to a career question.

If your client asks a specific question to which there is a negative answer, you can follow it with a broader question. If they ask about purchasing a particular house and the answer is no, you can direct them to ask if they'll find a suitable house within three months. If the answer is still no, you can direct the client to ask another question, such as, 'Is it wise to remain where I am currently living?' or 'Is it wise for me to rent a place until I find what I'm seeking?'.

Almost anyone can accept a no if they are shown what else is available to them. Sometimes I tell people they won't achieve their desired goal because they won't want it in two years' time. As we grow and develop our goals change, and the Tarot will predict and confirm these changes.

Claire came to confirm that she was about to secure a new job interstate, but instead received information about two new men, a change in career direction and verification that she was not likely to have a solid future with Ferdi.

I met Claire again about four months later, and she told me she had never heard back from the interstate company and Ferdi had found someone else. Standing beside her was a Knight of Cups. The slender man with soft eyes and long eyelashes was introduced as Neville, and even his handshake was gentle. He was a poet in his spare time.

It appeared that exchanging Ferdi's phone calls for Neville's writings had enhanced Claire's wellbeing; she was positively radiant.

'Thanks,' she said.

'Don't thank me. You're living it. I only saw it ahead of time. Enjoy.'

Helping your client formulate appropriate follow-on questions gets easier with practice. Your task as a reader is to remain objective so you can ask the questions they can't because they're too emotionally involved.

With practice you become adept at simplifying client's questions, breaking them down into a clear, concise form. Confused questions lead to confusing answers and as your client is already likely to be confused about the possible paths to take, it is your task as a reader to clarify things. Keep it simple. If you have a client who insists upon complicating each question, simply take a minute to determine what the underlying issue is with your client. Answer their underlying questions and they'll settle down immediately.

Sandra was a psychologist who had written a book, and she consulted me to see if it would be wise to attend a seminar in London at which she had been invited to speak. If she accepted the invitation she could gain valuable experience speaking internationally and sell copies of her book.

The problem was that although the book had been published in Australia it had not been republished in London. If she organised for her Australian publisher to send copies to their London branch she could not expect a London publisher to purchase the rights and republish the book there, as it was already available. Also, she would miss two weeks of paid work by being in London for the seminar, and have to pay her airfare, accommodation and other travel expenses.

Her questions were as follows.

Will my book be republished in England before the seminar next year?

Before I detailed the cards to Sandra I requested an additional card to accompany the Queen of Cups in the near future, as I didn't see it as representing Sandra.

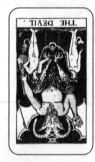

Past: Five of Cups reversed

'Although there have been disappointments in the past, you have overcome them. These could have been writing disappointments or, in a broader sense, career disappointments.'

Present: Six of Wands

'There is success around you at present, being either the success of your book in the Australian market or a successful contract to republish your book in Europe or elsewhere. Things look very good around you presently.'

Near future: Queen of Cups

'There is a tenacious and yet quiet woman supporting you in having your book republished in Europe. She has faith in you and she is emotionally supportive.'

Additional card: Seven of Cups

'With the help of this woman you'll be able to reassess your inner and outer needs regarding this book and your life. You may decide republication is not as important as you once felt it to be.

'Her influence increases your faith in yourself and in your work as a writer. Don't give up that belief in yourself.'

Surrounding energy: Three of Pentacles

'Are you studying at present?'

'No, but I run self-development groups.'

'That's it. And do these groups help you in your writing somehow?'

'Well, yes, I guess they do. You see, I implement my theories in the groups and then write about them afterward.'

'Well, this card suggests that teaching is also learning and that it's all building a solid platform for your writing future.'

Attitude: The Devil reversed

'You're hopeful an opportunity will come your way, and you're aware that being republished in Europe is only one alternative.

'Perhaps after this question you can ask if the book will be republished outside Australia generally, or in another specific market such as the US or Canada.'

Outcome: Strength reversed

'It seems to me that as time draws near for you to go to Europe, the book has not been republished and you're losing your inner strength and confidence.

'The reversed Strength card suggests that you need to reacquaint yourself with the previous card, the Chariot. The Chariot is the act of not giving up on your goals.'

Answer: The Wheel of Fortune reversed

'Opportunities for republication are likely to diminish as the time draws near for you to depart for Europe and the conference.

'It seems unlikely that your book will be republished in Europe, especially before the seminar.'

Sandra appeared despondent and numb, and I knew that to help her to leave the reading feeling clear-minded, confident and aware of the most likely course of events I'd have to present her with some other possible questions.

'You don't have to abandon the seminar just because the book hasn't been published in Europe.'

'Yes, I know. My publishers tell me they can airfreight copies over for the seminar, but I receive a reduced royalty on copies sold that way.'

'Okay. Let's come back to the book being published later. Would you like to ask if it's wise to accept the offer to speak at the conference next year? It could lead to all number of other possibilities.'

'Like what?' she said despondently.

'Like a tall, dark stranger with a bottle of chilled French champagne and a well-tuned mandolin to serenade you on a gondola in the heat of a summer's evening.'

'What?' she said.

I had to shock her out of her despondency so that she could focus on other questions she'd later realise were important.

I knew that in a few days when she'd accepted the book wouldn't be republished before the seminar, she'd want to ask other questions. It was my task to guide her towards asking those questions to give her value for her time and money.

That way, when she replayed her tape of the reading she'd have valuable information about several aspects of the European seminar, the book and her life generally.

'How about this for a question? Is it wise for me to attend the seminar in Europe next year?'

'Okay.'

Is it wise for me to attend the seminar in Europe next year?

Before I detailed the cards I asked Sandra to select an additional card for the answer position as I was uncertain about the conflict between the outcome (positive) and the answer (negative). The additional card was the Ten of Cups reversed, making a total of three Tens in the layout.

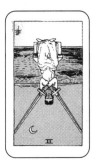

Past: The Tower reversed

'Has there been a sudden shock regarding a seminar in the past?'

'No. Not that I can remember. Why?'

'I have confirmation of a sudden shock regarding a seminar. It may not be related to this particular seminar; I sense that it is longer than two years ago. Can you recall a situation where sudden changes occurred in a seminar setting?'

She pondered this for a moment and I knew the importance of helping her make sense of each card before moving on to the next one. If clients cannot relate to what you've said, it's better to reword your description or broaden the scope for interpretation before proceeding. This helps them to have confidence in your predictions, and they realise the reading is a two-way situation where they can help you to clarify what you see.

'There was one situation, but it was a seminar I organised, and not one I was speaking at.'

'Okay. What happened there?'

'I organised a seminar with two colleagues and although it was a great success they walked off with the profits.'

'Were their actions unexpected?'

'Completely. I was stunned.'

'Okay. Has this left you uneasy about seminars you want to attend?'

'Yes, I guess so.'

'Okay. I'd like you to add another card to the Tower card, please.'

Additional card: Eight of Swords reversed

'This additional card describes the act of releasing yourself from the restricting beliefs you held regarding seminars. Have you attended seminars since then which have had positive outcomes?'

'Yes. I've spoken at perhaps ten or twelve seminars and conferences since then, and they've all been pretty positive; if not financially, then in feedback and contacts made at the time.'

Present: Two of Swords reversed

'You seem to be reluctant to make a decision regarding the seminar and it appears you haven't released some of your beliefs since the shock of your colleagues' actions some time ago.'

Near future: Four of Cups

'In the coming months you appear to be asking yourself what you need to do to reconnect to your work and the fulfilment it once gave you. I'll put it to you this way: if you don't go to Europe for the conference, what will you do instead to reconnect yourself to your work? What alternatives do you have that will fulfil you instead?'

'I don't know. I haven't thought about it, really. I guess now that I do think about it,

I usually travel to Europe every three years for study or a holiday, and I was due to go this year but I've been too busy. I could go next year and the conference will pay for part of the trip.'

In discussing the issue with Sandra I was giving her the opportunity to speak her hopes and fears aloud, and in turn she was able to decide for herself what she would do regarding the seminar.

Surrounding energies: Two of Pentacles

'You're currently weighing up the costs of travelling to Europe and examining what else that money could be used for. Travelling to Europe won't bankrupt you, but at the same time it's a large enough sum of money to warrant reflection.'

Attitude: Ten of Wands

'Your attitude is one of knowing the work involved in speaking at this seminar, and you realise you'll have to prepare everything yourself. You're confident you can achieve the level of success you hope for, yet you know it all depends on your own efforts.'

Outcome: Ten of Pentacles

'The outcome suggests that attending the seminar will prove financially rewarding or at least good for your long-term business plans. Perhaps you'll be invited back, or if you write another book those who have heard you speak will become a ready-made market for you in Europe.'

Answer: King of Cups reversed

'Although it looks financially positive it's likely to be emotionally unrewarding for you to attend this seminar. This King reversed can describe power struggles with a man who is undisciplined creatively and who could feel the need to thwart you in your endeavours. I'd like another card for the King, please.'

Additional card: Ten of Cups reversed

'This Ten confirms you'll feel somewhat excluded from the group of people speaking at or attending the seminar. It may become a clique to which you have no admittance. In summary, there are three Tens in this layout, suggesting contracts or legal paperwork if you attend the seminar. It appears to be worthwhile from a financial standpoint but not from a creative or emotional one. Does this make sense to you?'

'Yes it does. They're paying me to speak, so there'll be papers to sign and I may be able to interest a publisher while I'm there.'

'Would you like me to make anything clearer for you?'

'Well, I'm still uncertain as to what to do, so can you make the answer clearer?'

'Sure. Can you select another card for me, please?' Sandra selected the blank card, which I added to the outcome position alongside the Ten of Pentacles.

Additional card: Blank card

'Well, it's in the hands of the gods now. The blank card suggests that life has plans for you which are greater than you have for yourself. I suspect that if you travel to Europe you're not only going to speak at the seminar but that life wants you there to meet someone or some opportunity. Allow the whole situation to turn out as it will, for life will direct you to where you belong anyway.'

'That's just great! Now I feel like I'm walking blindfolded into next year. Why can't it just be simple and straightforward?'

'It can be, but it isn't for you at present.'

'Couldn't you just tell me that it will be fine?'

'I could, but lies cost extra. The fact is that with the blank card, you'll look back at your decision about the seminar and be happy that you did what you did, realising that it led to an opportunity you could not see this year. You're asking me if it's wise to attend this seminar but the blank card is telling me there are issues and opportunities involved which are bigger than you can see at this time.'

'So, what's the answer, then?'

'Can you afford to go?'

'Yes.'

'Are you still prepared to go if you'll feel emotionally excluded from those speaking or attending?'

'I guess so.'

'Are you prepared to keep your eyes open for your true purpose when you travel?'

'Yes. When you put it that way it sounds rather exciting.'

'The blank card is exciting. You prepare yourself for one opportunity and life offers you a different one. If you're adaptable it can be an enlivening experience.'

'Okay, now I have another question about the seminar. They've offered me only one space to talk but I'd like a second space. I want to know if they'll give me a second space to speak if I ask them.'

I folded the cards on the table back into the pack and shuffled briefly. After fanning the cards across the table, I asked Sandra to think of that question as she selected seven more cards.

'Will they offer me a second space to speak if I ask them?'

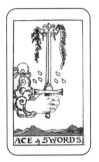

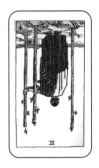

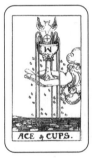

As I scanned the cards it appeared things looked very positive for the seminar in the coming months but that when the time arrived it might not go according to plan.

Past: Ace of Swords

'It appears you've been successful in the past with seminars, due to clarity of thought and careful planning. Does this make sense?'

'Yes. The last two have been very successful for me and I've enjoyed them. I like the group contact and the excitement which fills the room at conventions.'

Present: The Chariot

'The Chariot suggests you feel confident enough to request a second speaking slot in the agenda, and that based on your past success you can negotiate and expect a fair hearing.'

Near Future: Seven of Pentacles

'In the coming months you appear to be expectantly awaiting news regarding the seminar. I see you planning your career and examining your opportunities, including speaking at other seminars while you are in Europe.'

'Now, that's a thought. It never occurred to me to speak elsewhere while I'm there.'

Surrounding energies: Ace of Cups

'It appears that in the next four weeks the news is good, as the Ace of Cups describes happiness. While you are asking, why not inquire about other similar seminars in other countries that you could attend before or after this one. It's a world trip after all, and you could travel via America, or other European cities.'

Attitude: Four of Wands

'You appear to be hopeful your request will be accepted and you'll be welcomed by the organisers and attendees alike. You are hopeful of a positive outcome.'

Outcome: Three of Wands reversed

'There may be delays in your receiving news as to the exact time allowed for your second talk. Alternatively, you may have to delay your flight to Europe due to other commitments.'

Answer: The Tower reversed

'The reversed Tower card describes the act of narrowly missing a time of upheaval, so it suggests you won't actually be given a second time to speak at the seminar. This may be a blessing in disguise. With both the answer and the outcome cards reversed, I don't see you speaking more than once at the seminar.'

'Oh, so what do I ask next?'

'You might ask, "Would it be wise for me to travel to Europe in August?", just in case your opportunity lies in Europe but not at the seminar.'

'Okay, I'll ask that then.'

'Is it wise for me to travel to Europe next August?'

Past: King of Swords

'This King suggests there has been a man around you who has supported or helped you in some way regarding talks and seminars. Can you relate to this?'

'Yes. I was taking acting lessons to help with my presentation skills.'

Present: Four of Cups

'You seem to be unsure that all the effort is worth the outcome.

'This card suggests you've lost your connection to your work and that you need to find this connection within before you seek opportunities to speak at conventions. A change of location is not sufficient to reignite your enthusiasm for your subject.'

Near Future: Death reversed.

'There are changes approaching which may lead you in another direction entirely. You seem to be resisting these changes because you cannot see what will replace them. Perhaps it is time to surrender thoughts of speaking at this seminar and allow life to take you where you need to go instead.'

'Yes, perhaps it is time,' she sighed.

Surrounding energies: Hermit reversed

'Are you presently working hard, and is your workload taking up the evenings and weekends?'

'Yes, it is.'

'The Hermit reversed suggests that a rest and a period of reflection is necessary so that you can regain a healthy perspective.

'Can you take a few days off soon?'

'I was planning to take a weekend away in the country at an old manor house, but I came down with a cold, and had to cancel clients and rest at home. Then I had to catch up with my workload, so I haven't had a chance to re-book the break.'

'I suggest you take that planned break; and soon. You won't regret it.'

Attitude: Three of Cups reversed

'This reversed Three suggests you are not hopeful of travelling to Europe in August. Instead you seem to be focused on the group activity, which I assume is the seminar. You seem to fear that it won't be fulfilling.'

This card appears to contradict the previous cards in this position in earlier layouts. This may be the result of Sandra's hope of travelling to Europe diminishing during the reading process. Sandra still had the free will to fly to Europe and attend the seminar, but my job as a reader was to advise her as to the wisdom of such actions and the consequences should she choose to go. The blank card in the previous layout proved to be a new relationship opportunity which Sandra may have missed had she travelled to Europe.

Outcome: Wheel of Fortune reversed

'Your opportunities to travel overseas in August next year are likely to slip away as other demands surface.

'These demands may be every bit as rewarding as your planned trip, but they may prevent you from travelling at that time.'

Answer: Five of Swords reversed

'This reversed Five suggests that you need to negotiate a preferred solution. Is there another seminar you could attend in Europe next year?'

'*Actually, yes, there is. They're running another one in November. Could I ask about that one?*'

'Can you ask if it would be wise to attend that seminar and select one card for me, please?'

As we had already asked several questions about the August seminar, I felt it suitable to ask about the November seminar with a one card cut. Sandra selected one card from those remaining face down on the table while thinking about the question. If the card selected had been vague I'd have asked Sandra to ask the question in a new layout, selecting seven cards as before.

Additional card for November seminar: The Eight of Pentacles

'Yes, it appears a November seminar would be more rewarding for you than the August one.'

'*It looks as though I should forget about seminars, doesn't it?*'

'Is the seminar to promote your book or to gain international experience?'

'*Both, really, but I'm writing another book, which is a novel, and if that's successful I'd like to give up the counselling work and pursue writing full time.*'

'Then why not ask what the future holds for you in fiction writing?'

'*Okay, that sounds good.*'

What does the future hold for me in fiction writing?'

Past: The Hermit.

'Well, I have to start by saying that it looks good. Very good indeed. The Hermit in the past suggests that you've spent time reflecting upon ideas, themes and stories, and that these will serve you well as a source of inspiration for your writing.'

Present: The Magician

'The upright Magician represents a focus upon your writing at present, so this is a good time to write or to pursue publication if you have a completed work. You appear to be focused, productive and effective at translating your ideas into a story at present.'

Near future: Nine of Wands reversed

'You appear to be self-critical in the next few months. When you review your past writing efforts, you seem to focus more clearly on those which were unsuccessful rather than those which went well. Writing is a combination of experience and reflection, and there is a need for some fun, play and direct experience in the coming months. The reversed Nine suggests a return to the upright Eight of Wands is necessary, and the Eight is a card of fun in the sun. It's a pity you can't take an extended holiday and write it all off as a tax deduction.'

'Yes, if only. Presenting it to the tax department would be my first completed work of fiction,' she laughed.

Surrounding energies: The Star reversed

'You appear to lack faith in your abilities. The Star is a card of faith in life's possibilities, and the ability to allow creative ideas to flow through you easily and naturally. What do you think you need in order to restore that faith in your work, or the ability to allow your creativity to present itself?'

'I need a holiday, I guess. Not much. Just a few days off to live and breathe again. A bit of time to kick over a few leaves under an enormous oak tree as I select a picnic site and read a book.'

'I'm hungry for it just hearing about it.'

Attitude: Knight of Wands reversed

'Your hopes and fears surround delays in your plans. It seems that you fear that if you are delayed in putting your ideas on the page you might lose your momentum or enthusiasm for the project at hand. It's also possible that you want to go out and live life and leave the writing for another day.'

'Yes. That sounds about right.'

Outcome: Seven of Cups

'Your writing can open up parts of yourself presently hidden from view. It is also likely to help you to discover who you are and what you want from your life. In short, keep writing, as it gives you a sense of purpose.'

Answer: King of Cups

'The King of Cups describes success through creative discipline. Are you disciplined with your writing?'

'Yes, I like to think so. I'm not one of those people who write for two hours every day at the same time, but I love to write and I'm disciplined enough to complete what I start.'

'In summary I'd say that you have a very positive future in writing fiction, and this is easily the most positive layout you've had so far today. Does this make sense to you or would you like me to make something clearer for you?'

'Perhaps I'm tempting fate but I'd like an extra card for the near future, please.'

'Sure. Close your eyes and concentrate on the question again as you select one more card.'

Additional card: Eight of Swords reversed

'The reversed Eight suggests that you need to surrender some of your negative attitudes to writing or to writing fiction. Past restrictions will fall away from you soon and you'll find that you can adapt your life to writing part time. A return to the upright Seven of Swords is called for, and the Seven is a card of mental adaptability. Adapt and thrive. Would you like me to make anything else clearer for you?'

'Yes. Could I have another card here, please?'

'For the outcome? Sure. Close your eyes and concentrate on the question as you select it, please.'

Additional card: Judgement

'The Judgement card confirms what I've been saying; namely that writing fiction is a part of your spiritual purpose. I can see it on the front cover of your first book of fiction, "God taught me to write and then he told me to write". Writing seems to distil your purpose here on earth. So write away and make sure to send me a free copy of every one of your books. It's the very least you can do.'

She laughed and we moved on to other questions. Sandra had come to hear about her attendance at a seminar in Europe, and through a series of questions I ended up telling her about her greater purpose here: to write fiction. She came to see me a year later to ask about how to have her first completed manuscript published, but that's another story.

———————————

Ben consulted me about his relationship with Rebecca. He explained that she was keen to be married but that he had been married previously and was somewhat resistant to marrying again.

What does the future hold for my relationship with Rebecca?

Past: Three of Cups

'Did you meet Rebecca in a group situation, such as a party, or a course of some sort?'

'Well, yes. We were both on a self-development course together a few months ago.'

'I see it as an enjoyable experience and you felt included in a group event.'

Present: Seven of Wands
'There seem to be some obstacles to overcome if you want to pursue this relationship. Are you busy with work or with other commitments?'
    'Yes, I'm flat out at the moment. Does it look good for us?'
'I'm coming to that.'

Near future: Nine of Wands
'In the next few months I see you hesitant to pursue this relationship more deeply. You are reviewing your past, and recalling difficulties and pain. That's not to say that this relationship will cause you any pain, but that you have memories of previous painful relationships.'

Surrounding energies: Nine of Pentacles
'This Nine describes a comfortable life financially. It suggests that you have taken care of your financial needs and now you are ready to extend yourself into a relationship. In short, you are successful but now you need someone with whom to share your success.'

Attitude: Ace of Swords
'You seem to have a clear vision of where this relationship will lead if you pursue it more deeply. You seem confident that you can succeed if you take the next step in your relationship with Rebecca.'

Outcome: Two of Pentacles
'I see financial decisions regarding your relationship. Perhaps you are planning to relocate or to change jobs and this may affect your finances and, in turn, your relationship. In simple terms this can signify the financial deliberation that precedes action. Can I ask you to add another card to the Two, please?'

Additional Card: Wheel of Fortune
'This suggests that if you pursue this relationship further you'll be happy with the outcome. It describes a period of growth and development in your relationship with Rebecca, so the outcome is positive for you both.'

Answer: Queen of Cups
'I see that Rebecca is sensitive, emotionally supportive and ready for a deeper relationship with you. She has been thinking about it, but it's not her nature to force

things so she's waiting for you to take the next step. In summary, it appears wise to pursue a deeper relationship with Rebecca; there is likely to be positive growth and development in your relationship if you do so. Does this make sense to you?'

'Yes.'

'Would you like me to make anything clearer before we move on to your next question?'

'Yes, please. I'd like to know more about the next few months, if that's okay.'

'Sure. Can you select another card for me, please.' The additional card was the Tower.

'Can you give me another card, please?' The additional card was the Emperor reversed.

Additional cards: The Tower — the Emperor reversed

'This seems unrelated to the earlier cards. The Tower suggests there could be sudden changes and, alongside the Emperor reversed, these changes could result from your lack of discipline. Does this make sense to you?'

'Er, sort of.'

'Well, to continue, the actions you are weighing up in the Nine of Wands may not just be about Rebecca, but also to do with other things in your life which may cause sudden changes and problems in your relationship with her. Have you been considering some course of action which may disrupt your relationship with Rebecca?'

'No. Not that I can think of.'

'Well, I'll ask you to reflect on this and we'll move on to your next question.'

'Okay. Now I'd like to ask about another girl I'm interested in.'

'Oh. Now it comes out. Can I ask you this? If you pursue this other girl, might that cause some upheaval in your relationship with Rebecca?'

'It might.'

'So, what's your question?'

'What does the future hold for Jenny and me?'

'Okay. There are several ways that you can ask this question. You can ask:

1.   What does the future hold for our relationship?
2.   Is it wise for me to pursue a relationship with Jenny?
3.   (or a more general question) What does the future hold for me in love relationships?

What does the future hold for our relationship?

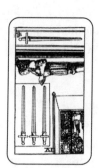

Past: The Star reversed

'Was there an Aquarian person around you in relationships in the recent past?'

'No, not that I remember.'

'Had you lost faith in love relationships for a period of time, preferring your freedom instead?'

'Yes. I didn't have a relationship for four years. I just didn't want one.'

Present: Ten of Cups reversed

'It seems you are keen not to repeat your family patterns in relationships, and that Jenny is from another social group. I don't think she mixes with your social set presently.'

'Yes, that's right. She's much younger than me and I guess her friends are very different from mine.'

Near future: Page of Cups reversed

'It seems you won't know where you stand with Jenny in the coming months. Could you add another card to this for me, please?'

'Yes. She's off overseas in a few weeks for a long holiday!'

Additional card: Nine of Cups reversed

'It's apparent to me this holds no fulfilment for you in the next three months. Pursuing this relationship is unlikely to feed you in your heart. The reversed Nine often describes addictive or compulsive behaviour. Is your attraction to Jenny compulsive in some way?'

'No, not really. She's just someone I met who I'm attracted to.'

'And what is it that you think Jenny can offer you that Rebecca cannot?'

'I hadn't thought about it really. I haven't been in a relationship with Rebecca long enough to know what she's like.'

'But you must have some inkling of her inner nature.'

'She's fairly secretive, really.'

'So that makes two of you then.'

'Oh, I'm not secretive.'

'So you've told Rebecca about Jenny then?'

'Er, no.'

Surrounding energies: Three of Cups

'Is Jenny already in a relationship or about to start one?'

'I don't know. We've only met a few times, so I don't know that much about her.'

'Can you add another card for me, please?'

Additional card: Page of Swords

'How old is Jenny?'

'I think she's twenty-one.'

'And what astrological sign is she?'

'A Pisces.'

'Then this Page confirms there is someone else around her at present who is also interested in a relationship with her.'

Attitude: Page of Wands

'You seem to be keen to pursue a love relationship with Jenny and you're confident it will give you what you want.'

Outcome: The Moon

'The Moon suggests that if you pursue this relationship it may have to be kept secret from others. Although this may increase the passion and excitement, it is also likely to restrict its development.'

Answer: Four of Swords reversed

'This reversed Four suggests you are becoming restless with the possibilities in your present relationship, and that you want to throw caution to the wind and pursue a relationship with Jenny regardless of the consequences.

'Can I have another card, please?'

Additional card: Justice reversed

'You may disregard the consequences now but you'll have to live with them later.

The reversed Justice card suggests ongoing arguments and disputes, which are likely to be in your relationship with Rebecca after she discovers your relationship with Jenny.'

'So, how can I stop Rebecca from finding out?'

'Don't bother. She appeared as a Queen of Cups, and this Queen is very intuitive so my guess is that she knows already.'

'But I haven't done anything yet.'

'True, but your energy and your commitment has strayed from her, and she'll know it immediately. It's really your choice what you do in your love life, but I'm here to tell you that you won't be hiding much from Rebecca.

'Can I have another card, please?'

Additional card: Seven of Wands

'This tells me you'll have an uphill battle on your hands if you pursue a relationship with Jenny, and there will be issues to resolve in your relationship with Rebecca, so, in short, do so at your peril.

'So what would you like to ask next?'

'I'd like to know if it's wise to pursue a relationship with Karen?'

'What's the story? Exactly how many girls do you have back there?'

Is it wise to pursue a relationship with Karen?

Past: Temperance

'There seems to have been peace and stability around you emotionally in the past. Perhaps you were able to see where you were heading long term in love relationships, or to know what sort of relationship suited you.'

Present: The Magician reversed

'This is not a good time to pursue a love relationship with Karen. The reversed Magician suggests you may be using a position of power to exert an influence over her. Is this so?'

'Er, well, we met on a meditation course, and I was paired with her to support her after the course finished. I'm more experienced than her with this particular meditation, so I guess she looks to me for guidance. In that way maybe I have a position of power, but it's not that important.'

'Perhaps not in the scheme of things, but does Karen look to you for help when she gets stuck with her meditation practice?'

'Yes, I guess so.'

'Then that puts you in a position of power.'

Near future: The Emperor reversed

'The reversed Emperor in the near future suggests that you need to be more disciplined where love relationships are concerned. More is not always better, and in this case more partners could translate into more demands.'

Surrounding energies: Page of Wands

'The Page suggests that you are eager to pursue this relationship, and that it could start in the next four weeks if you want it to.'

Attitude: The Chariot reversed

'The reversed Chariot suggests that you are torn between your heart and your head regarding pursuing a love relationship with Karen. It also hints at you looking forward to a new relationship as a way to avoid past emotional issues regarding relationships. Is there a particular relationship you have yet to resolve emotionally, aside from the relationship with Rebecca?'

'No. Not that I can think of right now.'

Outcome: Queen of Pentacles reversed

'The reversed Queen may describe Karen as practical, realistic and currently lacking in confidence. Is she an independent woman?'

'Yes, I guess so.'

Answer: King of Cups reversed

'The reversed King confirms to me that you have unresolved emotional issues from past relationships which are driving you forward to seek new opportunities. These issues may make it difficult for you to stay in one relationship when deeper commitment beckons, due to past betrayals. Does this make sense to you?'

'Not really.'

'Okay, I'll break it down a bit more. How is your ability to trust in relationships?'

'Not very good, I guess.'

'Is your lack of trust related to a particular incident in a past relationship?'

'Not that I can think of, no.'

At this point I tuned in clairvoyantly and was given the year 1988.

'What was happening in relationships in 1988?'

'Let me see now. Oh yes. My girlfriend at the time had left and moved interstate.'

'Why did she move?'

'I guess she was restless for something new.'

'And did she ask you to go with her?'

'No.'

'Did you want to go?'

'I never thought about it, really.'

'Thinking about it now, would you have liked to have accompanied her interstate?'

'Not really. All my friends are here and I like it here.'

'Did you discuss her intended move?'

'No. She just decided one day and she was gone a few weeks later. It was all a bit of a surprise, really.'

'And how have your love relationships been since then?'

'Well, I was married for three years, and then she left and went overseas.'

'This is starting to look like a pattern to me. Have any other partners moved away as they ended their relationships with you?'

'No, just those two.'

'So, do you feel that you've resolved the issues from the two relationships you've described to me?'

'Yes.'

'Then you're not carrying any emotional baggage from the past and you're ready to commit yourself to a long-term relationship?'

'How do I answer that?'

'Honestly, I hope.'

As I observed him, Ben seemed to grow weary, and heavy with the realisation he was about to impart to me. The self-assured young man who had entered the room forty minutes ago was ebbing away before my eyes, to be replaced by someone who appeared tortured, and bruised by life. As the facade crumbled, we approached the real issue behind his consulting me.

'The thing is ...' *he said, and paused as he searched for the words: 'Just when you think things are going well, they up and leave. I don't get it. I'm sick of being left by women, and so I decided recently that if it was a choice between leaving or being left, I'd leave every time.'*

He sighed, having admitted to himself and to me his real issues underlying the relationship questions.

'So, do you have these extra women like Karen and Jenny in case you have to leave suddenly?'
  'I guess so,' he muttered, and nodded.
'So let's return to what I said about your relationship with Rebecca. In that layout she appeared to be loving and supportive, and I couldn't see that she had any intention of leaving. By your own admission she wants to get married.
  'Doesn't that suggest that she wants to be with you for a long time to come?'
  'Yes, it does. But my first wife wanted to get married. She thought it would be for life but where is she now?'
'So the issue here seems to be one of trust.
  'Can I suggest a question to ask the cards?'
  'Sure.'
'What do I need to do to rebuild my trust in love relationships?'
  'Okay, that sounds good.'

It had taken several question to arrive at Ben's underlying issue; trust in love relationships. If I had lectured him about the need for monogamy and his apparent cavalier attitude to love relationships, we might never have arrived at his deeper issue. When dealing with deeper issues, a Tarot reading is often only the start of a long journey of self discovery.

This is where it pays to have the business cards of counsellors you trust, to recommend to your client so that they can complete the inner work you have highlighted to them. You are better off having a list of male and female counsellors, natural therapists, etc., so that your clients have a wide choice of person, and locality of practitioner. Ensure that you have personal experience of anyone you recommend and if you have not met the practitioner, tell the client so that they may reserve their judgement.

What do I need to do to rebuild my trust in love relationships?

Past: The Tower

'There has been a sudden change in the past which may have swept a relationship away from you without warning. The resultant shock may have left you with a period of upheaval in your life. Does this make sense to you?'

'Yes.'

Present: Eight of Pentacles

'You seem to be more committed to making the most of your life currently; although the emphasis may be in favour of career or financial things instead of emotional fulfilment, with the three Pentacles cards in the layout.'

Near future: Nine of Wands reversed

'When it comes time to review your emotional commitment in the coming months you are likely to examine the past closely, ignoring those things which worked out well in favour of those things which ended badly. I ask you to keep a balanced view of your emotional past, so that you can make unbiased decisions for the future. With the Nine reversed you have to return to the Eight of Wands to master the lesson contained therein before returning to the upright Nine again. The Eight of Wands is a time of uncomplicated fun, so perhaps you need to take each day as it comes, enjoying your relationship and your life opportunities as they approach you.

'I see the Eight of Wands as one of those halcyon summers you remember fondly over a glass of chilled white wine with friends. You are overdue for one of those summers, so don't take things too seriously. In playing and laughing you are also growing.'

Surrounding energies: Ace of Pentacles reversed

'The reversed Ace of Pentacles suggests you may currently be more focused on career and financial issues than on emotional ones. It also suggests that you feel you cannot have a deep love relationship until you have sufficient money to support you in the lifestyle you desire.'

His eyes filled with tears at this, and I paused to allow him to absorb my words and to recollect himself. This wasn't what Ben imagined when he came for his reading, but I have only one policy when I read: 'There are no secrets at my table'.

Attitude: Five of Wands reversed

'The reversed Five suggests you are hopeful you can include your partner in your life, and not lead two separate lives with diverging interests and goals.'

Outcome: Temperance

'If you keep the bigger picture in mind, finding a suitable partner is easier as they will share your spiritual path. Remembering your spiritual and emotional needs, you can receive some of the spiritual support you require. This may take the form of spiritual and emotional support from those who share your spiritual beliefs, or simply the knowledge that if your relationship ends, your spiritual path continues.'

Answer: Ten of Pentacles reversed

'This reversed Ten suggests that you need to rely less upon material and financial structure for emotional fulfilment, and more on people or spirit.'

'How do you mean?'

'Perhaps you can find some of the support you need through meditation to re-centre yourself. More support might be found through friends and your partner, through nature or through growing a garden. The choices are endless when you look closely. Can you select another card to go beside the Ten of Pentacles, please?'

Additional card: Six of Wands

'I see that you will succeed in overcoming your trust issues within the next two years, and you are likely to be enjoying a supportive love relationship at that time. The upright Six is a card for triumph and it confirms that your energies are congruent. You are not scattered in your focus and if you have a close partner it is likely that you are both focused on the same goals. Does this make sense to you?'

'Yes, it does,' he said and sighed.

In his mind, Ben came with questions about several women and his best emotional opportunities. Beneath these questions lay the real issues. I was fortunate to be able to address both his immediate questions and his deeper issues, but it's not always the case. Sometimes clients don't want to know about their deeper issues, preferring instead to have their fortune told.

The hard part comes when there is precious little ahead of your client they might consider to be good, and they don't want to hear about what they are doing to contribute to their current circumstances. Sometimes I see clients stand up to leave feeling disappointed with the reading, and it is hard to accept as a reader. From an emotional point of view, I like to know I've given the best reading I can for that day; from a business point of view, I realise that clients who are pleased with what they have been told will spread the word about me to others. However, I still refuse to give false hope. What is the point of making someone feel hopeful for a few days or weeks when their hopes are built on fantasy? Sooner or later they'll come to realise that the predictions were wrong and then I'll have lost a long-term client.

Although not all the news was good for Ben, he left with information about his relationship with Rebecca, details of possible relationships with Karen and Jenny, and an understanding of why he was afraid of long-term commitment in love relationships. It's up to him what he does with that information. Your task as a Tarot reader is to give your client the necessary information upon which they can base their decisions. Clients have free will and they sometimes need to be encouraged to use it.

Your part of the agreement is to put aside some time, and focus on your client's questions and the issues behind them. Clients think they are paying only for an hour of your time (if you give one-hour consultations) but in fact they are also paying for the months and years you have spent honing your Tarot-reading skills. They are paying for all those good habits you developed along the way, such as not drinking when reading the following day, meditating regularly, attending courses to further your knowledge, and perhaps even training in counselling to enhance your readings.

As a professional reader you owe it to your clients to enhance your skills and your knowledge continually, and, in return, your clients will support you financially to continue learning and improving. In this way everybody wins. As you become a better reader your clients receive clearer and more accurate information, and in turn they are prepared to pay more for your skills, enabling you to see fewer clients but to give them a higher standard of service.

In many ways the purpose of the Tarot reader is similar to that of a story teller. You tell your client a story, which is a metaphor for their life or current circumstances. Through listening to your story, the client can come to realise where they came from, where they stand now and where they are heading in life.

As a Tarot reader you are there to help others to review their steps and to reassess their purpose. This can mean pointing out to the client what they are doing that prevents them achieving their goals. Chances are you'll be telling them what they already know on some level, and what their friends have longed to tell them but could not, for friendships are often based on what we do not say to one another.

Part Five

★ The Four Approaches to Life ★

There are, of course, four suits of the Minor Arcana: Wands, Cups, Swords and Pentacles. The two stories which follow show the fundamental differences between these four types' approaches to life. The four Kings and Queens have been given names commencing with the same letter as their suit: *W* for Wands, *C* for Cups, *S* for Swords and *P* for Pentacles, to help you to identify them immediately. The men are spending a weekend away at a cottage and the women are planning a wedding.

It had seemed like late afternoon all day, with clouds obscuring the sky like a thick blanket. The weatherboard cottage seemed to huddle between the bushes to escape the constant wind which roared across the lake.

Will arrived first, with Steve in the passenger seat of the mud-splattered four-wheel drive, which hurtled towards the south wall of the cottage as though Will planned to drive straight through it. Steve stopped talking momentarily (a feat in itself) as the wall approached, but then the thought that he might die at any moment was sufficient to silence even him. After stopping, Will laughed heartily at Steve's expression and leapt out onto the sandy soil to explore the surrounds.

Steve sat in the car and read his book until Peter arrived with the keys, followed by Charles, who was conspicuous by the fishing equipment strapped to the roof of his car. Peter had all the supplies as usual, having carefully planned this weekend for three months. He was strict about the details, and insisted on bringing all the necessary utensils since they had once spent a whole holiday without drinking glasses because Will had left them in the driveway of his home when he departed.

They went inside and sat down, and Charles poured a generous quantity of Scotch into some tumblers. The night drew in as the fire sprang to life at the hands of Will. Conversation turned to the activities ahead as the four friends settled into the yearly routine of unwinding with their favourite pastimes.

Charles talked of fishing and the joy of sitting as still as the water around his small boat while he awaited a bite.

'I'm up early to climb the big one,' stated Will.

'Not that damned mountain again. Haven't you learned anything from your last experience?' laughed Steve.

'I would have made it if the sun hadn't set so early,' said Will defiantly.

The following morning after breakfast Peter prepared for dinner that night by chopping enough wood for a day or two and topping up the oil lamps. He preferred to be busy rather than simply sitting around on the lake with Charles. As Peter attacked the woodpile, Steve stood by talking and collecting the odd piece of kindling which happened to land nearby.

Will strode off into the distance in search of the mountain's peak, carrying his provisions and whistling. Steve shook his head and turned to Peter. He said: 'Where does he get the energy from? Hasn't anyone told him how tall that mountain is?'

'Hasn't anyone reminded him of his age is more to the point,' said Peter.

Meanwhile, four women sipped champagne as they discussed Wendy's wedding. Wendy asked if it was considered good form for the bride to arrive in a tow truck or on the back of a motorbike. The others laughed, but she was seriously contemplating it.

Clarissa was already sentimental about the wedding, and it was still three weeks away.

'Don't reminisce about it until it's over,' chided Sally when she caught Clarissa's expression.

Phoebe had the list of expenses and a small notepad filled with the quotes for the photographer, etc., that Sally had gathered over the past week. She said, 'Okay girls, let's get the practical stuff over with before Wendy opens another bottle'.

However, it was too late, as Wendy was already in the kitchen removing another champagne cork. There was a resounding pop, followed by the sounds of breaking china as the cork collided with a teacup hanging in the rack.

'Er, sorry Clarry, but this cork just had to get out and about. Bit like me really,' she laughed and appeared in the doorway, eager to pour another glass for everyone.

The above stories are simple illustrations of the four approaches to life detailed through the Minor Arcana. Alongside practical Peter (Pentacles) are talkative Steve (Swords), patient and water-loving Charles (Cups) and Will (Wands), who spent the day wandering off up the nearby mountain. We also saw outrageous Wendy (Wands), sentimental Clarissa (Cups), organised Sally (Swords) and realistic Phoebe (Pentacles).

Examples of the Tarot personality types appear around us constantly. Even brief observations of people can confirm this. I experienced the directness of a Wands approach in 1986 when I was studying hypnosis. One of the teachers, a psychiatrist, arrived in a wheelchair and started the lesson. He was an enthusiastic speaker and we were in fits of laughter throughout the evening.

I mentioned to a friend who was a Wands type, and who was also attending, that it wouldn't surprise me if the teacher was perfectly healthy and able to walk, but had decided to appear in a wheelchair to teach us not to form opinions about our clients before we knew the whole story about them. My friend mentioned this to the teacher during a tea break in the third week, and he roared with laughter. He said: 'I can walk a bit but I use the chair because I have multiple sclerosis. Some days are better than others. But it's a good version of events'.

I wanted the earth to open up and swallow me whole when I realised how tactless I had been to suggest it and my friend had been to mention it to him. She didn't mean any harm; she simply had the directness natural to Wands people.

Another example of Wands, and also of Pentacles, behaviour occurred while I was teaching a course some years ago. It was mid-winter and we had an open fire going all day. During the lunch break two students decided to head for a local café for a bite to eat.

'Is it cold out there?' asked the Queen of Pentacles.

'Not really,' replied the Queen of Wands.

They left, but the Queen of Pentacles returned a minute later, shivering.

'It's freezing out there,' she muttered as she collected her coat. The Queen of Wands reasoned that if she was cold she could walk faster and speed up her blood circulation, whereas the Queen of Pentacles wanted to be comfortable for the whole journey.

'Which Court card am I?' is often asked during introductory Tarot courses. As I describe the qualities of each Court card, many students can relate to more than one.

In a recent course a softly spoken girl asked which Court card she was and her blue eyes and blonde hair suggested she could be a Queen of Cups. I observed her during the course and later suggested she might be a Queen of Wands instead, as she sometimes displayed a fiery temperament. She disagreed with me, until another student reminded her of her actions at lunch in a local café. She had stood up and shouted for service, declaring she was '... bloody starving over here!', to the amusement of the other diners.

Often we share the qualities of two Court cards, but it's likely we will display the characteristics of one particular one.

From seeing the little Page of Wands throwing a tantrum in the supermarket, to seeing the Knight of Swords sitting with a list of questions in the second row of a lecture theatre at a talk on politics or philosophy, it is easy to understand the meaning of a particular card when you see it in action. For the aware Tarot reader the world is their classroom.

★ The Minor Arcana ★

The fifty-six cards of the Minor Arcana are divided into four suits, similar to the playing cards. Unlike the playing cards, the Minor Arcana of the Tarot have a fourth court card in each suit, being the Page. The Knight in the Tarot is equivalent to the Jack in the playing cards.

The Minor Arcana deals with everyday events and actions, and their consequences. If a client is travelling overseas, the Minor Arcana cards are likely to detail the preparations, the stress involved and the people around the client. For a deeper glimpse of the client's spiritual lessons, you need to look to the twenty-two cards of the Major Arcana.

The four suits of the Minor Arcana are the four elemental approaches to life. They are Fire (enthusiasm), Water (emotions and creativity), Air (thought and understanding) and Earth (practicality). The four suits represent four paths to understanding. Each of us treads one of these paths, sometimes taking a second path for a period of time before returning to the one we prefer.

Each path is equally important and, despite appearances, no path offers a short cut to understanding. All offer opportunities and contain obstacles to be overcome if you want to reach your goals. Those around you who tread a different path can sometimes help you to master your current lesson, as they have a different viewpoint to you because of their path or perspective.

Although each suit offers a particular path, we are individuals taking our own steps at our own pace, making a unique personal journey. History is filled with stories, books, films and plays about the challenges offered by the different paths and how particular people have triumphed over obstacles to reach an enlightened understanding of life. These books or films may inspire you or you may choose instead to write the story of your own journey one day.

Unlike *The Tarot Revealed*, this book groups each Minor Arcana card number together to help you to see the similarities of the cards and the different approaches of the four suits. In simple terms, all of the Threes in the Tarot have a similar meaning; only the approach to that meaning differs according to the suit to which the number Three belongs.

The Aces

The Aces represent the beginning of new projects, and each Ace shows a different approach to starting new things. Like the number one in numerology, the Aces show the need to forge ahead, to take charge and to lead from the front.

Three or more Aces in a layout suggest a fresh start or a change resulting in a new environment. Three or more reversed Aces in a layout suggest that opportunities are presently blocked and the client may be unable to see or to pursue new opportunities at this time. This inability to pursue new opportunities often results from being overloaded by present commitments.

Ace of Wands

This Ace represents urgent physical action. Wands people consider that plans are for other people; they like to transform their ideas into action before they lose the essence of the inspiration or impulse. From inspiration to action is a simple description of the Ace of Wands. When this card appears in a layout your client has sufficient energy to start new projects or to initiate action.

In this card the hand extends from a cloud, suggesting inspiration for action has come from a spiritual source. In a relationship layout it can suggest a new relationship or a new stage of an existing one, or simply that your client will meet a new partner while travelling, as the Ace of Wands is also a card for travel. In a career layout the Ace of Wands can suggest the start of a new job, or a new position within the client's current organisation. Sometimes, if the job involves project work, the Ace represents the start of a new project.

Reversed

When reversed, the Ace of Wands represents your client's inability to transform their impulses or ideas into reality because they have too many outstanding commitments. They need to return to the lesson of the Ten of Wands in order to resolve some things, to allow the time or opportunity to pursue the new project.

Wands people don't like delays, as they are innately impatient; they favour honesty over tact as it allows them to go to the heart of a matter quickly and efficiently. Wands people often pace around, bite their fingernails and tap their fingers on the desk when they are delayed or frustrated in their attempts to start a new project. Delaying gratification does not sit easily with them.

A friend named Brian exemplified this on a day he sat with me in a café, awaiting an important telephone call. He repeatedly checked his telephone, fiddled with his empty coffee cup and asked me the time, despite the watch on his left wrist.

Unable to contain himself, he started scrolling through the names and numbers saved in the phone memory until he came to a name he remembered. He made a call, throughout it fiddling continuously with a teaspoon, and eventually said goodbye. About thirty seconds after he'd hung up, his telephone rang. The call he'd been expecting had come while he was on the other call and it had gone to his message bank. He was even more frustrated when he returned the call and the man had left for lunch.

'Arrrgh!' he shouted, drawing the attention of everyone in the café. Ignoring them all he glared at his telephone. I felt my enjoyment of lunch fading, so I confiscated his telephone until I'd finished eating (another Wands action).

Ace of Cups

The Ace of Cups represents a time when your client feels connected to life emotionally and spiritually. On the type of days represented by the Ace of Cups, I awaken with ideas for a story for a book I'm working on, and I am unable to remain in bed a minute longer as I'm so excited about the possibilities of the day ahead of me.

In this card the hand extends from a cloud to hold a cup flowing over with emotional and spiritual fulfilment. The red flowers depict the passion accompanying the emotional and spiritual components of this card.

If this card appears in a career layout, your client is likely to be motivated to pursue their career, and emotionally fulfilled by its day-to-day duties and responsibilities. In a relationship layout this Ace can suggest a new relationship or a new stage of an existing one. It also suggests that your client has a great deal to offer a partner at this time as they are connected to their source of spiritual and emotional fulfilment. (If you feel complete and fulfilled before starting a new relationship, chances are you'll feel secure enough to bring out the very best in yourself and your partner.)

Being connected to your spiritual source of energy can sometimes allow others around you to centre themselves also. However, the secret here is to remain aware that long-term fulfilment comes from within, not from others. With this in mind, if others decide to leave, although you will experience feelings of loss, you still have a spiritual source of fulfilment available to you.

Reversed

The Ace of Cups reversed suggests that your client has lost that spiritual connection and is relying too heavily on those around them for fulfilment. This often leads to disappointment.

The reversed Ace can indicate a time when they momentarily gain and then lose their connection to spiritual and emotional fulfilment. For example, your client's partner doesn't know whether they really want to be in the relationship, and your client's mood swings from high to low.

This is a time for them to return to the Ten of Cups, and be surrounded with friends and family who can include them and support them. It is time for your client to remember that love, recognition and support come from many sources. The Ten of Cups is the perfect antidote to the aloneness experienced with the Ace reversed.

If they cannot be surrounded with friends or family, it is time to go within for fulfilment. Meditation may benefit them at this time. If it does not, they will benefit by seeking out those things which feed them emotionally and spiritually. These may include music, drawing, wholesome food or an afternoon spent in the garden or by the ocean.

Ace of Swords

The Ace of Swords depicts the intellectual approach to beginning something. It represents an idea or concept and the plan to carry it through to completion.

Swords types like to plan, or at least to come up with an idea which can then be discussed with others. This discussion is not necessarily for the purpose of refining the idea, but simply for the sake of talking about something, as Swords people love a good conversation. However, through conversation about their plans, Swords people can enlist the help and support of others. Sometimes it is only through talking about their intentions that Swords people's intentions become real to them. In simple terms, they tell so many people what they intend doing that they are then obliged to do what they have said they'll do.

In this card the wreath and the crown represent the ability to make an idea work in the physical world, for ideas alone are cheap. All of us know someone who is filled with creative ideas they insist are going to make them wealthy beyond their wildest dreams. However, taking those ideas all the way to their completion is another thing entirely.

The Ace represents a clear vision of the path before you. Jade, who showed me her outline for a novel she was writing, demonstrated she had this kind of clear vision. On a large, white sheet of paper she had pasted around sixty small bright-yellow stick-on pages on which were each scene or part of the story. The beginning, middle and the end were all laid out before me and Jade was systematically working her way to the end. She was, in effect, writing sixty short stories, using the same characters throughout, and it was so clearly laid out that writing a novel appeared deceptively simple.

'Almost anyone could write a story with this system!' I exclaimed and she laughed.

'Yes, they could, but don't tell them, or I'll never find a publisher.'

The double edges of the sword represent the realistic vision of what it will take to turn your idea into reality. (In simple terms this card represents clarity of thought.) The cloud represents spirit, from which all ideas derive, and the hand firmly grasping the sword represents firm grasp of an idea. With this firm grasp of an idea or a thought you are able to turn that idea around and play with it, leading to new applications for existing concepts.

An example of playing with a concept occurred recently with my six-year-old son. I was putting him to bed and he started into his routine of extending his time awake.

'I'm hungry.'

'No, you're not. You couldn't finish your dinner only an hour ago.'

'Then I'm thirsty,' he continued.

'Look. You've had enough to eat and to drink. In fact, you've had enough of everything, so just go to sleep,' I said firmly. As I closed the door, he said, 'I haven't had enough of tomorrow'.

Reversed

The Ace of Swords reversed shows a loose grip on a concept. It can reveal a half-baked idea or poor planning resulting in failure. It sometimes describes the act of trying to apply old logic to a new problem. Your client can expect delays in the commencement of new projects, and it is time for them to re-think their plans. A return to the lesson of the Ten of Swords can show them how ideas and beliefs can shape their reality.

Ace of Pentacles

In simple terms the upright Ace of Pentacles represents a practical opportunity to start a new project. It symbolises your client investing their resources (such as money, effort, time or energy) in a project, and the possibilities of that opportunity.

The card shows a cloud with a hand issuing from it, which contains one pentacle. The five-pointed star within the two circles points upwards as a reminder that our purpose in life includes keeping our minds above, or in control of, our passions. The five points of the star represent a person's head (top), two outstretched hands and their feet. The upright person keeps their head closer to the heavens.

The garden beneath the hand shows flowers in bloom, the rewards of practical application and effort. Pentacles people know the value of hard work and are usually happy to do what is necessary to achieve their objectives in a practical manner.

The two lines encircling the star represent the need to contain your energy and to direct it toward a useful purpose. In answer to a question about starting a new project, the upright Ace suggests that your client has the finances to start it, or that financial assistance will be forthcoming.

Pentacles people understand the importance of practicality, believing that it is pointless to be so 'heavenly' that you are no earthly good. 'What's in it for me?' is the Pentacles person's question. These people are unlikely to tell you that 'Money is only energy and we need to share it without thinking'.

The following is an example of the Pentacles attitude to money. It took place in a weekend workshop in the late 1980s.

The workshop coordinator asked each of us to produce a banknote for an exercise. Some produced five-dollar notes, some ten-dollar notes and then, of course, some hero waved around a crisp $100 note. The exercise went like this.

We were to exchange our notes for others' notes of any denomination continuously for a period of ten minutes. After ten minutes the teacher asked us to stop and to pocket whatever note we had in our hands and sit down.

The energy in the room slowly changed from excitement, to anger, to rage. I looked for the man who had started with a $100 note and he was sitting staring at a two dollar note in his hands.

Ten minutes later as we were starting another exercise, a man stood up with some banknotes in his outstretched hand and said: 'I'm uncomfortable about this. You see, I started out with a ten dollar note, and now I have two twenties and a five in my hands'. Before he could say another word, a man behind him stood up and snatched the notes from his hands, saying, 'Problem solved'.

I burst into laughter and the man standing glared at me. Everyone started talking at once, intending to find the note they started the exercise with, and the teacher silenced us before he spoke: 'So, money is only energy, eh? Seems to me you all have a lot of your own energy invested in something that is only energy'.

Everyone had verbally agreed that money was only energy but few of us actually felt it to be true.

Pentacles people know that money is important, and they usually have few doubts about wanting their share of it. It goes without saying that it was a Cups person who stood to declare his discomfort and a Swords person who saw a chance and swiped the notes from him.

When the Ace appears in a career layout, a new job or a new position within the current company is shown. In a health layout its appearance indicates that your client has a practical approach to their physical health.

Reversed

The Ace reversed indicates a time when money is slipping through your client's fingers. It could be that your client has poor financial discipline or simply that they are spending more than they are earning. This happens to all of us at certain times of the year, particularly when annual or monthly bills arrive and must be paid. It also occurs when we go away on holiday, so the card reversed does not always indicate a difficult time.

The reversed Ace appearing in a relationship layout can suggest financial issues are causing problems. In a career spread it can suggest that your client is leaving a job or that the job in question is not well paid.

The reversed Ace appearing as an answer to a question about a project suggests that the plan is unlikely to be financially rewarding, possibly costing much more than anticipated.

Twos

Aside from the Two of Cups, the Twos generally represent decisions. The Two of Wands indicates a decision about an action such as moving home or changing jobs. The Two of Swords represents the process of weighing up two alternatives mentally, while the Two of Pentacles suggests financial and practical decisions. The Two of Cups differs, in indicating a close relationship. This relationship involves shared decision making, so, in a way, the Two of Cups is still partly a card of decisions.

Three or more Twos in a layout (including the High Priestess, the Major Arcana Two) suggests there are important decisions looming for your client. They indicate that your client needs to take time to make important decisions, or that they are confused about the possibilities offered and need to focus on only one direction.

Two of Wands

The Two of Wands is about the act of deciding between staying in an environment which is familiar and no longer stimulating and making a change which holds promise but which may not deliver what you expect. This is the card which appears when your client is considering leaving their home, or a job, or even a relationship, which they feel is constraining them.

The figure on the card is wearing an orange tunic, which represents an enthusiastic approach to life; he also wears a red hat, denoting a passion for adventure and for mastering the physical world. The world in his hand suggests that his own world feels small to him now, and he is keen to pursue adventure and challenges elsewhere. Those low walls which initially offered him security, now only hem him in and curtail his need to have real contact with life.

The figure in the card will make a decision in his own time, leaving when he feels that circumstances have little to offer him. (This is a typical Wands approach to life: if it isn't challenging, something is wrong.) The water in the distance offers fulfilment, but if the figure is a true Wands person, he will also grow tired of that in time.

Reversed

The Two reversed indicates a time when decisions to act are being thwarted through fear of the new. Your client may be avoiding the fact that their world has grown small now, and that they need some new friends and challenges in order to grow. They are spending too much time weighing up the risks and not focusing enough on possible rewards.

It is time for them to return to the Ace to focus their energy in one direction; to decide what single goal is enough to inspire them to make the necessary changes in their circumstances. The goal must be sufficiently rewarding, and just out of reach so that they have to go in pursuit of it. By the time your client achieves the goal, they will look around and notice that they have moved on from their previous home or job, or other environment.

Two of Cups

In simple terms the Two of Cups signifies a productive union between two people. Whether it be a business or a personal, or even a musical, union, the Two of Cups upright shows that it is a fruitful one.

In similar positioning to the Lovers card, a man stands to the right and a woman stands to the left, facing one another. (This echoes the Major Arcana number Two card, the High Priestess. The two pillars in that card depict the masculine (right) and the feminine (left), or the logical, and the intuitive or creative.) The union between the man and woman results in the winged lion above the two snakes around the rod, or the Caduceus. This represents the great strength resulting from their friendship or relationship.

In most relationships or interactions between people, one partner takes the active role while the other takes a passive role. In this Two the man takes the active role, reaching for the cup and taking one step forward, while the woman takes the passive role. (In reality it might just as easily be the woman who takes the active role, and the man a passive role.)

Reversed

The Two of Cups reversed represents the imbalance often resulting from losing our connection to spiritual fulfilment. When we lose this connection, we may rely too heavily upon others, often those close to us, to fulfil us. To ensure this supply of fulfilment we may seek to control those around us, for fear of being alone or unable to fulfil our emotional and spiritual needs.

The reversed Two can describe a relationship or a partnership where both parties are emotionally unfulfilled as individuals; it is a relationship where each person believes that they are not fulfilled without the other. The reversed card indicates a partnership or relationship which is complicated, but which can be sorted out if the will to address the problems exists.

In simple terms the Two of Cups reversed can indicate two people struggling to find a source of love which does not exist for them. If they wish, they can return to the lesson of the Ace of Cups and reconnect with their own source of fulfilment within, before returning to the upright Two.

Two of Swords

In simple terms the Two of Swords is a card representing decisions. Its appearance in a layout can indicate a time when your client decides where they fit in in the world and what they believe about life.

The figure on the card sits on her stone seat, and holds two swords close to her for protection, despite the fact that she is blindfolded. In order to see the real threats, if any, around her she must remove her blindfold. That is, before you can release yourself from those unresolved fears and past hurts you hold deep within, you must see life for what it truly is. You must peel away the blindfold that is prejudice, opinion and partial fact, to see life clearly, without judging.

The figure's yellow shoes suggest that she is examining life through her thoughts (yellow representing clarity of thought) as she attempts to make sense of all those emotions symbolised by the water behind her. The Hanged Man also has yellow shoes, symbolising his use of thought to free him from circumstances. In the Two of Swords the figure feels restricted by her heart and her feelings. The moon above her also confirms the presence of emotions, increasing with the onset of night. The moon in the Two of Swords is a link with the High Priestess, the Major Arcana Two, revealing that creative solutions to problems can sometimes come from within.

Now and then when this card appears in a reading I add two cards to it, one either side, to clarify what the two alternatives are in the particular situation. For example, in one general reading the Two of Swords appeared as the third card (for the next three months), and I added the Ace of Pentacles and the Page of Swords either side of it, to determine what the client's alternatives were. She agreed that she was undecided about whether to save to take a holiday overseas soon (Page of Swords) or to continue to save her money (Ace of Pentacles) in order to have a longer holiday later.

Reversed

The Two of Swords reversed can highlight mental confusion resulting from too much thought and too little direct experience; you client needs to decide whether to re-enter life emotionally. Sometimes it can suggest they have been attempting to make sense of several emotional issues for a while and need to tackle one issue at a time.

They can return to the Ace of Swords to select one direction and one set of beliefs about life. Tackling one issue at a time is, in effect, a return to the Ace.

You can still ask them to add two cards (one each side) to highlight what issues are confusing them at this point.

Two of Pentacles

The Two of Pentacles indicates a time for your client to put some money aside with a view to being able to pay their way when their income is low. (Pentacles people think ahead to ensure stability for the future and peace of mind for the present.) So, in simple terms, this Two suggests financial decisions being made.

The figure on the card juggles two pentacles, meaning that he is dividing his time, energy and money between several projects at one time. We all do this on a regular basis. We are often juggling, organising which accounts to pay now and which to pay later, or how much to save now and how much to spend. The figure is dressed almost entirely in red and orange, suggesting a strong connection with the physical world and a practical approach to life.

The infinity symbol extending around and linking the two pentacles is a reminder that when you give money away you create a vacuum and that vacuums do not exist for long in the universe. The vacuum may not be filled with more money, but instead with opportunities, possessions or other forms of energy.

The blue skies overhead suggest that at this time finances are stable. However, your client is aware of the ebb and flow of the financial tides (the boats in the background sail on heavy seas, suggesting that money comes and goes in tides), and this may be an opportune time to prepare for the future.

You can add two cards, one each side (for each pentacle), to determine the financial alternatives your client has at present.

Reversed

The Two of Pentacles reversed can suggest being overwhelmed by financial demands. Decisions are crowding in on your client and they cannot decide which bill to pay first. It is likely that their expenses are greater than their income at this time.

To rebalance their financial situation, they need to return to the Ace in order to formulate goals and make clear plans. The Two reversed suggests that they have no clear long-term financial or practical plans due to the pressures of short-term demands. The water is above the pentacles when the card is reversed, suggesting that emotions are influencing or clouding financial issues.

For example, Miranda was trying to study and work part time, and raise her three-year-old daughter, Amelia. Miranda felt guilty about not being there for a part of every day, but she could see no alternative but to work to feed and clothe them both, as her former husband did not support them in any way financially. As the reader, it was my task to help Miranda examine her financial options, while not making any of her decisions for her. I suggested she defer her studies until Amelia was at school, and take another part-time job she had been offered which paid more than the position she then had. I suggested Miranda resume her studies when Amelia started school, in preparation for full-time, well-paid work later on.

When the Pentacles Two appears reversed you can add two cards, one either side, in order to clarify what pressures are bothering your client.

Threes

The Threes in the Tarot describe development of your client's plans. There is the Wands type of development (action, travel, and goals achieved) and the Cups type of development (a deepening of trust between friends or lovers). A Swords development would be an increased understanding by your client of their own self and of life, and a Pentacles development might take the form of a financial investment returning interest, or even the growth of a garden. (For example, a Pentacles friend took me outside one afternoon to show me the apricots on his trees. He beamed with the pride of a man who is about to become a father.) Three or more Threes in a layout suggests that plans are coming to fruition. This is a sign of growth in whatever the layout relates to.

Three of Wands

The Three of Wands indicates a time when any plans your client may have had are now under way and progressing steadily. In simple terms, it is a card depicting travel.

The figure in this card stands on a ridge overlooking the sea, with three wands firmly planted in the ground. He steadies himself with his hand on one wand, and in doing so connects himself with the earth. The fact that we view the figure from behind suggests that he has moved forward from an initial planning phase, to put his plans into practice.

That it can be a card for travelling is indicated by the way the figure stands; planning which boat to take for the next part of the journey he is on. Long travels often contain journeys within journeys, and every major journey can be broken down into its smaller journeys or parts. He has completed a journey by foot, and now contemplates a journey over water. His red cloak highlights the passion he feels for life in the physical world as he plans the next steps on his journey.

This card can also represent a move away from physical challenges and one towards emotional opportunities for growth and development. The figure is moving away from the journey on land (the physical world) and towards one over water (the emotions).

In a relationship layout the Three of Wands suggests a connection between two people which is growing and developing. In a career layout this card implies a job involving travel; perhaps one in the travel industry itself. In a health layout it indicates current good health, a return to health, or travel for health reasons. Its appearance in answer to a question usually suggests success and the fulfilment of your client's plans.

Reversed

The Three of Wands reversed represents delays in plans and a lack of growth. It requires your client to return to the Two in order to decide which path or approach to their goals is most appropriate.

When the card is reversed the water depicted is above the figure, suggesting that emotional issues need to be resolved before real growth can occur. In some cases it means that unresolved emotional issues are urging your client onwards when they need to be at rest in order to reflect and to decide what they need.

In a health layout the Three of Wands reversed can represent the need to return to the Two in order to find a new path towards health and wellbeing.

Three of Cups

The Three of Cups is a card of celebration. Weddings, reunions, birthdays, and Christmas or New Year's celebrations are all indicated by it.

The three figures in this card are seen dancing together in celebration at a fruitful harvest. Blue skies above them hint at a continuing growth and halcyon days ahead. The colours in their clothing represent their different motivations for participation. The white robe suggests pure, altruistic motives; the red robe reveals a more passionate, earthy approach; and the earthy tones of the third robe indicate a need to be grounded and to receive earthy rewards for efforts.

Traditionally, men compete with others whereas women seek community. Therefore, there are only women in this card, which represents support from those in your community in both good times and bad.

The appearance of this card may mean that those around your client have helped them towards their goals and are present to celebrate their achievements. In a career spread it signifies a group project where all the participants benefit from the success of the project, that is, a team effort resulting in success.

In simple terms the Three of Cups can signify that your client is surrounded by like-minded people, and that they feel loved and supported. Having friends to share in your successes is as important as having friends who support you through your trials.

Reversed

The Three of Cups reversed reveals a lack of support from those in your client's community. Perhaps they are being ignored, or those around them are simply too busy with their own goals and problems to notice your client's issues.

The Three of Cups reversed is the other kind of Christmas celebration, where the family gathers together to finish last year's ongoing argument. After a few drinks, words fly and, fuelled by a few more drinks, the festivity soon looks like a wild pub at closing time.

The solution here is for your client to return to the Two, select one person with whom they share particular views and spend time with them. Carrying on the Christmas theme, at Christmas gatherings it could pay for your client to spend their time with one particular family member, and stay out of 'the line of fire'.

Regarding family situations, the appearance of the card reversed can suggest a person causing tension by their words or actions. For example, it could indicate there is a relative living with a newly married couple; perhaps a child from a previous relationship, who resents the current situation.

In terms of your client's love relationship it can suggest a third person is involved. This could mean one party is having an affair, or that a relative or close friend is influencing the thoughts and actions of one of the partners. If there is a love triangle the Three reversed suggests a need to return to the Two in order to rebuild trust and intimacy.

The appearance of the card in a career layout can point to the presence of a team that is more competitive than cooperative. Each person in it seeks a reward or promotion at the expense of the others. There is a lack of respect for each other and plainly a lack of team spirit.

In a general sense the Three reversed can suggest that your client is among people who do not 'fit' with them. In essence, they need to return to the Two of Cups to find one close friend or partner before expanding their circle of friends.

Three of Swords

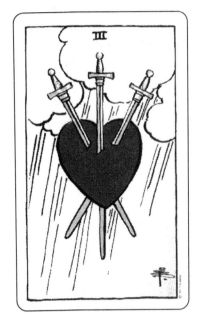

The Three of Swords is a card representing grief, emotional pain and loss. If into every life a little rain must fall, when the Three of Swords appears in a layout the person is centred deep within a storm. Some readers shudder at the appearance of this card, but grief and loss are a part of life.

This card shows a storm and three swords plunged into a heart. The implications of this vivid picture are immediately evident, even to the beginner.

Regarding health, the card's appearance can suggest heart trouble, or illness resulting from unresolved grief and loss. Like those things that bring us joy, the things that cause us pain cannot be compared to what brings other people pain.

The lesson of the Three of Swords is for your client to accept the loss or sadness and in doing so, allow it to pass; only when grief is accepted can it subside. For some, it is not the loss itself which is the source of the greatest pain, but the powerlessness to do anything about it. However, being powerless in the face of life and circumstances is a part of the human condition. In the case of the death of a loved one, accepting that there is, or was, nothing you could do to change the course of events is the first step towards eventual healing.

Reversed

The Three of Swords reversed indicates your client's inability to accept or deal with their pain or loss. It can represent a past grief that is being supressed or current circumstances that do not allow your client to grieve.

An example of the kind of situation represented by the Three reversed was that of Holly, who was left to raise three young children alone when her husband died suddenly, aged thirty-eight. She wanted to grieve but she had to feed and house the children. Her time for her own grief was non-existent, until fifteen years later when she collapsed into despair. Until the children were old enough to look after themselves she had felt unable to remove her focus from simple survival.

Suppressed pain rarely goes away of its own accord and, as more pain is suppressed, stronger techniques are required to avoid facing it. Greg had a business, and this functioned as his way of avoiding a tragic past. In time, working hard wasn't enough to enable him to avoid his feelings, so he took to gambling and then to alcohol. After he lost his business, he had plenty of time to examine himself and how he felt.

So the reversed Three of Swords can describe a suppressed grief from the past which, although unconscious, affects every choice and action of your client in the present. Suppressed emotions require a great deal of energy, both to have the emotions and to suppress them, leaving limited energy for new experiences and for life in general. As a reader, your task is to determine what has led to these feelings of pain and loss, and to encourage your client to face and experience them, and move forward into their life. It is time for them to return to the Two to examine their options.

Three of Pentacles

In simple terms the Three of Pentacles represents the growth which is possible with solid foundations. A tall tree with shallow roots is liable to blow over in the first strong wind, and Pentacles people realise this. Hence this card shows the four elements combining to build something lasting. This is a card for study and learning; for steady growth resulting from careful planning.

The card shows a scene involving an architect and a clergyman examining the plans for a church as a tradesman sets to work on the structure. They are building a monument to God and a reminder of our purpose in this world.

The three pentacles in the arch above them remind us that all success, material or otherwise, comes from God or spirit (the source of energy and life). To enjoy the fruits of the earth we must remain connected to both the earth (the pillar supporting the arch stands firmly in the earth) and to spirit.

Two smaller arches stand within one large arch, representing the Holy Trinity: the Father (God, the source) the son (Jesus, Buddha, etc.) and the Holy Spirit, which is the invisible life force and depicted in all the Aces in the form of the clouds. This multiplicity of three appears in many schools of thought, including the Kahuna teachings of Hawaii. They teach that each of us has a physical self, a mental self and a spiritual, or high, self to which we can direct prayers.

The clergyman represents Water (Cups) in the form of the person who meditates upon the hidden side of life. The architect represents Air (Swords), with his plans or drawings, and concepts. The tradesman represents Fire (Wands), being the person who

will actually construct the building. The building itself represents Earth (Pentacles) and stands as a reminder of what is essentially important in life.

Reversed

The Three of Pentacles reversed can indicate a lack of growth resulting from insufficient planning and/or poor foundations of a project. It shows your client's reluctance to learn from experience and that they are likely to repeat current patterns until they learn the lessons contained therein.

In a relationship spread this card suggests a repetitive pattern of behaviour that prevents the relationship from reaching its full potential. The four elements contained in the card are not combined harmoniously, and growth cannot occur until they are in harmony once again. The reversed Three can also indicate mediocre work or lacklustre living due to insufficient planning or destructive habits.

Your client needs to return to the Two in order to decide which path to take. Perhaps they are trying to do too much or have lost sight of the details of a project.

Fours

The Fours in the Tarot describe consolidation, from the Wands' need to settle down in a home or work environment to the Cups' need for emotional stability. The Swords approach is to take some time to make sense of things, through reflection, and the Pentacles approach is to save money in order to have a solid financial footing for any plans. Three or more Fours in a layout suggest a period of stability and consolidation. Your client is making solid, tangible progress.

Four of Wands

The Four of Wands is a card representing moving to a new home or workplace. Wands people enjoy new experiences and when they decide to change something they usually do so rapidly. (The planning is usually left to the Swords people, who like to glimpse the consequences of their actions before taking the first physical step towards carrying them out.) The Four of Wands indicates the community is showing signs of benefiting from the good times or success at hand.

On the card a wreath of welcome is tied to four upright wands that stand firmly in the ground. Two figures wave flowers and another group stands in the background, outside the castle walls. The fact that they are outside the walls of the castle suggests that they feel secure.

If the Four of Wands appears and a home or work move is not forthcoming for your client, it can describe a refurbishment of present surroundings. It represents settling into a new environment or re-settling into the present one. In any case, it suggests a stable home or work environment, and the number Four is a number of consolidation or practical application of the element of Wands (or Fire). That is, directing enthusiasm and restlessness toward a purpose benefiting the community.

Wands people can be self-absorbed, especially when you consider that in order to compete with others they need to remain focused on what they have to do to win. This means that those around them are often required to help them achieve their purpose. This works if the other people share your client's vision or if your client can inspire the community to help them; it can become problematic if all of your client's goals are personal ones.

Reversed

The Four of Wands reversed suggests a lack of stability or consolidation. It can still represent a positive time, but the positive time is transient. It may be that your client is working on a project that brings together compatible people with harmonious ideas, but that they'll each go their own way when the project has concluded.

In a relationship spread the Four reversed suggests that your client will be in a short-lived relationship before they return to the Three and decide where to move on to next. Thus, your client is experiencing a time of growth and joy but, like all festivities, it will be over soon, so they need to make the most of it.

Perhaps the stability your client is temporarily enjoying is the result of the hard work of others, and they are only passing through; for example, during travel when you spend a few days or weeks in a town before moving on. The community is, for example, responsible for the maintenance of parks and gardens, and you temporarily enjoy the results of these efforts.

Four of Cups

In simple terms, the Four of Cups is a card about taking a step back in order to ask yourself if the external things life is currently offering you will be fulfilling. It indicates that it is time for your client to remember the Ace of Cups and the joy it offered them through being connected to their spiritual purpose.

In this card the figure sitting in contemplation is aware of external opportunities but realises that inner fulfilment is paramount.

The cup in the hand extending from a cloud is the key to him enjoying the opportunities offered by the three cups standing in front of him. He is aware that pursuing the chances represented by the cups before him will require commitment, time and effort.

All outer fulfilment is fleeting, and only a reliable source of inner peace and happiness can bridge the times between external accomplishments. The Four of Cups indicates your client is consolidating their connection to inner peace (the cup from the cloud) and to outer fulfilment (the three cups).

From time to time we must take a step back from exterior things in order to nourish ourselves from within. Meditation is one reliable way to access spiritual nourishment and to rebalance our physical, emotional, mental and spiritual selves.

Reversed

The Four of Cups reversed suggests that your client is no longer connected to their source of inner fulfilment and that their exterior opportunities are also unrewarding. It is time for them to return to the Three of Cups to associate with people who may show them a path to inner peace or to new opportunities.

For example, Ellie had spent fourteen months struggling to write a book. During this time she had declined all social invitations in order to focus on the task at hand. At the end of this period she was exhausted, and unsatisfied with the results of her work.

I suggested she ring her friends and arrange to meet them for coffee, lunch, etc., and in a month she was back in the swing of things socially. At a friend's house-warming party she was given the name of an editor and mentor who worked one to one with writers. Two months later she had rewritten her book with the help of her new editor and was satisfied with the results.

In returning to the Three of Cups and re-integrating socially, Ellie was able to access the help she needed to move forward with her writing project. Returning to the Three allowed her to return to the lesson of the upright Four on her way to completing her creative project.

Sometimes the return to the Three of Cups is a chance to pursue another direction entirely. This opportunity often comes through friends or social situations.

Four of Swords

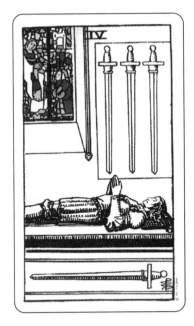

The Fours are cards of consolidation, and the Four of Swords represents mental consolidation. It represents a time for your client to reflect upon past conversations and actions, and the consequences of those words and actions. It can be a time for them to clarify their plans or their direction; to make sense of life. Learning from past actions through reflecting upon them can save time and effort in the future, if they come to realise which approaches work for them and which are fruitless.

The leadlight window on the card contains a scene of a disciple receiving a blessing from someone more senior. The figure laying in the foreground is receiving this blessing mentally, while meditating. His body being entirely yellow suggests that his mind is active despite his body being at rest.

Some of us meditate, while others of us enter into counselling with another person. Reflection time is still required after a counselling session, as your client examines what was brought to light by the therapist. Quiet time spent in reflection is especially necessary in the Swords suit, where thoughts about the future can excite the person, scatter energy or cause disturbance and pain.

Reversed

The Four of Swords reversed indicates disregard of contemplation, usually resulting in pain. There is a need for your client to return to the Three of Swords in order to experience the pain that separates them from life. When it subsides, they will be left with the upright Four as they attempt to make sense of what happened.

For example, Robert's mother died when he was six years old. Robert decided that all women leave sooner or later, and chose to avoid romantic relationships as an adult in order to elude the possible pain of loss. After some encouragement, he allowed the pain of the loss of his mother to sweep through him, reducing him to emotional rubble for nearly a year. When the pain eventually subsided he was in a position to learn to trust again.

The appearance of the Four reversed can suggest a person who is rushing around, doing a hundred things at once to avoid reflecting on past actions or experiences. Eventually, when they tire themselves out, those issues will be waiting for them. Scattered thinking and little regard for the consequences of thoughts or words are also shown by the Four reversed.

Four of Pentacles

In simple terms the Four of Pentacles indicates your client can afford (financially) to put plans into action. They have the money to build a house, take a holiday, or to finance a project, or are currently saving this money.

The figure on the card is cloaked in red and black with a thin line of pale blue. He is grounded in the material world, confirmed by the pentacles in his hands, beneath his feet and on his head. The pentacles represent money or material possessions, and separate him from the earth (beneath his feet) and from the heavens (above his head, covering his crown chakra or energy centre).

The pentacles blocking his heart can leave him feeling that things are more important than people. He surrounds himself with material things and must guard against allowing these things to come between him and other people; between him and life. If that happens, he moves into the emptiness shown in the Five of Pentacles.

In general terms the Four of Pentacles shows financial discipline. Regarding relationships it can indicate someone who barters their affections. In terms of health, this is also one of the cards for the sign of Taurus. Taureans tend toward problems in the neck and throat area, so this Four can represent neck and throat tension.

Reversed

The Four of Pentacles reversed can indicate depleted financial reserves and/or the inability of your client to save the money necessary to achieve a goal. Money is slipping through their fingers now.

However, if the Four reversed appears in a relationship spread it can represent the ability to give wholeheartedly in order to build a solid and lasting relationship. Sometimes it represents the need to place more value on those things you are giving to others. The Four reversed takes your client back to the Three of Pentacles, which indicates the need to build something lasting through establishing strong foundations.

Fives

The Fives in the Tarot depict change, and the four suits show four different approaches to change. The Wands suit indicates eagerness for change, whereas the Cups suit suggests the loss that accompanies it. The Swords suit is about how the need for inner change can lead to arguments that force outer transformation, and the Pentacles suit shows how limited your ability to determine the changes in your own life becomes when you lack financial stability. Three or more Fives (including the Hierophant, the Major Arcana Five) in a layout highlight a period of change. If the Fives appear reversed, your client is open to the changes.

Five of Wands

As mentioned, the Five of Wands represents an enthusiastic approach to change. The approach of Wands people is to force change in order to appease their restlessness. The appearance of this Five indicates a need for a purpose behind action; the scattered energy resulting from undirected enthusiasm can be exhausting even to those watching.

The card depicts five people enthusiastically waving wands around with a disregard for each other. This represents the Wands person's enthusiasm and recklessness, which, although deserving of admiration, can leave you with bruises if you get too close to the action.

The card can represent the several different parts of one person, with each part having a different purpose. I have a friend named Angus, who typifies the Five of Wands. In the morning he can be full of beans and impatient to change the world. By lunchtime he is pensive, sitting quietly while preparing to write a short poem. After lunch he's on the phone to eight people back to back, and by early evening he is highly critical of those around him, telling them in no uncertain terms what he thinks about their efforts as he beats some eggs and waits for his socks to dry in the oven.

In a relationship spread the Five of Wands can describe juggling of work, social and family commitments, resulting in two people who are rarely spending undisturbed time with one another.

For example, there is a couple I know who e-mail one another when they are both at home. As she eats breakfast and he showers, rather than walk into the bathroom to tell her husband what she needs to say, she leaves a message on his e-mail so that he can read it on the way to work in the morning. They must have the quietest arguments of any couple around.

In answer to a question about achieving a specific goal or purpose, the Five suggests a lack of success due to too many other commitments. It can describe those times when everyone is screaming at you, demanding your time and attention, and leaving you lacking in real focus.

Reversed

The Five of Wands reversed indicates a realisation by your client that focus is essential to achieving a goal. Perhaps due to sheer physical and emotional exhaustion, they are sitting and reflecting upon the appropriate path to take to realise their objectives. After a period of confusion or scattered focus, they are able to regain their sense of what is important.

The different coloured tunics worn by the figures on the card represent physical, emotional, mental and spiritual needs, all crowding in to be met at once. When it appears reversed, this means your client is able to meet each need with the attention and energy it deserves.

Also, when the card is reversed, the earth appears above all the scattered energy of the wands, suggesting that material or physical (earthy) concerns are forcing your client to become more realistic at this time.

The Five of Wands reversed shows the need for your client, after realising they must focus to achieve a goal, to return to the Four of Wands in order to regain stability. In that situation, a team of like-minded people can work together toward a common goal for shared success.

Five of Cups

The Five of Cups represents your client spending time looking back. Before they can embrace the new they must grieve that which is gone forever.

In this card heavy, grey skies blanket what might otherwise be a tranquil scene. The overturned cups hold the attention of the figure in black, who is grieving for lost opportunities for fulfilment. The figure is blind to life around them; thus, the Five of Cups can represent narrow-mindedness. Their environment is offering the figure little that they are prepared to receive, and they isolate themselves from the river, the source of renewed fulfilment. The card depicts the way most grief is an isolating experience.

In simple terms this card can represent grieving the loss of a job, a relationship, or even the loss of wasted years spent with a person, or in some other fruitless situation. For example, Jasmine fell into a deep depression soon after she left her abusive husband of thirty years. Before she could face the task of rebuilding her life, she had to grieve the years she had spent in what she described as a lifeless relationship.

Remember that while this card depicts grief or loss, it is only a step towards your client's ultimate destiny. Grief is unavoidable if you become emotionally attached to people, animals and things. In time, when the grief has passed, your client will be able to regain their awareness of life and all it offers them. When awareness of life's opportunities returns, your client may see the bridge over the river, leading to the stability offered in the castle. This castle is shown more clearly in the Six of Cups.

Reversed

The Five of Cups reversed indicates the release of loss and grief, and the desire to return to the Four of Cups in order to become reacquainted with inner sources of spiritual and emotional fulfilment. The grief and loss represented by the upright Five ensure that your client will appreciate the stability of the upright Six of Cups when they arrive there.

The Five of Cups reversed indicates a time for your client to realise that there are other cups aside from those which have been overturned, and that there is a bridge over the river (the emotions) leading back to the castle, which symbolises stability. Regardless of how long ago your client's loss or separation occurred, the

Five reversed shows the release of any sense of grief or isolation. They can walk back into life now.

The Five appeared reversed in a relationship layout for a client who had recently reunited with his former wife after they had resolved their differences. In other cases I've seen it signal the extinguishment of a flame kept burning for a past lover and an increased awareness by a client of what their current relationship offers.

Five of Swords

The Five of Swords represents the mental acceptance of change. It can also show change occurring through words, such as in disagreements where each party speaks their mind. Therefore, in simple terms, it can be a card for arguments. Its appearance in answer to a question about the resolution of a dispute suggests ongoing disagreements or a parting of the ways.

The energy-charged clouds scattered across the sky in this card represent angry or aggressive thinking resulting in arguments and tension. The figure in the foreground wears red under his green tunic, suggesting that he is easily roused to passionate discourse. He speaks his mind, forcing the issue with his three swords (thoughts, arguments and passionately held beliefs) and, although he wins the argument, he loses the war.

The three swords represent the pain he has experienced in the Three of Swords, and now he turns this pain outward in the form of words and actions that hurt those around him. He responds inappropriately to his inner torment, venting his anger to hide his fears about being powerless in life. He cannot engage the cooperation of the others in this card, as they feel betrayed or brutalised by his actions. He will be left alone or ignored by those around him, giving him plenty of time (in the Six of Swords) to reflect on his past words and actions, and their consequences.

Sometimes when we cannot accept change in our lives we fight against it. This fight can be with those who appear to bring the change to us, or simply with those close to us for allowing the change to happen. In some cases the Five represents different parts of the one person, being angry, hurt, abandoned and vulnerable all at once. If you disturb this person you could be on the receiving end of one of their swords, in the form of sharp words or actions.

Reversed

The Five of Swords reversed represents a more open-minded approach to change. Perhaps the arguing is over now, and there is an opportunity for real negotiation as the parties involved have a chance to be heard by one another.

For example, Maree's husband had been harassing her and disputing the division of property during a nasty divorce settlement. Having found a new partner, he suddenly gave up arguing with Maree, and they reached an agreement in six weeks that they had not previously arrived at in five years. Another example of a Five reversed situation is when parliament passes a bill at 2:30 am. After hours of disagreement, exhaustion suddenly makes the MPs more agreeable.

In effect this reversed card shows a need for your client to return to the Four to listen to their inner needs. They may then be less threatened when hearing the needs of those around them. The tranquillity of the Four gives an air of order to proceedings when groups or families get together to negotiate a change.

Five of Pentacles

The Five of Pentacles suggests that a change is necessary before your client can find their proper path again. Perhaps they are too focused on one part of their life at the cost of personal or spiritual development. In simple terms the card represents the material approach to change. Poverty can force us to change or simplify our lives in order to re-evaluate what is important to us.

The couple on the card need to experience poverty so that they will know the other side of the coin. If they remember these days of deprivation clearly when they are wealthy again (in the Ten of Pentacles) they are likely to be more generous towards and understanding of those in need. The toughest steel is forged in the heat of a raging furnace, as character is strengthened by challenges met.

Perhaps a period of poverty is required for your client to have full appreciation of wealth. This poverty may be financial, emotional, mental or spiritual. Whatever type it is, your client feels excluded from a source of fulfilment, as the figures in this card feel excluded from the church by the thick wall.

In a career layout the card can suggest that your client is currently working too hard.

It can imply that their career is leaving them unfulfilled, or that the pursuit of financial or material success is clouding their awareness of their spiritual path.

As well as poverty, the Five of Pentacles can suggest poor health, low vitality and a spiritual emptiness. The figures in this card don't only need financial success to improve their lives; they need to reconnect with their spiritual paths.

Reversed

The Five of Pentacles reversed can suggest a departure from a work environment or a living situation that has been holding your client back. The card shows the need for your client to return to the Four of Pentacles in order to consolidate their financial or physical approach to life.

Darryl was working full time as a waiter when he really wanted to return to wood carving. He resigned from his job as soon as he was accepted into a wood-carving academy. His leaving an unrewarding situation and moving toward something more fulfilling was shown in the Five reversed that appeared in his layout.

Sometimes the Five of Pentacles reversed symbolises the return to well-paid work after a period of unemployment. It can also suggest a separation which is inevitable; both parties realise that they will not be fulfilled if they continue the relationship and they part without regret.

Sixes

The Sixes in the Tarot depict stability, and the four suits show four approaches to stability. The Wands suit represents stability as the period soon after a goal has been achieved and before the urge to achieve another goal presents itself, whereas the Cups suit is about the emotional contentment longed for by Cups people. The Swords suit shows stability as the gradual change of beliefs after a period of mental or physical turmoil, and the Pentacles suit is about financial stability stemming from each participant in a project knowing their place. When three or more Sixes appear in a layout, general stability is indicated and, when they appear reversed, growth is suggested.

Six of Wands

The appearance of the Six of Wands indicates your client is harnessing their energies to pursue a particular direction, usually resulting in success. Gone is the confusion shown in the Five of Wands, as they have realised that to achieve their objective they need to avoid distractions, and inspire those around them to support them in their quest. In simple terms this is a card about achieving your goals.

The card shows a figure riding a horse in a victory parade. His win is the result of the confidence and enthusiasm Wands people have in abundance. Clothed in red (suggesting passion and physical application to the task at hand) he is enjoying his success before the next challenge calls. The clear skies over the figure suggest that there are few obstacles to his path at this point. This is an example of confidence and application resulting in success.

The figure in this card shares his victory with others, as they have helped him achieve his position. It was his belief in himself that inspired those around him to help. Wands people often possess an infectious enthusiasm that can make the impossible seem close enough to be just reachable, with effort.

In a relationship layout the Six of Wands can mean a new commitment in your client's relationship, whether it be moving in together, marriage or the birth of a child. The appearance of the card in a career layout can mean a promotion, a new job, a successful conclusion to a project or a new position within your client's present company. As the answer to a question generally, provided that there are no conflicting cards, the Six of Wands means 'yes' to the question asked.

Reversed

The Six of Wands reversed shows a return to the Five of Wands and to the confusion shown there. Perhaps your client is attempting too many things at once or giving up on their goals long before they achieve them. Their confidence is waning, and with it the support of those who need to be inspired to commit themselves to the goal. It can also signify your client is confused about their real purpose in life.

For example, Jerome was unsure of what was really important to him. He was working longer hours at work in order to secure a promotion, and his relationship was suffering. He was studying at night to gain further qualifications and trying to keep fit by jogging early each morning. At weekends he was trying to renovate his house, and it was evident to me that Jerome was attempting too much in a short time. This was confirmed by the three telephone calls he took during the reading and his short attention span.

Your client is spending too much time resolving problems involving those around them in their career or relationship for them to be able to take any concrete steps toward their goals. In simple terms the Six reversed can signify losing a job, leaving a relationship, missing out on a promotion or a general lack of success.

Six of Cups

The Six of Cups can represent returning to familiar places, such as the home or the town where you spent your childhood, or to a familiar career, in order to collect yourself. It can also be a time of bringing together those spiritual or emotional parts of you that you have left behind. In simple terms this is a card representing continuing stability and comfortable routines.

The two figures on the card itself are at once big and little. They are adults and share an adult relationship, but are safely surrounded, and somewhat dwarfed, by the castle. Their mature faces and bodies are at odds with their children's clothing. They are repotting flowers in a garden; the woman wears a gardening glove. The couple are nurturing the plants and one another at the same time. The tenderness between the figures in this card shows a time to recreate purity and innocence, as do the white flowers being transplanted. The figure walking away in the background suggests that others are helping things to run smoothly, providing some of the structure or the stability this scene illustrates.

We often, especially after great change or upheaval, need a period of time where life is reassuringly familiar. The Six of Cups is about the emotional approach to stability, showing a time when the incidental things are taken care of as your client heals, or re-collects their reserves of energy.

It is a rest on the path to the Ten; this rest is as valuable as the growth represented by other cards, as it lets them experience a brief glimpse of the Ten and reaffirm what they are seeking long term.

Reversed

The Six of Cups reversed suggests that your client is feeling hemmed in by the constraints of familiar routines. They seek change and growth, and in order to achieve these, they must return to the Five, leaving behind their comfortable, secure environment for new horizons.

For example, James, at nineteen years of age, was feeling frustrated with living at home with his parents. He wanted to share a house with other young people and to experience life as a young man first-hand, without the rules of his parental home. He saved some money, and moved out of home and into a flat by the beach with two friends.

Leaving the security and familiarity of his family home for the freedom of the flat by the sea was both a loss and a liberation. For some months he hovered between the two, returning to his parental home for meals and support, and using the flat as the base for his new lifestyle of surfing, partying and meeting new friends. The reversed Six had shown his need for new horizons.

In short, the Six of Cups reversed shows that new patterns of behaviour or unfamiliar territory are about to be embraced as the desire for change replaces the need for security.

Six of Swords

The Six of Swords represents your client's mental approach to the need for stability. The card indicates they are retreating from disagreements in order to reflect; they recognise the need to have stable emotions in order to think clearly.

In this card a family steers its boat away from turbulent waters into calmer surrounds. The six swords, or beliefs about life, are firmly planted in the boat, suggesting that we take our view of the world wherever we go. They weigh heavily as the figure manoeuvres the vessel, just as our beliefs can weigh us down in daily life. Heavy cloud depicts confused thinking.

In a relationship layout the Six of Swords can signify the settling of differences which had caused tension, as a new understanding allows for a more stable relationship. In a career layout it represents stability resulting from your client understanding why things have gone the way they have for them. In a health layout the card symbolises a slow, steady healing after difficult times.

When placed alongside the Death card in a health reading the Six of Swords can signify a tranquil passing from this world to the next. An example of this came up in a reading for Zoe, who shook her head when I mentioned a recent quiet passing. It was her mother's death, and Zoe explained the way it had happened: 'I don't believe it. She fought with everyone her whole life and then she dies peacefully in her sleep. She was causing trouble with all of us right up to the end. When I heard that she had died peacefully I wanted to slap her'.

The Six of Swords shows the act of moving away from a source of conflict in order to make sense of your beliefs about life. In simple terms it is about allowing life to settle emotionally or removing yourself from an emotionally challenging situation. It can also represent travel over water, as shown by the image on the card itself.

Reversed

The Six of Swords reversed indicates a need to return to the Five in order to bring issues to the surface. Having an argument can sometimes clear the air to allow negotiation, and the Six reversed represents the act of seeking emotional upheaval in order to get the energy of a situation moving again so that it can be resolved.

In a travel layout the Six reversed can signify travel resulting in upheaval. An example of this came up in a reading for Michael, who was planning a trip home to visit his parents to tell them that he was gay. He expected some emotional conflict as a result of the visit, and the Six reversed confirmed this would be the case. However, Michael felt that it was necessary to tell his parents in order for them to have an opportunity to have an honest relationship with him.

Sometimes the Six reversed can show that your client is not satisfied with their stable life and that something within them is driving them toward conflict. This might be a good time for them to examine their beliefs about life and stability.

Six of Pentacles

The Six of Pentacles represents the earthy approach to stability, as Pentacles people know the value of money in making life materially stable. To this end they are prepared to make sacrifices in order to enjoy the stability which money affords them. In simple terms this card depicts the community looking after its members so that everyone can have a reasonable life. It can also signify your client getting a new job or a loan of money to pursue their plans.

In this card we see a wealthy man giving some coins to one of two people kneeling on the ground before him. The figures from the Five of Pentacles are gratefully receiving a portion of what the wealthy man has to offer. He shares his abundance so that stability is preserved; if he did not share with them, they might die or become lawless in the pursuit of enough money to survive. Therefore, his generosity, in fact, preserves his comfortable lifestyle.

In a relationship layout the appearance of the Six can signify that one partner has the role of the wealthy man, dispensing a small portion of the money/love/energy they have to the others (partner and children) in the relationship. This person controls the relationship and its direction, while the other partner has the passive role. The roles of the relationship are clearly defined, leaving the partners unequal; however, if you look closely, you will often find that both partners agree to this arrangement to ensure stability.

The appearance of the upright Six of Pentacles in answer to a question about a legal matter can represent a sum of money being awarded to your client. In a health layout, the Six depicts the act of spending money to ensure stability in health. Perhaps your client is regularly attending a gym, or having a weekly massage or bodywork session to maintain their physical fitness and reduce their stress.

Reversed

The Six of Pentacles reversed suggests that your client is presently controlled by their financial circumstances. In simple terms it describes a lack of control over financial matters, leading to a lack of stability. They may be experiencing difficulties meeting their financial commitments. Perhaps there are too many people depending on them financially at this time and their resources are being stretched thin.

Its appearance in a relationship layout suggests that your client is being dominated by another person and that a separation (a return to the Five) is necessary to reclaim their personal power. In a career layout the Six reversed can suggest that your client is leaving their job or that they are unemployed at present. It can also highlight the fact that they are putting too much into their work for what they receive in return. In answer to a question about a legal matter, it can suggest that a sum of money will be awarded against your client in favour of another party.

Generally, the Six reversed describes your client's return to the Five in order to re-experience being cut off from their financial security or pushed out of their comfort zone. This is a financial winter time but it, too, will pass. Change is required before they can return to stability once again.

Sevens

The Sevens in the Tarot symbolise the realisation by your client that a new approach is required in order for them to achieve their goals. When three or more Sevens appear in a layout it suggests that while their method of obtaining their goals may have to change, they should not give up on their ambitions.

The Wands suit signifies having too many irons in the fire, whereas the Cups suit indicates someone searching within themselves. (Cups people regularly look within themselves for a greater understanding of their motives and to reassess their feelings about people and situations, so their task in the Seven is easy.) The Swords suit represents the adaptability of the mind, and how fine the line is between changing your view of the world and deceiving yourself about circumstances. The Pentacles suit indicates an opportunity to reflect upon your goals because current projects are taking care of themselves.

Seven of Wands

'Don't give up' is the theme of the Sevens, and the Seven of Wands concerns the need to stay on top of physical challenges. In simple terms this Seven can indicate your client having to channel their energy into one purpose to avoid obstacles that may prevent their success.

In this card a man defends himself against the opposing forces represented by the six wands before him. He stands upon higher ground and is completely focused on the task at hand. Blue skies above him confirm that this is not a fight to the death, but rather a self-imposed challenge he carries out to maintain or improve his skills. He wears odd shoes, suggesting that he has dressed hastily, rising to a challenge that arrived without warning. The shoes also highlight his transition from the Six of Wands to the Eight; one foot rests in the stability of the Six, while the other rests in the strength of the Eight. As he moves through the Seven to the Eight of Wands, he must face more challenges and streamline or delegate responsibilities before he can accept the rewards of the free-flowing energy of the Eight.

For example, Brett wanted to compete in an international rowing event. This required fitness training, dawn practice with his rowing team and a full-time job to earn money for airfares. There were cold, dark mornings in winter when he didn't want to get out of bed, let alone row into the low mist over the icy cold river, but he didn't give up. He forced himself to perform the task at hand one day at a time, and this attitude eventually led to his triumph in an international championship.

Reversed

The Seven of Wands reversed indicates your client is becoming overwhelmed by challenges or responsibilities, and needs to return to the Six in order to focus on fewer things at one time. (The Six represents the projects or goals you can adequately handle at once.)

The odd shoes worn by the figure on the card are highlighted now, signifying a lack of careful preparation, which is resulting in chaos and the need for short-term crisis management. Your client needs to return to the stability offered in the Six before they will have time to prepare for the additional responsibilities offered in the Seven.

In career layout the Seven reversed can indicate a person who has a job for which they are unsuited. Perhaps they are not coping with a recent promotion and feel that everyone is demanding something from them continuously. A return to a more familiar, and less demanding career position in the Six may allow them to find a suitable place among the team.

Too many people or situations are demanding their attention now, and they are losing focus. If they pursue their present direction they could be swamped by life's demands. That is why they need to return to a simpler, more focused path (as shown in the Six). Don't hold on is the message of the Seven reversed. Don't release yourself from life's demands, but focus on the important things only at this time.

Seven of Cups

The Seven of Cups represents the emotional and spiritual need not to give up the search for purpose. It is about the quiet moments when we look within ourselves to find out who we are. In coming to terms with who you are, you can gain an understanding of what fulfils you. It enables you to know what career suits you, what type of relationship might help you become more fulfilled, and what weaknesses need to be overcome as you pursue your true spiritual purpose.

On the card a figure in silhouette examines the contents of seven cups contained within a cloud. The person depicted is searching among the different aspects of themselves to discover who they are spiritually.

In simple terms the Seven represents the search within for fulfilment. As you search you glimpse those unresolved issues which prevent you from maintaining inner peace. These issues may include: others perceiving you in a limiting way (shown by the cup containing the face), according to your persona or to the mask you wear in life; and matters relating to your home environment (shown by the cup containing the castle), your self-worth and your material worth (shown by the cup containing the jewellery), your inner strength and self-confidence (shown by the cup containing the wreath), your subconscious connection to your true spiritual purpose (shown by the cup containing the demon) and your sexual and creative energies (shown by the cup containing the snake).

So, essentially this card depicts the search for your true self as found under the shroud in the centre cup. This card represents the act of not giving up in the search for your spiritual self. In simple terms it can describe a time where your client asks what makes them happy. They are reflecting upon past choices, and deciding about their future regarding work, relationship and interests that might bring them fulfilment.

Reversed

The Seven of Cups reversed denotes refusal to examine yourself, and to ask yourself what might fulfil you. Instead of taking a few quiet moments to reflect, your client is filling every waking hour with the pursuit of things which may or may not satisfy them. They won't know if these pursuits will offer them any real fulfilment until they rest awhile and consult those different parts within to determine what they truly want.

The Seven reversed shows your client is holding on to what they are familiar with, or on to what once fulfilled them, and refusing to update their information about life and their new needs. This indicates that they need to return to the upright Six, in order to have enough security to reflect without the fear that their life will collapse around them if they do so.

Seven of Swords

The Seven of Swords signifies deceit, a lack of clear communication or the presence of hidden agendas. However, it can also suggest that your client should not give up on their goals, as they may find a way of reaching them through a new approach to overcoming any obstacles.

In this card golden skies suggest sunrise or sunset as a figure steals away with five swords belonging to those in the military camp in the background. The people in the camp are foreigners and he is using their swords (ideas, plans or military information) for his own ends.

In a relationship layout the Seven can suggest deceit, but other cards are needed to confirm this. Perhaps your client is being dishonest with themselves about what they want from their relationship.

For example, Taylor appeared to be happily married with two small children. Each Sunday afternoon he visited his aged mother in a nursing home for a few hours, until his wife Athena discovered that his mother had died two years before. It turned out that Taylor had a male lover in another part of town, whom he visited each Wednesday morning and Sunday afternoon. Taylor clearly wasn't being honest about what he wanted in a relationship. The Seven of Swords and the Knight of Cups alongside the Three of Cups reversed confirmed this.

Alternately the Seven can suggest a new approach to a problem is available, through thinking about it in a different light. For example, Stephen often complained that he needed $300 a week to rent a small house to live in, but he did not have enough money. A friend suggested that he really only needed a small house to live in, not $300. Five months later we received invitations to his housewarming party. He had been asked to caretake a large, fully furnished waterfront home for fifteen months for a friend who had been transferred overseas. Stephen sought a house rather than the sum he thought he needed to rent one, and his house was forthcoming.

So, as mentioned, the Seven of Swords suggests 'Don't give up'. Don't rule out reaching a solution to a problem; think the problem through, and think of alternative approaches. An unusual viewpoint can produce the solution that has been invisible to those who thought along traditional lines. For example, some of the greatest advances in science have resulted from people applying the teachings of one field to another area, and arriving at concepts later hailed as discoveries.

Reversed

The Seven of Swords reversed suggests that your client's old beliefs are leading them to repeat old patterns of behaviour. It can indicate that your client is engaging in self-deception, refusing to see life for what it is, and may be stuck in a rut, unable to see viable alternatives. It requires your client's return to the lesson of the Six of Swords in order to leave behind all those unworkable beliefs that have been holding them back.

Seven of Pentacles

In simple terms the Seven of Pentacles refers to the need for your client not to give up on their financial and career plans. However, it signifies a period where less effort and more vigilance is required as their labours bear fruit. It can be a time when they are thinking about where life is leading them regarding their career or financial success, or their relationship.

In this card a man stands casually, watching his money tree growing. He is contemplating possibilities now that the fruits of his labour are about to reward his efforts. His blue clothing suggests that he is also rewarded spiritually; yet he remains torn between the security of the Six and the challenge of the Eight, as shown by his different coloured boots. The Pentacles nature is to become comfortable with what they already have, but passion, symbolised by his orange boot, pushes him towards the opportunities offered in the Eight.

The Seven of Pentacles depicts a time your client will have money to invest and they are planning their financial future. In a career layout it can show plans by your client for further study to enhance their current skills.

Reversed

The Seven of Pentacles reversed can indicate your client is unaware that the fruits of their labours are about to be delivered to them. Perhaps they have lost sight of their long-term plans and need to return to the Six of Pentacles.

The return to the Six of Pentacles allows you to enjoy safe routines and lack of responsibility. It can, however, frustrate you by the lack of challenge into moving forward to the upright Seven in order to become that wealthy man as depicted in the Six when you reach the Ten of Pentacles.

'Don't hold on' is the watchword of the reversed Sevens, and in the Pentacles Seven it refers to not holding on to material things. Perhaps your client is holding onto a job which is not helping them achieve their goals, and a return to the Six would be the act of securing a new job.

The Seven of Pentacles reversed can also suggest that your client has lost control over their finances, and returning to the Six offers them a chance to regain it. With the Seven reversed making an appearance, their dreams are unlikely to be achieved until they regain control of their finances or of their life generally.

Eights

The Eights in the Tarot represent strength and the four suits show four different types of strength. The Eight of Wands is about having the strength to flow with life and to see where it leads you. The Eight of Cups indicates the strength to leave an emotionally unfulfilling situation. The Eight of Swords is about the existence of inner strength despite the restrictive beliefs of those around you and negative learned attitudes, and the Eight of Pentacles represents strength of commitment achieving results.

Three or more Eights in a layout suggests your client's inner strength is being tested. Three or more Eights reversed suggests they are currently not learning the lessons they need to, and that they are likely to be operating from a position of weakness.

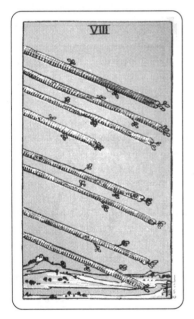

Eight of Wands

The Eight of Wands depicts a period of freedom; the desire of most Wands people. Life is good and the summer days are long when this card appears.

In this card eight wands, without hands to hold them or the ground to encase them, sail freely towards their destination or goal The castle in the distance is visible but still far enough away to engender anticipation and excitement. The river suggests travel over water (overseas) and the clear skies overhead confirm a continuing stability. In simple terms, the Eight is a card for travel which is exciting and rewarding.

The Eights are cards of strength, and the Wands strength is shown at its best in freedom of spirit, enjoyed during travel, sports, competition and the pursuit of achievable goals. The moment of sailing unhindered towards goals shown on the card is the one that Wands people live for and remember vividly. All the struggling and physical efforts in the past were in the hope that these moments might be achieved. In travel, Wands people love to have a destination to look forward to (and an alternative destination in case the desired one doesn't measure up to expectations). In fact, they prefer travelling to arriving.

In short, the Eight of Wands appears when your client is steadily rising in their career, signifying few obstacles to their success and achievement of their goals. It can also indicate they have the benefit of an uncomplicated romantic relationship and/or one in which they and their partner have shared goals.

Reversed

The Eight of Wands reversed indicates there are some restrictions now, but not enough to prevent the wands from reaching their destination. That is, your client will reach their desired goals, but not as quickly as they may hope.

When the card appears reversed it is time for your client to return to the Seven, in order to take charge of those things slowing their progress in the reversed Eight. It is time to make decisions and resolve issues that will have to be dealt with later if they are not resolved now.

An example of a typical Eight reversed situation occurred with a friend of mine, Tony. On the spur of the moment, Tony decided to travel overseas. He wanted to spend five months in Europe, and there were ten weeks between his decision and his departure. In that ten weeks Tony was too busy working and saving the money for the trip to think about his possessions and where they would be stored when he left.

He drove his car to the airport, stopping only to collect a load of washing from the laundromat and to pack his bags in the airport car park. Handing his keys to a friend he asked that the car be sold and the money transferred overseas to wherever he was at the time.

Having spent his money seven weeks later, Tony had to postpone his visit to Europe and work in England in order to have enough money to live on until his car was sold. The car didn't sell, and Tony returned having only seen a few countries in Europe.

By not dealing with all his possessions before he departed, Tony lived through the Eight of Wands reversed. He was not prevented from travelling altogether, but his trip was shorter than he had planned.

Eight of Cups

The Cups strength lies in knowing when a situation has offered you all that it can for now. Although Cups people have a tendency to live in the past, they are usually aware of what a present situation holds for them because they have sensed the energy of that situation. They know within themselves if it is right for them to stay or to leave.

On the card a figure in a red cloak and boots is seen walking away from eight cups arranged to allow for a ninth one. He recognises that although the Seven of Cups offers a glimpse of life in many of its variations, the picture is incomplete, and in the Eight he walks away in search of the ninth cup. The search requires energy, passion and commitment, shown by his red cloak and boots; it takes up both days and nights, signified by the presence of the sun and the moon in this card. Through searching, reading, asking and noticing during the daylight hours and through dreams at night, he seeks what is missing within himself.

The Eight is not a promise of happier times nor a guarantee of success. It simply means your client needs to act on their awareness that they have outgrown their present circumstances. Perhaps after ten years of working and living with their partner, the two of them have ceased to grow together; the Eight is the realisation that what they seek cannot be found where they are presently. In simple terms it can describe the steps involved in your client walking away from a job, a relationship or a lifestyle, reasoning that it holds nothing new for them.

Reversed

The Eight of Cups reversed can indicate confusion resulting from indecision about where your best opportunities lay. While one part of your client wants to explore new possibilities and horizons, another part fears that in doing so they'll miss out on what their current circumstances have to offer.

The Eight reversed points to your client's uncertainty about whether it is better to stay with or to leave a person or a situation. For example, on Monday they are determined to stay; on Tuesday their resolve has weakened. On Wednesday they are ready and willing to leave; by Friday staying appeals to them once again. Knowing their needs would help them to identify what circumstances might best meet those needs.

A return to the Seven of Cups is the answer here, to allow your client to reassess their needs and to see first-hand what feeds them physically, emotionally, mentally and spiritually. Through identifying their requirements, they can determine whether their current circumstances or new horizons would serve them better.

Eight of Swords

The Eight of Swords symbolises that brute force is no match for clear thinking,

In this card a figure stands bound and rigid, blindfolded and surrounded by swords that point downward and are rigidly placed in the ground. This suggests that her beliefs are rigidly fixed, allowing her few options mentally. Clouds suggest confused ('clouded') thinking, so the grey skies above her suggest that even with her eyes open, she may be confused or restricted in her thoughts.

The figure cannot see the path before her. She cannot raise her hands to defend herself and she cannot even raise her hands to pray for intervention from above. (Although if she were to look within herself she may recall the Hanged Man, who knows that all prayers are silent longing, and that the clasping of hands actually counts for nothing.) Her silent longing, her prayer, is for the inner strength to face the torments of her own thoughts which, fed by fear, create a worse reality than actually exists outwardly.

However, the figure is dressed in red, suggesting that she has passion and courage. The Eights are, of course, cards of strength. The Swords' strength lies in the mind's ability to seek new solutions. Where Wands people have to attempt an action physically to determine if it will work, Swords people are able to examine an action mentally, seeking possible problems before they test it.

Therefore, the figure's power lies in her ability to think coupled with her inner reserves of strength. Those around her (in the castle on the hill) can restrict her movement, her sight and her arms, but they cannot restrict her thinking unless she allows them to do so. She is blinded but so are they. Everyone has blind spots, and if you know someone's blind spot, you can approach them without being seen. If the figure knows the blind spots of those who seek to keep her captive, she can turn the wardens into prisoners.

A simple example of outwitting brute force occurred in my own life when I was in Year 9 at school. Our mathematics teacher was a brutal man, better suited to hunting big game than to teaching thirty boys. He was living testimony to Oscar Wilde's saying that, 'Those who call a spade a spade should be made to use one'.

For the fun of it, he'd often pick a boy and beat him about the head until he heard the answer he sought to some obscure mathematical question, and I took it upon myself to distract him from this task as often as possible. To do this I'd ask him a question about his favourite subject: the difference in light and heat reflection of the different colours of the spectrum.

More than ten lessons of each term were spent listening to him repeat stories about how most people where he grew up in the outback knew that a white car could be 10° cooler than a black one. At the start of each lesson I'd pose the same questions in a different way, and often he'd be content to ramble on about light and heat while all my classmates completed the lesson without bruising to their heads.

In a health reading the Eight of Swords can suggest asthma, chest and lung troubles and physical stiffness resulting from mental rigidity.

Reversed

The Eight reversed suggests your client needs to return to the lesson of the Seven, in order to find a solution through their own deliberation.

When the card is reversed it shows the swords falling out of the ground, indicating that thoughts are less rigid now, allowing for unexpected solutions. Solutions may arrive in your client's dreams while they sleep at night, or while they are completing some menial chore and their subconscious mind sifts through the possibilities.

The Eight reversed shows that through her thinking, the figure cuts her bonds with the swords (representing her thoughts). She approaches her situation as a puzzle, and puzzles are solved because they tease the mind to search for possibilities. The solution is all in her mind, just as a person may walk on water by thinking that, like a boat, they are made of wood.

In short, when the Eight is reversed, the return to the adaptable thinking of the Seven allows for unusual solutions. The Eight of Swords is, in effect, a more positive card reversed.

Eight of Pentacles

Pentacles people's strength lies in their practical, commonsense approach to life. When problems arise, they are prepared to work hard to restore balance. The Eight of Pentacles represents the benefits of hard work and self-discipline. In simple terms it is a card about commitment to goals.

In this card a man sits at his work, focused upon the task at hand, with his wares or finished products (the six pentacles hanging up) before him and another one lying incomplete below his workbench. A path leads off to the city where he sells his goods, but his reputation is such that he can live away from the city and still make a solid living. His blue tunic suggests that he invests his work with his spirit, making each pentacle more than just the work of his disciplined hands. His red tights and boots confirm the physical energy required for his work and that he has abundant physical reserves.

The wealth the figure generates benefits his family and others in his community. However, he is focused entirely on the work simply because it brings him pleasure to see a job well done. If problems arise, he is practised in breaking down the task of restoring balance into smaller parts, and tackling each of these with steadfast determination.

In a relationship layout the Eight of Pentacles suggests your client has a commitment to a fulfilling relationship. In a career layout it often shows your client is adding skills to their existing qualifications, in order to specialise in some particular type of work. In a health layout it indicates a commitment to maintaining or returning to good health.

Reversed

The Eight of Pentacles reversed represents a lack of commitment by your client; that is, it often reveals lack of direction or lack of a goal worth working towards. It suggests the need for a return to the Seven of Pentacles to reflect upon what is important to them.

In a relationship layout the Eight reversed suggests your client is not committed to a future with their partner or that the two of them have lost sight of their shared goals. In a career layout it indicates shoddy workmanship, or poor concentration and a lack of motivation.

A return to the Seven of Pentacles allows your client to stand back and decide if their work, relationship or lifestyle is worth the effort.

Nines

The Nines in the Tarot represent a period of reflection before you give a final commitment to a goal or purpose. The Nine of Wands shows a weary figure examining his past decisions and actions. The Nine of Cups displays a contented figure reflecting upon his past actions. The Nine of Swords depicts a figure unable to sleep because of all the unresolved issues crowding in upon her at once, and the Nine of Pentacles shows a figure whose sense of routine allows time for her to reflect on how to ensure her present stability continues.

Three or more Nines in a layout suggests a cycle or a chapter in your client's life is ending, and that it is a time to reflect upon these changes.

Nine of Wands

The Nines represent reassessment before the completion suggested by the Tens, and the Nine of Wands represents re-examination regarding commitment to projects or to people. Because Wands people like to look ahead toward new challenges they can miss the perspective available to those who also look back to past actions. We are all products of our past circumstances and decisions, and realising which decisions gave us the results we desired can help us to plan things more carefully. In simple terms the Nine of Wands is about weighing up past successes and failures prior to making a lasting commitment.

The figure in this Wands card examines the past to assess the consequences of his actions. The bandage around his head hints at past strife. He looks warily back at previous challenges, hesitant to make any new commitments before he is aware of their consequences. He no longer has an easy way out if things don't go well for him, and knows that if problems arise he'll have to stay and sort them out. This is hard for Wands people, who love nothing better than to move on to greener pastures when things get too difficult or too slow for their liking.

The figure is aware that lasting success lies in his pacing himself for the long haul. Whereas in the past his life was a series of short sprints, he is now looking at a long-distance marathon. The prize will be more than he's ever achieved before, but the risks and the demands are also greater. To achieve the rewards offered by the Ten of Wands, he must first become the King of Wands (if he were a woman he would, of course, need to become the Queen of Wands).

To achieve success your client needs to find a new way to resolve conflict so that they can work well in a team. Wands people are better suited to working alone or being team leaders due to their naturally competitive tendencies, but your client needs to curb some of these tendencies in order to make a long-term commitment.

Reversed

The Nine of Wands reversed can indicate your client is hesitant to make a long-term commitment. It is often a card for those who feel that life is all work and no play. They feel overcome by responsibilities or a lack of support, and so are hesitant to make a commitment.

To remedy this they need to return to the Eight of Wands in order to experience a period where life flows easily and pressures are few. Perhaps a holiday or living some kind of simpler life for a while can rejuvenate them at this time. When reversed this Nine is a card that represents dwelling on the pain and the frustrations of the past, and a period of joy is the antidote to this.

Nine of Cups

The Nine of Cups is a card representing emotional reflection on a situation prior to commitment. (Knowing the value of the love you have to give is one thing, but knowing that love is really of little value until you actually give it away is another thing entirely.) In simple terms this Nine represents the fulfilment which comes from a job well done, or an idea seen through to completion. It can also signify feelings of self-love and self-respect.

Although the figure in the card wears a red hat and socks, or stockings, their dress is grey. This suggests that they are surrounded by love but need to connect emotionally with those around them in order to give and receive it. The bright yellow background represents clarity of understanding regarding the value of love and of being loved by others. The blue behind the figure signifies the security that is derived from knowing that you are loved spiritually and knowing your spiritual value.

Some students I've taught have a problem with this card, finding the figure smug or filled with self-importance, but I've usually observed that those who feel this way about this Nine lack an awareness of their own self-worth. They mistake self-respect for smugness. Knowing what you are truly worth is the first step to knowing what you don't want in your work, in your heart and in your life generally.

The figure protects his cups from those approaching him until he is sure that their motives are sincere. Past pain has taught him that others do not necessarily have his best interests at heart. However, he knows that life is a banquet to which he has been invited. It has taken him almost until the Ten of Cups to realise that which he knew as a small child: that he has a place in his community and in the world.

The appearance of the Nine of Cups in a relationship layout indicates your client feels happy and fulfilled. These feelings may be due to a close partnership, their family or to a stable home life generally.

Reversed

The Nine of Cups reversed suggests your client has forgotten their place in the world and in their community, and hunger is the result. This hunger burns deep into their heart and soul, and they may seek to satiate it through worldly distractions. This inner hunger is both difficult and simple to feed, but the first step is that your client's heart and soul be open to being fed.

The Nine reversed indicates your client is reaching for worldly things to satisfy their hunger. They may be engaged in addictive and compulsive behaviours, including anorexia, bulimia, drug and alcohol addiction, gambling, and the addiction to anything that creates a buzz. This is very draining spiritually and emotionally for those around them as their unconscious hunger can pull others off-centre.

In simple terms the Nine reversed suggests your client is unhappy about how things are turning out for them. Their spiritual and emotional needs are not being met at present, and they may feel isolated from their friends and their life generally. To remedy this your client needs to return to the Eight of Cups to see what they have to leave behind in their life. This would be a good time for them to plan an adventure, a holiday, or to take up some courses or interests that will feed them spiritually and emotionally. Regular meditation may benefit your client at this time.

Nine of Swords

In simple terms the Nine of Swords represents a time when your client needs to question their commitment to their beliefs about life. These beliefs shape a person's life completely, allowing them to see some opportunities or keeping them blind to others. If their belief system does not support them, then they must consider whether they want to support it.

The figure in this card has been awakened from sleep by a disturbing dream, which reflects her life at present. Her subconscious mind is attempting to make sense of her life and to present her with solutions to her daily problems. The blue squares on the bed cover suggest a connection with her spiritual self through sleep and in dreams, and the red roses (also on the bed cover) show her heart being revealed in its purity at night when she is asleep.

The struggling figures carved into the bed represent the skirmishes that sometimes take place in dreams. The dotted outlines of the planets and the signs of the zodiac suggest that planetary influences are also at work, and that certain periods in each calendar year are more suitable for clarity of dreams than others.

Fear, doubt, and worry over present or future circumstances are shown by the Nine of Swords. In a relationship layout it can suggest that your client is unsettled on a deeper level about their relationship. At this point their dreams might hold the answers they seek. In a health layout it can signify disturbed sleep at night and problems with headaches, the neck and the upper back and chest. That is, problems may be occurring wherever the swords penetrate the body of the figure in this card.

Reversed

The Nine of Swords reversed can show that your client is aware of their dreams at night. Although their sleep may be disturbed, they are making sense of what their subconscious mind is trying to tell them. Worries and fears are subsiding now, either through resolution of the problem or through resignation to circumstances as shown in the Eight of Swords.

A return to the Eight allows your client to access their inner strength to overcome their limiting beliefs or attitudes. It can also be a retreat into themselves, allowing life or others to have control over them, until they find the strength and commitment to make the necessary changes to move forward again.

In a health reading the Nine reversed can still signify sleep disturbance, headaches, neck, shoulder and upper back problems. It can signify a time when your client takes their worries to bed at night, only to awaken exhausted in the morning.

Nine of Pentacles

In simple terms the Nine of Pentacles is a card symbolising financial and material success. It signifies your client has a comfortable life, which results from practical planning, discipline and commitment to their goals.

The figure in this card stands outdoors; she is relaxed, and secure in her surroundings. She has taken all the necessary steps to ensure that her life is stable, and this allows her time for her hobbies, and for the simple routines by which the days, weeks and seasons are measured. The snail at the figure's feet suggests that building things of value takes time; slow, steady steps are required to develop solid wealth and fulfilment. The fruit on the vines is ripe and represents the fruits of her labours.

The figure has been disciplined throughout the past eight cards and now she finds herself contemplating herself and her life. She has secured her future to the best of her ability and now she is ready to extend her talents and her abilities to a wider circle of people. She is considering group projects and goals, such as a family or plans relating to her local community.

Although the castle in the background of the card represents stability, the figure is happiest outside among nature, for it replenishes her. This is often the case with Pentacles people. They can rejuvenate themselves by walking in forests, in fields or anywhere in the countryside, as nature calls them out of their routines to remember their place in the world.

In a relationship layout the Nine of Pentacles can indicate a materially comfortably life but one that involves periods of aloneness. Perhaps your client's partner is too busy working to spend time sharing their interests and pursuits. However, often the Nine appearing in a relationship layout suggests that your client has taken care of practical and material concerns, and is now ready to find someone to accompany them on their path in life. In a health reading it suggests good health resulting from a balanced attitude to life.

Reversed

The Nine of Pentacles reversed suggests your client lacks understanding of their place in the world and the need for time among nature. Walking, hiking or simply having a picnic may help to restore their energies at this time.

In a career layout the Nine reversed signifies your client is working too hard for the lifestyle they desire. This can mean working evenings and weekends, two jobs or simply being paid poorly for their efforts. It can also describe someone who is working full-time and studying to improve their career prospects. The card leads your client back to the Eight in order to gain further skills so that they can charge more for their efforts.

Clara looked exhausted even as I told her that she was working too hard for her lifestyle. She worked six days and three nights a week at two jobs in order to save for a house deposit. Her husband was twenty-five years older than she and he was content to rent a house. Clara knew that she wanted her own home, and she realised that it was necessary to save for it now while she was young enough to borrow the money from a bank.

The aloneness reflected in the Nine is often increased when it appears reversed. In Clara's case she felt unsupported by her husband and alone in her pursuit of a financially secure old age.

Tens

The Tens in the Tarot describe completion of the lessons of the suits. The Ten of Wands shows the grand challenge being realised, whereas the Ten of Cups depicts a complete family unit and the fulfilment that it brings. The Ten of Swords illustrates how beliefs lead to results; that although beliefs themselves are invisible, they can be traced by the results they bring to you. The Ten of Pentacles indicates a stable home and work environment where the results of your efforts are visible in the material world. When three or more Tens appear in a layout, contracts, legal documents or the purchase or sale of a home, car or business are suggested.

Ten of Wands

The Ten of Wands indicates your client reaching their goals, but not smoothly. Wands people have difficulty saying no to offers and opportunities, and the result is often the Ten of Wands, where they are overloaded but still struggle towards their goals. The Ten is a card of achievement, but more energy is used reaching goals than is necessary.

On the card a figure carries ten wands towards his destination: the castle in the background. He feels that he alone is responsible for his success and that if he wants to achieve his goals he needs to remain aware of each of those wands.

In a relationship layout the Ten of Wands can represent issues within the relationship or shared goals, such as buying a house, travelling overseas or saving for retirement. It can also signify that one partner feels fully responsible for the success or failure of the relationship. If so, it is your task as a reader to point out that if two people are in the relationship, then both parties are responsible for its outcome.

If the card appears in answer to a business question, the wands can represent parts of the business: for example, the accounts department, the sales force, the products and the business premises. In a health layout the Ten can suggest stress or back trouble from taking on too many physical or mental responsibilities.

It is a card indicating your client is successfully reaching their goals, but that things might be easier if they were to delegate some of the responsibilities to others. This in turn would allow them to focus on the important issues, while keeping their goal in sight.

In simple terms, the Wands Ten depicts a life filled with goals, challenges and commitments. Your client is likely to be juggling deadlines and to feel pressured to perform.

Reversed

The Ten of Wands reversed indicates a person who is unlikely to reach their goals, as they are weighed down by their commitments and responsibilities. Your client needs to return to the Nine of Wands so that they can decide which things in their life warrant their commitment. By discarding or delegating those things of lesser importance, they will have more time and energy to focus on the steps to their goals.

The Ten reversed can also mean your client is using their career to avoid emotional issues. This is illustrated by the story of Ross. Starting or expanding a business can demand all of your attention, which suited Ross as he didn't even want to be aware of the problems in his marriage. The twelve-hour days and the weekends he spent at the office kept him away from his family, as well as the conflicts they presented him with.

Instead of the issues between him and his wife being resolved Ross suffered a heart attack, and the time he spent in bed recuperating helped him to notice that his wife and children no longer knew him. He was a stranger in the midst of his own family because they had learned to live without a man who was always working.

Ten of Cups

The Ten of Cups represents finding the right workplace for you to achieve emotional and spiritual growth. It can also indicate a harmonious family life or the existence of a peaceful love relationship built on commitment and trust. In short, this Ten signifies emotional completion; that your client has found their place in a community or a family.

On the card a couple stand together enjoying their abundant surroundings as children play nearby. Ten cups appear above them in a rainbow. These figures represent people who know the value of time spent together as a family, and that real understanding of others comes from unplanned precious moments in life and not the 'quality time' which is factored into a busy schedule. They have a less adventurous life than some, allowing room for sentiment and emotional fulfilment.

In a career layout it indicates that creative opportunities and emotional support from those around your client are more important to them than financial rewards, and that they are well supported in their chosen work. In a health layout the Ten of Cups suggests balanced health and emotional stability. In simple terms this card shows your client has an emotionally balanced home or work life, and feel that they are where they belong in life.

Reversed

The Ten of Cups reversed can describe a lack of support from those around your client. Its appearance can also signify that your client has a pattern of retreating from groups when they can.

Oliver's childhood was spent avoiding others from a fear of being teased. As an adult he still managed to blend in, by keeping silent, and to hide away, both physically and emotionally, when group activities took place. The appearance of the Ten reversed showed that Oliver felt excluded by those around him. However, he was, in fact, excluding himself through his reluctance to participate.

On the other hand, the Ten reversed can signify that there is a clique from which your client is excluded. This sort of situation sometimes occurs in country towns, where a newcomer may be considered a visitor ten years after their arrival. However, this exclusive group may be part of your client's work environment, peer group, or be any group imposing a particular code of dress or behaviour on its participants. In a relationship layout the Ten reversed can signify that your client feels excluded or ignored by their partner. It can suggest they are repeating a family pattern of being physically close but emotionally distant.

Ten of Swords

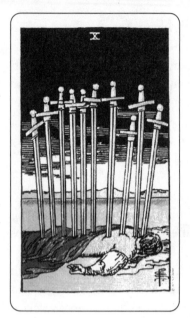

The Tens are cards of completion and the Ten of Swords shows how your thinking determines who you become. When our lives end we are the sum total of all of our actions and decisions; as you think, you become.

On the card a figure lays face downward on the ground with ten swords in his back and neck. The red cloth he is draped in indicates his passion and physical energy, which, in this case, is insufficient to change his situation. The dark sky over the figure shows the heaviness of his burden but the glimmer of light heralds the dawn approaching.

In a health reading the appearance of this card may represent back and neck problems. It can also indicate low reserves of energy due to your client's negative beliefs about life.

When this card appears the relevant situation is at its lowest point; however, from death comes rebirth. That is, from the death of one situation appears another opportunity. As forewarned is forearmed, you can compassionately tell your client that things are reaching, or will reach, a low point. Your client's knowledge that winter will be colder than usual allows them to stock up on food and fuel to see them through, pacing themselves for the long haul.

The best course of action for your client to take with the upright Ten of Swords is to surrender to circumstances. They can take this time to re-examine their beliefs about life, as these beliefs have contributed to their current circumstances.

Reversed

When the Ten of Swords is reversed the swords are falling out of the figure, who appears above the darkness and the burden. This suggests that your client's difficult period is now over, but that they have not realised that they are free once again.

Old beliefs or attitudes are holding your client back now, and it is time for them to stand up and take charge of their life. The Ten reversed suggests your client can return to the upright Nine to listen to their inner voice through dreams at night or through their intuition, and to accept that changes are necessary before stability can return.

The Ten of Swords reversed represents the act of carrying an open umbrella when it has been sunny for days. Your client is reacting to life as it once was even though things have changed.

Ten of Pentacles

The Ten of Pentacles is a card representing completion through material things. Pentacles people place great emphasis upon the physical comfort that often results from financial security, and they are prepared to work hard to ensure that their old age is spent doing those things they want to do and they can afford to do.

The card itself shows things that make for material stability. There is a solid house, with family crests on the wall confirming that it is built with old money. The business in the background provides the income for a comfortable lifestyle and the family to share in this.

The dogs are focused on the man who is seated; they know who is the real leader of the household. Being pack animals they seek out the leader of the group or family, and look to that person for guidance, attention and approval. The man was once the Page and then the Knight of Pentacles before becoming the King of Pentacles. We see him sitting patiently surveying his domain, clothed in the fruits of his labours.

However, to the left of this card, and just above the head of the man seated, is a small image of the Tower, suggesting that this situation has the appearance of stability and permanence but that like all other things in life, it is only transient. The Tower represents change, reminding you that you have a spiritual purpose and that those things you cling to for security are impermanent.

In a relationship layout the Ten of Pentacles can signify your client places a strong emphasis on wealth building and financial security, and that career and financial goals cement their relationship with their partner. In a career layout it represents stability and success.

In simple terms the Ten of Pentacles is a card representing stability and financial security. Despite the image of the Tower, the blue skies shown on the card confirm that things will be stable for some time to come.

Reversed

The Ten of Pentacles reversed can suggest that the tide is receding financially for your client. For example, in a career layout it can represent a large corporation which is tightening its belt, leading to financial cutbacks and redundancies, and often, in a bid to save money, a policy of not replacing the staff who have had to leave.

In a relationship layout the card indicates financial difficulties are damaging or undermining your client's relationship. (Financial issues are one of the most common reasons for relationship breakdowns.) In answer to a question about borrowing money the appearance of the Ten reversed suggests that the loan will not be forthcoming.

Perhaps your client is counting on stability which is ebbing. An example of this was Bernard, who invested heavily in his business, counting on the economy to remain in a growth cycle and the demand for his products to remain high. Five months after he had borrowed $600,000 the economy slowed, and demand for his exclusive outdoor furniture halved, leaving him to service a large debt with high interest rates.

Part Six

★ Becoming Professional ★

After you have given 100 practice readings you may be ready to look at becoming a professional Tarot reader. (Starting out as a professional reader can be daunting, and it is recommended that you charge less than the standard rate until you have sound experience.) There are many avenues for a Tarot reader. Be realistic when you examine them, for it requires arduous effort to achieve the pinnacle of Tarot reading.

During a recent advanced Tarot course I placed a range of professional reading possibilities in a line on standard A4 pages on the floor and asked the students to stand beside the page where they then were as readers. I then asked them to stand beside the page which listed their aims as readers and two students stood alongside the top page: to be paid to tour the world speaking about and teaching the Tarot. I asked one of them, Jeremy, how long he expected it to take for him to move from reading at markets to touring and teaching and he replied, 'Four years'. 'It has taken me over twenty years and I'm only just arriving,' I replied, but he was determined. Since that course finished he is becoming aware of how hard it is to reach the top of Tarot reading.

However, not everyone wants to be at the peak of their profession; some might find it too demanding. Finding where you fit is what the Tarot is all about; after all, it's a tool to help us to navigate life's storms. The possibilities for reading include:

- at a market
- at an alternative book store
- at a natural health centre or alternative healing centre
- in a café or restaurant once a week
- from your own premises in a shopping centre
- from a home office
- in a shared house rented as an alternative centre
- on a cruise liner
- at a public or private function
- on the telephone.

Each of these avenues for working as a professional reader offers possibilities but has its limitations also.

Markets are popular, but they limit the number of readers allowed so as to give each reader renting a stall enough business. Also, stallholders offering Tarot readings can be very territorial about sharing their market with newcomers, which is unnecessary if it is a popular market. I used to work at a market with six or seven readers in a row. Instead of making for unhealthy competition, it became known as the place to shop for the right reading for you. The readers varied from astute professionals to one young man who offered I Ching readings and read passages aloud to clients in an appalling speaking voice from a thick, tattered book. I was often tempted to tear the book from his hands and complete the passage he was crucifying in his expressionless tone, but I restrained myself.

Clients usually select the appropriate reader for their needs. With my short, spiky hair I was considered perhaps too young and edgy for some people, whereas the woman beside me with her incense, beads and nose rings was for others just what they expected a reader to look like. In a market you often read for people who have never had a reading before, and their only exposure to the Tarot is through books, magazines and movies. They expect a reader to be a woman in her fifties with an exotic accent and a black cat close at hand; some particularly like the gypsy look, with a scarf and gaudy earrings. (For a man this can increase your set-up costs, when you factor in the make-up, woman's clothing and having your arms waxed to remove unsightly hairs!)

However, after a while people sought me out, looking for the guy with the 'flat top' (I kept my hair mown like a freshly cut lawn). One day, another reader in the row of seven cut his hair to look like mine, and his business increased rapidly for a few weeks until word got out to look for the guy with the flat top and the business cards. As he didn't have business cards and I did, people could identify me easily.

Alternative book stores offering readings usually have different readers for each day of the week, and the shop sets the fee and takes a percentage (this is typically 40–50 per cent. Tapes are usually included for an extra fee). As a Tarot reader you have the added benefit of no rental outlay, and regular passing trade in the book store.

Rental for rooms in healing centres is usually on a daily basis (paid one month in advance) and often involves a bond or refundable deposit of four weeks' rent. Renting a room in a healing centre is a long-term option, as it can cost $1000 to start at a centre and every four weeks you have to find another month's rent. This option is better suited to those who already have an established clientele, as it is up to the reader to find their own clients.

To ensure the word gets around that you are there, offer a free reading to the receptionist and to fellow practitioners. It is essential to get the receptionist on side as they can make or break your business, being the first person the client speaks to when they call. I worked in one healing centre for seven years and I'd built up a good reputation, so my returning clientele and word-of-mouth recommendation were enough to fill my appointment sheet for the one day I was there each week. However, a new receptionist arrived and my services conflicted with her religious beliefs, so she did not recommend me.

In two years I found that all my clients had disappeared and I was diverting my home office clients into the healing centre to keep myself busy on my day there.

(One day I sat down and decided that I could save myself the hassle and $4000 per year simply by leaving the centre and working solely from home. I did so, and I've never looked back.)

A potential downside of working from a healing centre is that you can walk into bad residual energy from previous practitioners. In another centre I rented a room which was used by a grief counsellor on other days, and each time I entered the room on my day there I found it filled with left-over emotional energy from his weekly clients. If I left this residual energy in the room (as I did on some occasions) 50 per cent of my clients for the day would usually cancel. This was because there was no room for any new energy to enter the room until the old energy was cleared out.

I soon grew tired of asking the counsellor to take responsibility for his left-over energy, as he often looked at me as if I was being a hippie. Tiring of having to clear the centre of negative energy before I could start work for the day, I left the centre and soon heard that the grief counsellor was ill, presumably from sitting all day in an uncleansed room since I was not there to cleanse it for him. (Energetically clearing your work space is important if you want to have a comfortable work environment: see 'Cleansing your Workplace'.)

Working from cafés or restaurants is a quick way to establish a clientele and it is also inexpensive. I used to read in two cafés in a trendy alternative neighbourhood in Sydney and the buzz in the café felt like a night out. I was welcomed by the staff, who all knew me after their free readings, and they often had friends and customers there who were waiting for readings.

I'd place simple A5-sized pages on each table explaining what I did and how much it cost, and even if customers didn't have a reading that day, they often took the fliers home and phoned me for a private reading later. Cheap, short readings with minimum risk (as I was only two tables away from their friends, not down some lane or up seven flights of stairs in an unfamiliar neighbourhood) appeal to many people who wouldn't otherwise consider a Tarot reading.

There are two ways to make the arrangement appealing to the café owner/manager. Firstly, you can pay a fee for the table for several hours a night so that they're not losing money on the one you are using. Secondly, you can give them a share of all your income (30 per cent or more) and offer to advertise in a local newspaper's classified section that you'll be reading at that café on that day. That way the café owner/manager should get some extra profit and some new customers.

Setting up your own shop requires more commitment than the other options outlined above, as you have to pay rent during the winter months when fewer people have readings. Spring and summer are usually the busiest months as many people want to know about their relationship possibilities in spring.

You'll have to advertise and to pay electricity and other bills, and decorate the place to make it inviting, so it is a long-term project for those with stamina and deep pockets. Also, if you open a Tarot-reading shop you'll have to find other reliable readers, and this can be challenging. Readers can be like artistic children: sensitive, moody, disinclined to turn up when it rains and apt to disappear at a moment's notice when their astrological planets are badly aligned.

I've worked with amazing clairvoyants in England, one of whom almost drove me crazy. As I didn't finish until 9 pm it was often easier for my dates to meet me at work, in the centre of London, as it was a short walk to restaurants and night-life. Sometimes a girl would be waiting for me, sitting beside Margaret. Margaret had the ability to tell me how many days or weeks each potential relationship was going to last, and she insisted on telling me, too.

A date named Charlotte arrived one night. As we were leaving, Margaret smiled and said, 'Three', meaning that the relationship was going to last for three days only. After four accurate predictions I told her to keep her insights to herself so that I might at least attempt to establish a relationship. She still smiled as I left with new potential partners, but said nothing.

One day two girls arrived to meet me and Margaret was smiling away as we left. The next day she quizzed me about them, as she was confused. She sensed that I was attracted to one girl whereas the other girl was attracted to me.

'Tell me about it,' I sighed.

'I know you've told me not to tell you what I see, but the girl who is attracted to you will be married in seven months.'

'What?' I asked nervously, and started to panic, not being remotely ready for marriage. 'I'm glad you're not my mother,' I said, shaking my head.

Offering your services from an office at home is the most inexpensive and practical way to start your business, provided you live somewhere accessible to the public. It has to be on a bus route, near a train station and easy to find. If not, you'd better have an international reputation unless you don't mind starving through the winter months.

The home office has the advantages of low rent and allowing you to do other things between seeing clients. It is frustrating arriving at a healing centre on your day to work there to find a 10 am, a 1 pm and a 6 pm appointment. Your day is taken up with having to be close by for your clients, and yet you are not busy. There are only so many books and magazines you can read before you start pacing about the place (who's a Wands type, then?).

As I now work from home, I write, instead of reading, books between seeing clients, and I do the washing, go shopping, clean the house and play the piano. Yesterday my first client arrived to find me gathering up tree branches I'd just pruned in the front garden. He helped me for a few minutes and then we went inside for the reading. I felt as though we had broken the ice, and it relaxed him when he saw that I was just another guy, and not a mysterious reader who might be a bit weird. (As you know from 'The Reading Process', putting your client at ease is the first step towards giving a good reading.)

Most clients are nervous, and if a client appears unsettled when they arrive I usually ask them to sit at my table in my office for a minute or two, telling them that I will be with them in a moment. This allows the client to survey the room, get their bearings and become comfortable in their surroundings. It also allows them to peruse my brochures on hypnotherapy, counselling and courses which may interest them.

By helping your clients to be more comfortable with the process you'll make it easier for them to refer their friends to you, especially those friends who have never had a reading and wouldn't normally have anything to do with a Tarot reader. By being practical, reasonable and without all the mysterious window-dressing such as crystal balls and elaborate rituals, you can concentrate on the readings and your accuracy. I'm always suspicious of elaborate ritual, as I feel it is often used to replace accuracy. History is littered with civilisations whose rituals masked the fact that they had lost their way. Keeping things simple is an art in itself, and your task as a reader is to help your client better to understand themselves and their lives.

So, in many different ways, you do need to consider appearances. A friend left her black German shepherd dog with me for three weeks some years ago, and it sat out on my front porch scaring all my clients without any effort on his part. It was the kindest dog I've known, but that big, black face and wolf-like features made all my clients think twice about entering the front gate. Don't put your clients off before they have a chance to hear what you have to say.

When reading from home, you have to have a designated room which is only for giving Tarot readings. I've heard appalling stories about clients arriving at readers' houses to be, for example, led into dark rooms filled with unfolded washing and petfood bowls in the corner, and then the reader starting to read above the sound of a television and two children playing at being soldiers in the throes of an uprising.

Your office is more appealing if its colours are subtle and relaxing. Most clients are nervous when they arrive, so if you can settle them with small considerations like this before the reading your job will be easier. If you have any certificates or diplomas these may be displayed on the wall. Don't overdo it, as it can be confusing. I used to have seven certificates on the wall and it looked a mess. I now have only one, and when the occasional inquiry about my training arises I tell the client that I have a box of dusty certificates in my linen cabinet and that they are welcome to peruse them at their leisure. There have been only three such inquiries in eight years.

A solid table covered by a subtly coloured cloth is required for the actual reading. Fold-away card tables can be wobbly, and this can distract from the reading process and make you appear less than professional. To put it another way (for the Pentacles people) when people are paying top price for a reading they expect professionalism. If you are starting out as a reader and expect to be charging top fees eventually, start looking the part now. It is a lot easier to build an image from scratch than to overcome a poor image you have already established. A marketing manager recently told me that research has shown that a satisfied customer tells an average of ten people about their experience with you, whereas an unhappy customer tells an average of twenty people. Your future business depends upon each and every client you have every day.

In full private readings such as you might offer from your home office, it is advisable to include a tape of the reading into which you can insert a business card, so that the client can find you again for their next reading and/or recommend you to others. (I purchase tapes in lots of two hundred, but there are magnetic tape suppliers who will supply tapes in smaller lots and deliver them to your door.)

If you include a tape in the price of the reading it adds value to it. The client has a record of what you have said which they can refer to when your predictions start to eventuate. Clients often say to me, 'I listened to your tape last week, and it prompted me to phone you and book another session'. Speaking of the price of the reading, you can have a price structure which allows for short and full readings. The short (half-hour) readings are usually more than half the price of the full (one-hour) readings: for example, you might charge $40 for a short reading and $70 for a full reading.

Launching a home office practice requires some referrals, and the process of referrals being given can be started by having a launch party. You set a date, invite everyone you know and ask them all to bring three friends. On the day of the party you set up your office as you want it to be when you are seeing clients, and close the door. The party is held in another part of the house. Throughout the party you offer to take selected groups on a tour of your office. Their curiosity will make them want to explore it, and it still holds its mystery by being closed off throughout the party.

When inside your office you give each person (five or six people at one time only) a brochure and a business card. Resist the temptation to give any readings on that day, but have your appointment diary handy to book clients who want readings. In such a case it pays to have a glass of champagne with the first guests to arrive and then tell those who request a reading that you cannot as you have been drinking, but that you can book them in for later that week. The launch party is an inexpensive publicity method. If you're careful with your budget, for around $100 to $200 you can tell 100 people, friends and strangers, where you are and what you have to offer them.

You could write a press release for a local newspaper and offer to give away five free consultations to readers. If the newspaper runs the story you, of course, would have to give away the five sessions but you would have had invaluable publicity.

Brochures need not be expensive, elaborate affairs. Simple brochures can be made up on most computers and folded to fit into plastic display stands so that the client can see them easily. Don't make up too many brochures at any one time as things change and you don't want to be left with 600 outdated ones. I must admit that my current palmistry course brochures include a photograph of me taken six years ago, and I look completely different now due to ageing and a different hairstyle.

You can also put a mailing list for a newsletter in the waiting room. Many people like to be kept in touch with what is happening with you and your colleagues. However, be careful about asking for too much information from clients, as some people can be resistant to give out their details in case they are bombarded with leaflets.

You might consider renting a house for the sole purpose of practising Tarot and, if so, you are better off sharing it with complementary practitioners. For example, an osteopath, a massage therapist or a counsellor would help increase your business, as they can refer clients to you and their clients can collect your brochures as they sit in the waiting room.

Work on a cruise liner is a good way to see the world and read for a wide range of people; however, naturally you don't build a lasting clientele, for at the last stop the clients return to where they came from. Another downside is that travellers who are addicted to having readings are likely to turn up almost every day to have another session with you. Still, this can give you practice in finding new ways to express the same concepts, if you need it.

Bookings of Tarot readers are becoming more popular as a way of breaking the ice at corporate Christmas functions, publicity launches and even at birthday parties. Such readings are usually between ten and fifteen minutes, with several readers working together if there are large groups. A drawback of function bookings is that they can be very draining because you often have to speak over music, and/or the sounds of laughter and talk, cutlery and the occasional ringing of a mobile phone.

Readers charge an hourly fee for reading at functions, and you have to be assertive about leaving on time or you'll find yourself working for five hours when you were only contracted to work for three. I make it a rule to tell the person who contracted me when it is twenty minutes until my finishing time, to allow them to fit in a special guest or to negotiate an extension of the time at a suitable rate. If the host decides not to extend the booking and there are still people waiting, I usually tell them that I cannot extend my stay as I have another booking to attend. It's best to have the host break the news to anyone waiting on line that you have to go, and, as a consolation, you can offer them your business card if they want to consult you privately.

The upside of function bookings is that you can meet the rich and famous. At publicity launches you often read for politicians, film stars, artists, musicians and famous sportspeople. Even though they are celebrities, they are still people with personal problems who require the advice of a Tarot reader and expect that their confidences will be kept; you treat a reading with a celebrity as you would any other reading and they'll respect you for your professionalism.

Some Tarot readers prefer working for telephone Tarot services as they can dress how they want to, and they have an anonymity which allows them to be more forthright. One of my former students, Carolyn, worked as a telephone reader and she had no intention of changing her job, as she loved it: 'I can sit in bed late at night, with hot coffee in a thermos and biscuits, and answer the phone while keeping as warm as toast'. We all laughed when we heard that, imagining Carolyn in her hair curlers, sipping strong coffee between layouts, with an airport novel opened face down beside her. I enjoy the occasional telephone reading, but, then, I usually enjoy telephone conversations anyway.

Lastly, it is inadvisable for women especially to attend a client's private home alone to give a reading. If you decide to give a client a reading in their home, take a friend with you for safety. Otherwise, it is better to insist they see you in your office at a mutually agreed time.

★ Stranger than Fiction ★

Those who read the Tarot for others soon realise that life is stranger than fiction. Just when you think you've heard everything, a client sits down to tell you of a jaw-dropping scenario in the hope that you'll find a clear path out of their maze for them.

Keiran was one of those clients. He told me that he was having an affair and had been doing so for six years. He assured me that his wife would never suspect him and I questioned this, saying, 'Partners often know about infidelities, even if only on a subconscious level'.

'Oh no. She'd never suspect me because I'm having an affair with my sister,' he said unblinkingly. I stopped and wondered if I'd misheard him at first. Then I wondered if I had imagined it all. Then I wondered if I was still breathing.

In another case, a woman named Emma consulted me. When she sat down her anger filled the room.

I laid the cards out onto the white linen cloth and the problem was immediately apparent.

'I see an undisciplined man around you. He's emotionally young, and physically old enough to know better,' I said to her.

'The bastard,' she snorted, glaring at the cards in front of her. Before I could continue, she explained, saying, 'I'm having an affair with a married man … and he's … he's … cheating on me. On me!' she repeated.

'Hey, wait a minute. Am I missing something here or is it safe to assume that you are both cheating on his wife?'

'That's different. He doesn't love his wife.'

'Oh, of course,' I said, wondering where I could go from there. Downhill, was where.

I tuned into her clairvoyantly for a clearer picture of the man and the situation, and Emma confirmed that he had an expensive imported car with tinted windows. I was loath to tell her that he was in fact cheating on everyone in this situation, as I saw him attempting to park his enormous car discreetly in an inner-city backstreet, prior to his weekly visit to his favourite rent boy.

'He's been seeing a male prostitute?' she choked. 'That explains it,' she said furiously. I didn't dare ask exactly what it explained; I simply completed the reading.

Giving Tarot readings to strangers allows you to scrutinise life in all its flavours. It therefore affords you the opportunity of observing humanity, which has led me to discover that, for all our differences, we humans have much in common. Most of us seek peace, fulfilment and a deep sense of belonging, and it is only the path we choose to achieve these which differentiates us from one another. Reading the Tarot involves observing people; not only their actions and the consequences of such, but how they perceive themselves.

For example, in a recent reading a woman named Shirley apologised that she was 'only a mother' and I corrected her immediately. 'You have the greatest responsibility of all. You are raising people. The effects of your actions will last for generations. How many businessmen can say the same thing?'. She paused for a moment and it dawned on her that being a mother was no simple thing.

Along with the chance of observing life, the Tarot affords the reader an opportunity to see any patterns which repeat themselves during a client's life. What sort of patterns do you need to look for? You are able to look for long-term relationship patterns, as shown in a reading for Tracy. She complained that she only fell in love with men who were emotionally lost, financially stuck and addicted to expensive substances. Seven successive men like these in a series of relationships was no accident; sixteen years of men who had the mistress of addiction.

I asked her where she might have first seen or established this pattern of behaviour. She couldn't tell me at first, so we talked for a few minutes. Together we traced the pattern back to Tracy's first relationship, when she was seventeen years of age. I asked her to search back even further, in case the pattern was with her before her first love relationship. I asked her about her first relationship with a man: the one she had with her father.

'Oh, he's an alcoholic. Mum was forever rescuing him from the front lawn at two in the morning. I made it a rule never to get mixed up with anyone who was addicted to alcohol.'

Tracy had kept to her rule and never been mixed up with an alcoholic, but each of her partners had an addiction. While the substances they were addicted to varied, Tracy's pattern had remained with her from childhood.

So, although the cards (such as the Three of Pentacles reversed) can suggest an unlearned repetitive pattern is occurring, as a reader you may need to have a conversation with your client to find out exactly what that pattern is. It doesn't matter that you don't always reach the underlying causes of their problems through clairvoyance; the point is that they leave with a clearer understanding of themselves and their lives. The best decisions are often based on good, clear information and if you can give your client the information they need, they can make their own life decisions. If you are unsure how your client can resolve their current dilemma, you can phrase a question to the cards; for example, what is the best course of action to resolve this situation?

Your client has responsibility for their own actions, as the Tarot does not replace free will. Some clients don't want to exercise their free will, like the woman who phoned me recently for the address of a clairvoyant who could foretell lucky lotto numbers. I laughed and explained a small but important fact that she had overlooked: 'If you were a clairvoyant and you could accurately predict lucky lotto numbers, would you spend thirty or forty hours each week giving readings when you could spend an hour at the local lottery office and make a million dollars a week?'.

'So, you don't know where that man lives then?' she continued. Not about to take any responsibility for her finances, she preferred to win her happiness instead. I have a theory that those who exercise no discipline in the gaining of wealth usually exercise no discipline in the spending of it.

Many people seem to hold a diploma in spending, like the client who wanted another reading three weeks after her previous one. I explained that we risked covering old ground and that there may have been more important things for her to spend her money on. She was undeterred. I asked her why she wanted another reading so quickly; she replied that she had money troubles. 'I've saved you the price of a reading already,' I laughed and she reluctantly agreed.

A small amount of logic goes a long way in this industry, as illustrated by my experience with a woman who rang up for a telephone reading. When I told her that I offered telephone readings by credit card, she told me that she didn't have one. When I offered to give her a 1900 telephone number where she could have a reading and have it charged to her telephone bill, she told me that she'd had a bar put on her phone for 1900 calls after spending thousands of dollars.

'I've had over fifty readings about this one problem and I'm confused.'

'I'm not surprised. What's the situation?'

'Is he coming back?'

'Who?' I asked, thinking that perhaps she was very religious and expecting an imminent Second Coming.

'My boyfriend. He left three months ago and I don't know what to do.'

I heard a small child crying in the background and my heart sank. I had a vision of a mother feeling too abandoned by her partner to care adequately for her little son or daughter, and I felt that everyone was losing in this situation.

'I won't give you a reading but I can tell you what to do. It doesn't need a reading as it is immediately apparent to me.'

'Yes?'

'Yes. Put the man aside and focus on each minute of each hour of each day, one at a time. Focus on your life and your child.'

'Children. I have two.'

'Then focus on your life and your children, and get your life back. If he comes back then you'll be happy, and if he doesn't you'll still be happy as you'll have your life back. You win every way.'

'Wow. You know, that makes sense. You're the first person to say that to me and it makes sense.'

'Good, then go and get your life back, and appreciate your children before they have children of their own.'

She thanked me and rang off. Two weeks later she called to thank me again.

'You were right. I was ignoring myself, my needs and my children. They are happier for me focusing on them and on what I have to do in my life.'

'That's great,' I said.

'And do you know what?'

'What?'

'He came back. And this time I'm never going to let a man come between me and my life, or between me and my kids again. Thanks for the reading.'

'I didn't give you a reading if you remember. I simply gave you a reminder.'

Sometimes in answering your client's question all you have to do is to ask them what they already know. In response to a question from a wife about her husband's repeated infidelities, I sometimes ask the woman, 'Do you think that this is the last time?'.

If she answers 'No', then I ask her what she intends doing about it. These are hard questions, but sooner or later she'll be asking herself the same things; if she waits she may be worn down by the situation and too tired to think clearly. It may be necessary to try to glimpse the long-term future for such a client in order to remind them that what they are experiencing will pass. This may give them the courage to pursue an outcome. They'll still have to take the necessary steps, but they will be aware that future happiness does exist for them.

Resist the temptation to cross the line and give them hope on credit, as this only wastes their time. An example of getting 'hope on credit' happened to me in my second-ever reading, in the 1970s. I was confused, depressed and at a crossroads in my life. Instead of telling me what the choices were, the reader decided to cheer me up. To this end she said: 'You're missing out on a large sum of money. It's in a tall building. About ten floors up you'll find a sum of money awaiting you'.

This distracted me from the problems at hand as I spent a few weeks searching for the money, but it did not change me or my life. Therefore, after I tired of the search I was still facing the decisions I had consulted her about. What this reader did is soothsaying: the act of soothing your client by saying something pleasant or predicting some exciting incident ahead for them. It doesn't help your client and it doesn't help your reputation; you may as well hand your client a romantic novel and tell them to escape from life into its pages.

Also, a reading is not always enough to change a person. Sometimes a reading can highlight a pattern of behaviour but it cannot change it. After years of referring clients to counsellors for further help in changing life patterns, I decided to become a counsellor myself. Ongoing counselling can take realisations about behaviour patterns to the next stage: to implementing change to help clients toward their desired goals.

In the case of one recent Tarot client I saw a pattern of relationships with abusive men, and I felt that it might take three or four years to change such behaviour patterns in order for her to have a rewarding and fulfilling relationship with a man.

I asked, 'Are you prepared to have a period without a relationship while you make the necessary changes?'.

'No, I can't bear the thought of being alone,' she replied.

'Not even if it means that you'll have more rewarding relationships afterward?'

'No. I need to be in a relationship.'

'Then what about staying with your current partner as you do the work on yourself?'

'No, I can't bear to be near him,' she said.

'Well, the only obvious alternative is to have a relationship with a woman until you feel ready to have one with a man.'

'Why?'

'Perhaps a woman can offer you the nurturing you seek.'

'I'd better have some time to think about that one,' she laughed.

This client was reluctant to be alone but my task was to find an alternative for her despite this.

In another case a woman named Chelsea phoned me in tears wanting a reading immediately. I offered her an appointment that evening, realising that it would be more a counselling session than a Tarot reading.

Five minutes into the reading she was crying again, explaining that the man she had been involved with had left her and gone back to his wife. It's a familiar story when you sit in the reader's chair. Men who are having affairs often return to their wives, especially when children are involved.

'But David had said that he loved me,' she sobbed, and I offered her some tissues and gave her room to feel the pain.

'I'm going to be forty-five in a few weeks and we had so many plans together. We were so happy together … so happy.'

'Just because he has returned to his wife and children doesn't mean that he didn't love you, only that he has decided to be with them,' I said as she composed herself.

She brightened at this thought and moved on to her questions. At the close of the reading she collected her tape and smiled. She said: 'You are very kind, you know. I feel much better now. I'm going home to have a good cry, and then I'll open a bottle of wine and pack his things'.

I realised that there was still a great deal of pain for Chelsea to go through before she resolved her relationship with David, and I expected her to call in the coming weeks for more support. Three days later that call came. I offered her a counselling session, but she insisted on a Tarot reading as she had a few more questions.

Once again Chelsea was in tears before asking the first question, and I offered her some tissues and a few minutes to compose herself. As previously, she appeared stronger toward the close of the reading.

'I don't know how I can go on living in that house. Everything about it reminds me of David,' she said mournfully. Suddenly she looked up at me and smiled.

'I know. I could move out and find another place to live. I could move in here with you.'

'Er … with me?' I asked.

'Yes. I don't have to bring much with me. I could put most of it into storage. You seem to have a nice place here and we get along very well.'

I was stunned. What had given her the idea that I wanted her to live with me? Ordinarily I am somewhat distant when giving a reading, almost reserved. As Chelsea had needed some support I had given it to her, through listening to her and helping her to see that this pain would eventually pass. She had mistaken this for something else, or perhaps she was given to believing that things were not as they actually were.

'What? Don't you want me to live here? I wouldn't take up much space, and you could use a woman's touch around the place.'

I was speechless, and that is no small thing for me. I kept waiting for her to laugh and tell me that she was joking and when she didn't, I became distinctly uneasy.

'Do you have one last question?' I asked her, and she moved on with the reading as though nothing had been said.

If you don't start out with a broad-minded approach to life, a few years of giving readings will probably expand your outlook (if not make you cynical). For example, in a recent reading a woman asked me about her career, and I could see from the cards that she had her own business.

After detailing what the cards on the table revealed, I tuned into her clairvoyantly. Then we started having a conversation.

'What sort of business is it exactly?' I asked her, as I was puzzled by the images I had in my mind.

'Why do you ask?' she inquired in return, obviously reluctant to reveal details about the business.

'Well, it's just that I see a room filled with items, none of which are used for what they were intended for. Does this make sense to you?'

'Yes, it could make sense. What do you see?'

At this point I thought that I might as well state exactly what I saw, so I jumped in.

'This may be symbolic but it's such a clear scene that it appears to be actual,' I said, preparing her for what was to come.

'So what do you see?' she asked again.

I took a deep breath and began. 'I see a wardrobe but it is not used for storing clothing. Instead I see a man bound and naked and locked inside the wardrobe, and you're standing nearby glancing at your watch. You seem to be thinking, "Oh, I'll give him another ten minutes," and then you walk away.'

I looked over at her to see her smiling.

'Yes, well, I think you know what my business is. Now, what other things do you see there?'

'I see a small table with an array of things lined up, including a horse-riding crop, some wooden spoons, an egg flip and a few other kitchen utensils, none of which have ever been near a kitchen.'

'Tools of the trade,' she said calmly.

★ The Client's Story ★

At some point during the reading the client may choose to tell you their side of events. This is their story; it is not necessarily fact but they will believe it is such. As a reader it is your task to be objective and therefore not take sides. This is especially the case with stories about relationships. Relationships are a dance and each dance requires two partners who both know the steps; I cannot waltz with you if you only know how to tango. That is, it takes two people to have a relationship and to share responsibility for what happens within it.

An example of variations in clients' stories or versions of events occurred with Hans and Ellen, who were married with three children. They came for readings, and at the initial reading Ellen went first: 'We're moving back to Europe as Hans has not been happy here in Australia. He wants to make a fresh start, and so we are taking the children out of school and leaving for good in ten weeks. I've already resigned from my job and although I'll miss it, it's probably for the best'. This was her story, or version of events. It sounded perfectly reasonable and I didn't doubt it at the time.

When Hans sat down and told me his story, a completely different picture emerged: 'Nine years ago I visited my family in Europe for my mother's seventieth birthday and I spent five weeks there. During that time I met a girl and we fell in love. We spent nearly every day together and then I returned home to my wife and the kids. In the past year the girl has been in my mind constantly and I've written to her twice. She is happily married now, but I can't help thinking we could make a go of things if only I lived closer to her'.

Two years later Hans and Ellen consulted me again.

'Are you over here on holiday?' I asked Ellen when she sat down.

'No,' she sighed. 'It didn't work out with Hans and work over there, so we decided to come back again.'

When Hans sat down later I asked him what had happened.

'It didn't work out with me and the girl, and then I became so depressed that I couldn't find a decent job and I missed Australia, so here we are.'

Two completely different versions of the same events reminded me that things are not always what your client tells you they are. After all, if things were clear and simple, your client would not need to spend time and money talking with you; they'd have solved their problems, and they'd be at the beach or using that money to order lunch.

Important clues which you, the reader, need to pick up on are often contained within your client's story. Readings are partly memory (of card meanings), partly intuition and partly observation (of your client). The observation part is more difficult during telephone readings, when, with no visual clues to assist you, you have to rely more heavily on the other two aspects.

As a reader, your task is to give your client enough information for them to make balanced decisions or to take appropriate action toward their particular purpose. This does not involve you doing all the talking and them all the listening. If you encourage the client to speak a little (not too much) you have a better chance of helping them to comprehend fully what you are saying to them.

★ Setting Boundaries ★

Gaining a good reputation as a reader is one thing and maintaining it is another. Once you develop a good reputation your services will be in great demand. Obviously this is beneficial, but when the public desires your services it can become quite demanding, and in order to have a life aside from readings you must have a sense of discipline.

This discipline involves setting limits with clients who want to see you when it suits them but not when it suits you. It makes sense that with a busy lifestyle the average person cannot consult a Tarot reader during their working hours, and the fact that they may have young children and therefore after-school responsibilities only complicates matters.

At the beginning of an introductory Tarot course I usually explain to students that the most difficult readings they will ever give are those for friends. This is because friends are not used to you in the role of the Tarot reader, and they are likely to challenge you, distract you, answer their mobile phone just when you get to the good bit or, as one student described, phone another friend from the reading table to relay the news as it is being given. (Also, reading for friends continuously can damage the friendships, especially when you consider that 'friendship is based on what we do not say to one another'.) Professional readers rarely have to endure such treatment, and they are better at setting limits with clients.

Setting your limits clearly and assertively without offending potential clients or surrendering your days off can be done with practice and tact. Having said that, while I was writing this book there were several occasions when clients wanted to bend the rules and, while I try to set boundaries, in a number of these incidences I did not. I hope the following will show you what to do and what not to do.

At one point my five-year-old son was visiting me, and I had kept the week free of appointments so that we could have a good time together. It was an exhausting but rewarding week, and at the end of it I had more respect for the effort his mother puts in full time. In any case, as I was tired I was less assertive when dealing with clients, and that led to my not setting boundaries in the following situations.

Shirley telephoned on Tuesday to say that she had missed the third day of an introductory Tarot course I had conducted about eighteen months before, and as her sister wanted a reading she wondered if she could obtain a discount for her. I asked Shirley what sort of discount she wanted and she replied that a half-price reading was what she had in mind.

It was not a type of arrangement I usually made, but I offered Shirley a discount of about 40 per cent for her sister's reading. Shirley asked if Saturday would be suitable and I told her that my next available appointment wasn't until the following Tuesday. Her sister, Olivia, phoned the following day to make an appointment. She also tried to get me to see her on Saturday, but I pointed out that the following Tuesday was my first available appointment.

That was just the beginning of the saga of that weekend. Things actually started to become stressful when another client, Lydia, arrived with her mother for a Saturday appointment. She wanted a palmistry reading about her long-term future and at the end of it she had a list of short-term questions. I had explained before we began that short-term questions were answered by the Tarot, and that I don't combine readings as I believe that combination readings are for those who do not have enough to say through one mode.

However, Lydia seemed so upset that I answered some of her immediate questions clairvoyantly despite my next client sitting in the waiting room, and this took me fifteen minutes over time. Lydia was still asking questions from the doorstep while she was leaving.

Later that night her mother phoned to ask if I could do a Tarot reading for Lydia the following morning before she departed for her home interstate. Lydia's plane departed at 9 am, so I would have had to start the Tarot reading at 7 am on a Sunday (my first day to sleep in for two weeks). However, on that occasion I did set a boundary, and offered Lydia a telephone reading in the following week or a face-to-face reading when she returned five weeks later.

Sunday morning arrived and my first telephone call of the day was from Zoe, who needed 'a reading today'. I offered her a day or evening during the week but she was busy. I offered her an appointment for the following Saturday but she was unavailable then, too. 'Sunday is the only time I have free as I am managing a busy office and can't take any time off at present,' she said. As a rule I don't read on Sundays anyway, and that Sunday I had planned to go shopping with a friend and to check out some potential snorkelling beaches, as we love to snorkel in summer.

I told Zoe that I'd telephone her in the afternoon if I was able to give her a reading that evening. At 3:15 pm I called her and she came for a reading in the evening. This was another boundary crossed.

It didn't stop there. Fifteen minutes before Zoe arrived for her reading I received a telephone call from Germany. The caller, Owen, explained that I'd read for him twelve months ago and that he needed a reading immediately: 'All I need is ten or fifteen minutes on the phone as I have only a few questions'. As the day was already turning out to be unusual, I said yes to Owen's request. I explained that I offer readings by telephone of thirty or fifty minutes and that they are paid for by credit card.

'I don't have any credit cards,' he said, and I laughed aloud before I could stop myself.

'Oh, of course you don't,' I said, as I realised that the evening was going to be surreal. 'What I can do is to send you a present from Germany. What would you like?'

'I'll think about it, and if you'd phone me back in ninety minutes I may be able to read for you then.'

After Zoe's reading Owen called, and I read for him for fifteen minutes. At the conclusion of the reading he agreed to send me an old pair of lederhosen as a present. Now, I won't agree to such an arrangement again as long as I live, but he caught me at a moment when I was tired and somewhat curious about his offer to send me a gift.

Late on Sunday evening Lydia telephoned me from interstate. She had just arrived home, and said she needed another reading. In this case, I asked her to listen to the tape of her reading from the day before, take a bath and have a good night's rest. I thought that if she still felt like a reading the next day she knew how to reach me and arrange a time for a telephone reading, and that if she didn't telephone me I could assume she had the answers to her questions and was perhaps spending her money on good-quality champagne.

The first point here is that many Tarot readers and clairvoyants don't always establish very strong personal boundaries between themselves and their clients. This is understandable when you consider that they penetrate the emotional and psychic boundaries of others for a living. The second point is that many clients also have weak personal boundaries, and they sometimes have to be gently but firmly reminded that you, the reader, don't necessarily solely live for reading for others.

Also, as discussed in *Limitations of the Tarot*, I prefer to postpone a reading when a client sounds emotionally distraught or 'un-centred', because it is difficult to be accurate when the client is in the eye of the storm. They won't hear what you are saying, sometimes insisting on interpreting what you say in a way which fits their desired outcome. It may seem cruel to delay a reading when someone is experiencing great pain, but if delaying your reading will make it more accurate and effective in showing your client the right way, it becomes the obvious thing to do.

A materially ambitious reader may, for the sake of a fee, read for the client immediately and insist that they come for another reading when the storm has passed (perhaps in a week or two) but this can make the client dependent upon the reader, which is unhealthy for both of them. Such dependence is likely to lead to strong psychic cords of energy existing between both parties, and these can pull the reader off-centre and imbalance their life as a result. (Psychic cords are covered in more detail in my previous book, *A Secret Door to the Universe*, Simon & Schuster (Australia) Pty Limited, Sydney, 1999.)

Even if your potential client is in urgent need of a reading you are not obliged to read for them. You can set boundaries for a variety of reasons besides those already discussed. For example, I never read for a client after I've consumed any alcohol. After I had had a glass of wine with dinner one night a client phoned for a reading, and it took me ten minutes to explain to her that my accuracy diminished after consuming alcohol and that I would not complete a reading for her that night.

Other reasons for refusing to read for someone are that they:

- have consumed a great deal of alcohol
- appear irrational
- are having too many readings in a row and risk becoming dependent upon you as a reader to make their decisions for them, or they
- are calling at an unreasonable time.

Regarding this last point, I receive at least two or three calls a month between 1 am and 5 am from strangers asking if I offer telephone Tarot readings. At present none of my advertising literature mentions telephone readings, and I do not have a 1900 number as the telephone Tarot services do. In the past I answered the telephone while emerging from a deep sleep (as my office is at home), but now I unplug it before retiring for the night and sleep peacefully.

You also have the right to refuse a client who asks you to do something illegal, immoral or downright seedy. This includes requests for negative magic spells or curses to be placed on people, advice on how to evade the law or to track down a partner who does not want to be found. Ten years ago I was telephoned by a man who wanted a 'reading' for himself and his wife. I sensed something was not quite right so I asked him a few questions. His hidden agenda soon surfaced. 'I have a sexual problem,' he explained. 'You see, I cannot become aroused unless I see another man making love to my wife. Can you do this in our session? I'll pay you extra for your time, of course,' he said. Naturally, I refused.

★ Difficult Clients ★

Not all your readings will be breezy affairs, punctuated by laughter, with you feeling confident about your accuracy and communicating with your client on a profound level. Sometimes you will simply have bad days, when making sense of the layout before you is more difficult than usual. However, at other times it will be the client who makes the process difficult.

An example of this occurred recently with a client of mine named Sandra. She telephoned me at 6:50 am for a reading, and I was still asleep so the machine took a message. She urgently requested a reading that morning as she was about to leave for the country in the afternoon. She asked that I call her back and leave a message on her machine.

I did so, but her telephone rang and rang, so I presumed that her machine was switched off. I telephoned Sandra again later, and after lunch she rang again, asking why I hadn't returned her call. It was a strange start to proceedings, and it went steadily downhill from there.

As I had put most of the day aside for writing I could fit her in at 5 pm. Sandra was excited, and desperate to have a reading until she asked my fee. When I told her what I charged the urgency cooled somewhat, and she told me that she'd have to call me back after she'd thought it over. She telephoned back an hour later and agreed to come at 5 pm. At 5:10 pm she called to say that she was held up by traffic, but according to my telephone readout she was ringing from home. She asked if she could come at 6 pm; I agreed to this and that was when she arrived.

From the moment Sandra came she took control of the whole reading process, forcing me to break rule after rule. She refused to fill out my client form. She then told me that she wasn't interested in hearing any bad news; once the reading began she gasped, and interpreted each card for herself as they appeared on the table.

However, even as I sat down at the table I had had a sinking feeling. I scrutinised myself to see if it was simply that I didn't like Sandra's energy, but it wasn't just that. Something was distinctly wrong. She was not my typical client and I studied her for a moment. She had arrived with two credit cards and a set of car keys, and my attention was drawn to the credit cards.

I sensed that they were not hers and probably stolen. I brushed away my thoughts as the product of my imagination, and then realised that I was a clairvoyant about to give a reading and sensing that the credit card she was about to use to pay me was stolen. If I couldn't trust my own instincts about that, then what sort of reader was I?

Sandra explained that she had recently had a Tarot reading from another reader and had been upset by what the woman had told her. The reader had predicted her relationship ending within twelve months, and she was consulting me in order to hear that this information had been wrong.

'Will my husband and I separate within twelve months?' was her first question. I offered Sandra some more positive alternatives to that question, as I sensed that with the emotional state she was in, the cards were likely to confirm her worst fears.

I said to Sandra: 'How about a more positive wording for that question? You could ask, "What does the future hold for our relationship?" or "What can I do to improve our relationship?", or even "Will we still be together in a love relationship twelve months from now?"'.

'No, I don't want you to tell me what to ask you. I want to ask the question.'

It was then that I realised Sandra wasn't hearing me anyway, as I saw her eyes scanning the cards searching for hopeful signs and confirming her worst fears at the same time. I took a deep breath and spoke: 'Look, I've been in this business for twenty-one years now and I have a set of rules which I work by. Since we first spoke on the phone this morning, I've broken too many of my rules and I'm not happy doing this'.

'Perhaps that's a good thing?' she countered.

'No, it's not, and I don't want to continue this reading. As a rule I never read for clients when they're in the eye of the storm emotionally, which you are presently. It reduces accuracy, which doesn't help anyone. So, I'll stop now, there'll be no charge for today and I hope that you find a suitable reader to answer your questions.' We were both relieved by this, and I put the cards away and she left.

I cannot recall the last time I refused to read for someone, but it is an important choice to have when you have exhausted other alternatives. If you refuse to read for a client there is usually no fee charged and the decision is often reached within the first ten or fifteen minutes. It is unlikely that you'd be fifty-five minutes into a one-hour reading and suddenly refuse to read for someone.

Sometimes you will clearly see a meaning for a particular card and your client won't be able to see it. During one particular reading, a woman in her early forties asked me about her love relationship. I saw two Pages in the layout and determined that they were two children.

'Do you have any children?' I asked her.

'Why?'

'Well, I can see two children here.'

'No, we have no children.'

'Well … I can distinctly see two children. I'll describe them to you.'

'Oh, he has a child from a previous marriage.'

'That's good, but I still see a second child.'

'No, we have no children,' she said impatiently.

'So, you have no children between you and yet he has one child.'

'Oh yes, I have a child, but she's sixteen years old,' she said off-handedly.

My eyes narrowed, and I sighed in order to prevent myself saying something we would both regret. It was like pulling teeth. I wanted to say: 'Perhaps I should have put it more clearly. Do you now have, or have you ever given birth to, a child or children of either gender, which, as your offspring, is, or are, still living and as such remain your child or children?'.

The client was so intent on hearing only about the direction of her relationship that she didn't think about the influence of the two children who lived with her and her partner; one full-time and the other at weekends. Two children will influence any relationship, but my client didn't seem to think so.

When you plainly see a meaning for a card and your client cannot (especially a meaning for a card representing the past or the present), do not proceed with the reading until your client understands what you are saying. If the client cannot see a future that you are predicting, that's okay; when we can see clearly where we're going, we don't need to consult a Tarot reader.

In a recent reading a client asked me about her career as an osteopath. The Three of Swords appeared reversed as the fifth card in a seven card layout (the energy around the question). I explained that she had some unresolved grief or negative feelings about a past career, and possibly about the one she had at the time of the reading, but she couldn't relate to what I was saying.

I quietly insisted that she reflect on her past career for a moment to see if any unresolved emotional issues were still there, and she still shook her head. Intuitively I picked up that the issue was six-and-a-half years old, so I told her this. I then traced back to the year and to the approximate month to help her to find the issue.

'What were you doing in the middle of that year?' I asked her.

'Oh yes, I've got it. I had just returned from a seven-month overseas trip, and the osteopath I'd hired to fill in for me while I was away told me that my clients had requested they remain with her and not return to me as we had arranged.'

'So, how did you feel?'

'I was devastated.'

'And did you check with those clients directly to confirm what the other osteopath had told you?'

'Er, no, I didn't. I just felt like I had been cut in two.'

'So, that explains why you want to return to your career as an osteopath but you have some reservations due to unresolved issues from the past.'

She was happy with my explanation and we proceeded with the rest of her reading. Had I skipped over the meaning of the Three of Swords reversed in her layout after she had not confirmed my initial interpretation, I would not have done my job as a reader: to leave the client with a clear awareness of the issues behind them and before them.

In some readings the client continues to dispute the outcome of the reading, saying that it is impossible. In the past I'd add extra cards until I had toned the meaning down, but these days if I feel that what I see is correct, I simply state: 'Well, what I've said is on the tape and I'll see you in two years. Then I'll ask you what has happened. I'm sure that you're aware that you have free will in all things predicted, but this is the most likely future from where you presently stand'.

★ Cleansing Your Workplace ★

Clients usually consult a Tarot reader when they have problems or have decisions to make. They are frequently tense or emotionally confused when they arrive for a reading, and as you read for them they release those pent-up emotions into your workplace. Therefore, it is wise to cleanse your workplace of these energies regularly after clients have left. If you don't, your workplace will soon develop a cold, negative energy and you will probably find yourself reluctant to spend time there. Eventually clients will also become reluctant to spend time in your negative workplace, and your bookings are likely to dwindle.

Just as a tradesperson maintains their workplace, tools and reputation, so must a Tarot reader.

Maintaining the positive energy in your workplace requires a few simple steps.

1. Keep a lighted candle burning during your readings. Fire helps to break up negative psychic and emotional energy. An open fire in a fireplace restores the energy balance to a room very quickly.

2. If possible, open the windows at every opportunity between readings to allow fresh air to pass through the room. Fresh air will sweep away negative energy. Obviously, if the outside temperature is -10° this technique is inadvisable.

3. Once a month place a bowl of water in the room to absorb negative energy, and replace the water daily for five days. You can disguise the water by placing it in a vase with flowers.

4.　Having cleansed your workplace you also need to cleanse yourself. This can be done by sitting beside an open fire, swimming in the sea or in a pool, or sitting beside the sea (sea breeze), having a bath, taking a long walk or some time spent gardening. In case you hadn't noticed, these methods include the four elements (as shown by the four Suits of the Minor Arcana), so one of them is likely to appeal to you.

5.　Regular meditation helps to restore your internal balance and centre you. Remaining centred is essential when helping clients resolve their issues.

6.　It pays to use some form of spiritual protection before commencing a reading, as you don't always know what you are dealing with in energy terms. Some readers surround themselves with white light, ensuring it covers the top of their head and goes under the soles of their feet. Others mentally ask for protection before they start. A simple request is: 'Please send me protection on all levels through the Father, the Son and the Holy Spirit. Thank you, thank you, thank you'. The three thank you's are for each level of protection you seek. (For more information on this, see Paul Fenton-Smith, *A Secret Door to the Universe*, Simon & Schuster (Australia) Pty Limited, Sydney, 1999.)

7.　The burning of incense or smudge sticks can also break up negative energy in a workplace. Smudge sticks are dried herbs, such as lavender, sage or rosemary, bound together with string; they are set alight and the smoke from them penetrates the room. A smudge stick can be about 15 cm long, and you only burn it for ten minutes and then immerse the glowing tip in water to extinguish it. You may choke and splutter when using a smudge stick, but they are very effective. Incense is available at alternative bookshops and some health food shops. Smudge sticks can usually be found where you purchase your Tarot cards, at crystal shops and some health food shops.

8.　Some Tarot readers prefer to use an oil burner in their workplace. Pure essential oils such as rosemary, lavender or sage can be used to cleanse the room without the side effects of smoke, which needs to be dispersed. The only problem with oil burners is if you slip with the oil bottle as you are about to sit down to a reading. I use orange oil, and when I slip and pour ten drops instead of three into the burner, it's like doing a reading in an orange grove.

If you read regularly but don't cleanse your workplace, you even risk problems with your physical health. Taking in negative psychic and emotional energy can eventually weaken you, although the actual health difficulties vary from reader to reader, according to their specific weaker health areas.

So, if you cleanse regularly your workplace remains a positive place to enter and to work. I see cleansing as routine maintenance. If you worked in a factory the routine maintenance might be servicing and cleaning the machinery. Carrying on the analogy, Tarot cards are simply waxed paper, so they wear out with use. After twenty-four months they are grubby and tattered, and the Court cards become quite faceless with the continuous shuffling action. I replace my pack every eighteen months, as they lose their 'spring' with time.

Maintaining your reputation as a reader is as important as psychic hygiene. More than 50 per cent of my clients first learn about me through friends, and a personal recommendation carries more weight than much of my advertising.

To maintain your reputation aim for consistently high-quality readings: no short cuts, no reading over a glass of wine at dinner with friends or attempting to impress strangers with your abilities when out socialising. When asked what I do by someone at a dinner party I usually tell them that I'm a counsellor. It saves an hour of 'So what do you pick up from me then?'. I'm proud of my work but away from it I enjoy talking about other things.

Also, not all publicity is good publicity, contrary to popular opinion. Avoid any media appearance where those inviting you are likely to slander you or your profession. Several years ago I was asked if I knew of any witches so that a sensationalist television program could generate some better ratings through a story. I told them (honestly) that I didn't but they invited me onto the program. I refused, knowing that they were likely to distort anything I said during the editing process. You are not always warned of a set-up prior to your appearance, however, but when faced with an antagonistic interviewer or fellow guest, you can leave the studio or have some standard replies rehearsed.

As you read for clients you may be giving them more attention than they have received in a long time. Sometimes they mistakenly equate this attention with love and they want a relationship with you. In such cases, especially if you also feel attracted to the client, it is standard procedure to sever all contact with one another for a minimum of three months. In this way, any attraction based upon what was said in your reading has time to dissipate and if you still feel the same way at the end of this time you can negotiate a relationship as two consenting adults.

Lastly, don't pass comment on other readers you know or who the client mentions. Unless you were present for a reading your client has received from someone else, you are in no position to judge that person or their methods.

★ Guidelines for Practising Tarot Readers ★

The following guidelines are really just commonsense, but I pass them on to all my students to help them with establishing boundaries between themselves and their clients and instituting suitable work practices. These guidelines are designed for professional Tarot readers and clairvoyants who charge a set fee for an agreed reading time, not for those who practise reading for friends over coffee.

Clients can reasonably expect that:

- You not engage in misleading or deceptive advertising.
- You have undergone basic counselling training to enable you to deal with clients in crisis.
- You maintain a basic psychic and spiritual hygiene, including regular psychic cleansing of yourself and your working premises.
- Where you are unwilling or unable to read for them, you offer them an appropriate referral.
- You are not working under the influence of alcohol or drugs.
- You are professional at all times.
- You do not use the reading time to sell the client products or other services. If you feel your client might benefit from one of your other services, or those of an osteopath or a nutritionist, etc., briefly mention it during the reading and give them details afterwards.
- You do not partake in any practices (such as drug taking to increase psychic awareness) which might harm yourself or others physically, emotionally, mentally or spiritually.
- You will show honesty tempered with compassion.
- You will ask them if they understand what is being said or predicted.
- The reading is not absolute, and that the client knows they are able to exercise their free will in all things predicted.
- You not give legal, medical or other advice you are not qualified to give, but instead refer the client to the appropriate professional for help (if asked for advice on financial investments (particularly shares) state on the tape-recording of the reading that you can only give a broad indication and the decision to invest is the client's).
- The fee and time quoted are adhered to.
- You will have an accuracy of 75 per cent or more.
- You respect client confidentiality, except where judging that the life or the welfare of others is at risk.

I felt it necessary to put these guidelines on paper after seeing outrageous advertisements for clairvoyants and Tarot reading which promised the impossible. The claims I've seen include 'Never fails to reunite the separated', 'Heals all bad luck and restores broken marriages' and 'Restores good luck and fortune'. My question to the reader who claims never to fail to reunite the separated is, how would the reader reunite a woman with her recently deceased husband without taking her life? When I see claims like these I'm tempted to join one of the sceptical organisations which set about debunking the myths and fictitious claims made by some people in this industry. However, this wouldn't be fair to those who are honest, hardworking and accurate.

In a recent reading on a hot day I left my office door open to allow the air from the airconditioner in the living room to cool us down. At one point I felt a gush of cold air sweep across my legs and I asked the client, 'Did you feel that?'.

'What?'

'The cold breeze across the floor.'

'What is it? A spirit?' she asked, wide-eyed.

At this point I broke into laughter.

'No, Just the air conditioner. I hope to impress you with my accuracy and not with amateur theatrics.'

There is no need to promise outrageous things, when, with practice, you can give the client what they have come for. Most clients come so that they will be able to see more clearly, for help with choosing the appropriate path or to see what they are doing to create the circumstances of their own life.

Part Seven

★ The Court Cards ★

As the Court cards can represent people or situations, they often cause readers a great deal of confusion. It is your task as a reader to determine when a Court card represents a person, a situation or an aspect of the individual sitting before you. Before you give up in despair, there are a few simple techniques which can help you to determine the appropriate meaning of these cards when they appear in a layout.

For example, if when you are answering a relationship question for a woman in her early thirties you are faced with the upright Page of Pentacles, there are several possible meanings for this card:

1. It represents a child or a young person. (If it lies in the outcome position it may herald the arrival of a child in the future.)
2. The client may be undertaking some study, or mastering new tasks at work.
3. It could signify her commitment to her relationship and to taking a new direction with her partner.

There are several things you can do to determine the meaning of the layout in that reading. These include:

1. Decide spontaneously. You might choose to state silently to yourself, 'That Page represents …' and conclude with the first option you think of.
2. Look closely at the surrounding cards to determine which meaning is confirmed by other cards in the spread.
3. Ask the client if she has any children or if her partner has any children. If so, then describe the Page to her as though it was a child. If neither she nor her partner have children, look for another meaning for this card.
4. Add another card to the Page. If it is another Court card, a person is confirmed. If you have a Major Arcana card it can signify that the Page represents an aspect of the client (unless it is a Major card for an Earth sign (Taurus, Virgo or Capricorn) as the Pentacles page can represent a young person of one of these signs so it would be the whole person, not just an aspect).

If you have determined that the Page is a child, and you tell your client this and they disagree, go back to your initial feeling. If you still believe that the Page represents a child, pursue a line of questioning to confirm your feeling (see 'Difficult Clients').

Court Cards — Elements Chart

Suit	Page	Knight	Queen	King
Wands	Air of Fire	Fire of Fire	Water of Fire	Earth of Fire
Cups	Air of Water	Fire of Water	Water of Water	Earth of Water
Swords	Air of Air	Fire of Air	Water of Air	Earth of Air
Pentacles	Air of Earth	Fire of Earth	Water of Earth	Earth of Earth

The four pure types are:

> Knight of Wands — Fiery part of Fire
>
> Queen of Cups — Watery part of Water
>
> Page of Swords — Airy part of Air
>
> King of Pentacles — Earthy part of Earth

Those who are represented by the above four cards exemplify the qualities of the element in its pure form.

Pages

The Pages in the Tarot can represent children or young people (up to twenty-one years of age). They can also represent the client at any age if they are feeling young as they approach a new situation or project. The Page of Wands represents the passionate, enthusiastic young person, filled with anticipation for life ahead. The Page of Cups symbolises the romantic, emotionally sensitive young person, anticipating loving someone special and being loved in return. The Page of Swords stands for the intellectual young person who wants to understand the why, what, when, where and who of life. (I've heard it said that 'Why?' is the question of the three-year old, but it is also the question of the scientist, the historian, the detective and the counsellor.) The Page of Pentacles embodies the practical, sensible young person; one who anticipates the material rewards that study, effort and commitment bring them.

When three or more Pages appear in a spread, news is imminent. When a greater number of these Pages are reversed, the news is likely to be delayed.

Page of Wands

The Page of Wands is an enthusiastic, energetic, self-motivated young person who needs to have a goal or a destination to motivate them. Without a goal they can become despondent, or restless and argumentative.

In this image a young man stands with one wand in his grasp, staring off into the distance and anticipating adventures ahead. Blue skies promise a clear path to his goal, and the fact that the predominant colour in this card is orange suggests that he is enthusiastic and passionate about achievement. The salamanders on his tunic represent the element of Fire, and the Fire signs in astrology are Aries, Leo and Sagittarius. This Page may not actually be one of those signs but will still possess all the Fire sign qualities in abundance.

This is the small child who loves direct experience and having the freedom to explore. When my son was fifteen months old we took him to the beach in winter. We thought a walk along the beach might do us all some good, and we rugged up against the wind. As we walked along the deserted beach he struggled to be released so that he could get into the water. He struggled and protested so much that

Amanda stripped off his clothes and allowed him to walk in. He stumbled toward the oncoming waves, free at last of the parental restrictions. As soon as he reached the water a wave engulfed him and he froze. The icy cold water gushed around him and he shot us a look which said, 'How could you let me walk into this cold water alone?'.

The Wands energy made him want to be free but he was unaware of the consequences of his actions.

When Wands people reach their goals they often find that they have had to overcome many more obstacles than they at first anticipated. However, this rarely prevents them from pursuing another goal.

The Page of Wands can represent the planning of a trip, moving house or changing jobs. It concerns that time in life when movement or change is required to make you feel alive again.

Reversed

The Page of Wands reversed can describe an impatient, restless young person whose attention span is short and who may be hyperactive. This Page reversed needs a wholefoods diet and plenty of regular exercise, preferably outdoors. They can become troublesome when kept indoors too long as they have a great deal of physical energy which needs an outlet.

It can signify the client has a desire to move on even though they have not resolved their present issues. Perhaps they want a new job so that they can escape their current one but they have not given enough thought to what it is about the current job that they dislike.

The Page of Wands reversed shows delays in plans. It may be a delay in news reaching the client or be due to other commitments which need to be fulfilled before something can take place.

PAGE of CUPS.

Page of Cups

When the Page of Cups represents a young person it is someone who is soft-hearted, imaginative and emotionally sensitive to their surroundings. Somewhat shy at first meeting, this Page opens up to others slowly, but values friendships and relationships greatly. The card can also describe a young person who is naturally nurturing, and therefore good with babies or toddlers. They are sensitive and creative, and they need some time every day to reflect in order to restore inner peace.

The Page on the card stands on the sand, staring into a cup in his hand. Cloudy skies above him suggest clouded thinking; this signifies that he is romantic and sentimental, his 'clouded' thinking softening reality for him. The fish in the cup represents the element of Water. This Page can represent a Water sign person (Cancer, Scorpio or Pisces) or someone with Water sign qualities, that is, they approach life through feelings, intuition and creativity.

The Page of Cups can also represent an offer, usually an emotional opportunity. There may be an offer of a relationship or a chance to join a group of people which may fulfil your client emotionally.

In a health reading this Page can suggest problems with the feet, or stress-related health problems which respond well to regular meditation. It also indicates a time of psychic or spiritual development through your client attending to their inner needs.

Reversed

The Page of Cups reversed describes a dreamy, passive young person who is content to imagine life as they prefer it to be, rather than face reality and actually do what they can to make a life for themselves. With encouragement this person may find a suitable outlet for their imagination through writing, painting or music, or through nurturing small children. In general terms, therefore, it can suggest that a more realistic view of life is required by your client before they can achieve their goals.

The Page reversed can also signify the dissolving of a relationship or a time when your client is uncertain as to where they stand in a relationship. They may be awaiting some kind of news to confirm their place in a particular situation, and when the Page is reversed, this news is delayed or unclear. When it appears in response to a question, the Page reversed is a 'No', suggesting disappointing news or delays in plans.

Page of Swords

PAGE of SWORDS.

The Page of Swords represents a talkative, curious, mentally restless young person, whose mind is ever searching for new information and understanding.

They might benefit from being away from a television or a computer screen, and outdoors doing something physical. However, Swords people are less inclined to physical pursuits, so supervision may be required to ensure that they discharge some of their excess mental energy physically.

A positive side to this Page (and to all the Swords Court cards) is that when they want advice, a discount on a purchase or some particular information, they are rarely shy in asking others for assistance. They know the value of communicating their needs to other people.

In this image the earth beneath the figure's feet is out of proportion, suggesting that the ground is a long way down and the figure is, in fact, up in the air. Birds fly overhead and clouds hover as the Page clasps a sword in both hands and looks wistfully off into the distance. The birds signify the mind's capacity to perceive challenges from an objective viewpoint (a bird's eye view) in order to locate an appropriate solution.

The figure's red boots suggest passion and his purple tunic shows the need to still the mind (purple being a colour for spirituality) in order to hear universal truths. His yellow clothing signifies mental energy and the trees in the background being bent by the wind symbolise that mental energy needs to be harnessed or disciplined to be effective.

If it appears in answer to a question, the Page of Swords suggests that your client is dreaming of solutions without solid grounding in reality. Perhaps they are dissipating their energy through talking about their goals rather than proceeding towards them. This Page can suggest that your client needs to make a list of ideas in order to arrive at the best solution for the challenge at hand.

The Page of Swords also represents the act of tossing ideas around, and playing with words and concepts until you have a different viewpoint. Sometimes a misheard sentence can make for a complete change in meaning.

This occurred recently when I overheard a four-year old state that, 'A lemon can't change its spots'. I immediately thought that, as the leopard risks becoming extinct, that saying may enter common usage.

Reversed

The Page of Swords reversed represents undisciplined thinking resulting in chaos or dissipate energy. It symbolises someone using words without thought of the power they have to hurt or to confuse others, and can describe gossip, or conversation for its own sake. It can also represent ideas which are poorly thought out.

An example of the kind of idea represented by the Page reversed is the concept a friend laughingly presented to me. It was that humankind is too obsessed with the pursuit of money, and that we should be more like the birds in a forest. The birds don't worry about money and yet still survive. This overlooks the reality that birds spend much of their waking time trying to feed themselves and to avoid predators. As humans have few predators we have more waking time to devote to other pursuits, such as learning to speak and to write, and travelling or building a house which is not 20 metres up a tree. Another example is an acquaintance of mine saying recently, 'I never repeat gossip, so listen carefully.'

In answer to a question the Page of Swords reversed suggests delays in news (similar to all the Pages), a poorly thought-out plan, or a presentation which is too wordy. (Such a presentation would be a twenty-three page résumé sent to a potential employer who has 280 applicants for one position.) Plans have to be revised now, and the Sword in this card needs to be used to cut out unnecessary words, ideas and concepts, distilling your client's plan into a useable form.

PAGE of PENTACLES.

Page of Pentacles

The Page of Pentacles represents a serious, responsible young person who is prepared to apply themselves to study and to work which will advance them in some way. Pentacles people enjoy material things such as food, and belongings which accord them status, and they usually maintain these things carefully.

In this image a young man stands in a field holding one pentacle and examining it closely. The bright sky above him suggests that all is well with the world, and that this is a tranquil moment spent planning the path to prosperity. His red hat and scarf depict the passionate pursuit of material things. His green tunic suggests awareness of the need for balance, for harmony between work and rest.

This is a card for an earthy young person and the Earth signs in astrology are Taurus, Virgo and Capricorn. (However, the person can be earthy in nature and yet still be another sign astrologically.)

When it appears in answer to a question the Page of Pentacles suggests that success will come after your client masters new skills, and indicates their dedication to developing the skills necessary to achieve their goals. The appearance of the Page shows your client as a novice at something and being dedicated to mastering it. For example, when commencing a new job you may feel like the Page of Pentacles again as you attempt to gain the new expertise it requires.

Reversed

The Page of Pentacles reversed represents a young person who is materially hungry; equating material wealth with peace of mind. (However, it can also suggest that they need to lighten their workload in order to realise their goals.) It can imply immaturity; perhaps this is the child who is given things in place of time, attention and love, and soon learns that they can play upon the innate guilt of parents to secure more possessions or material gain.

The image in this card shows an upright pentacle containing a star with the tip pointing upward, depicting the need for your client to keep their emotions subordinate to their mind in pursuing goals. When the card is reversed this star points downward, suggesting that their desires presently dominate their thinking. In the short term, they may decide that their social life is more important than their studies or other long-term goals.

It shows a lack of commitment to mastering the necessary skills to achieve particular goals. Perhaps your client has taken on too much or is unclear about the right path to take to achieve a goal, or their desires are simply taking them in another direction.

When it appears in answer to a question the Page of Pentacles reversed suggests that your client will be unsuccessful in the pursuit of their goal because they are only intermittently committed to their purpose. Time spent in the country or in a garden or doing physical things may help to rebalance the type of person indicated by the Page reversed.

The Knights

The four Knights of the Tarot can represent people or situations. As people they are usually young men between twenty and thirty years of age. When a man in his fifties appears in a reading as a Knight and you are confident that the card represents him, he is usually emotionally still in his twenties.

The Knight of Wands is enthusiastic and forthright, the Knight of Cups is romantic and sensitive, the Knight of Swords is talkative and curious, and the Knight of Pentacles is serious and responsible. In terms of situations, the Knight of Wands stands for movement and travel. The Knight of Cups represents an offer or an emotional opportunity. This Knight can also symbolise the choice between the Cups and the Wands paths in life (see the Knight of Cups for more information). The Knight of Swords can represent the need to act swiftly or to 'carpe diem' (seize the day). The Knight of Pentacles signifies remaining aware of the long-term consequences of actions.

Three or more Knights in a layout represents academies, study and learning. Their appearance may therefore signify your client is undertaking or will undertake university study, a part-time course or even a correspondence course.

Knight of Wands

The Knight of Wands is an enthusiastic and forthright man, usually under thirty years of age, who is impatient and therefore quick to act. The Knight of Wands is better suited to short bursts of activity than to prolonged application, as his attention wanes when goals seem too far away. He doesn't yet have the discipline to pace himself for the long haul. When he has developed this sense of self discipline, he'll be the King of Wands.

The image on the card shows a young man straddling a horse which is rearing up. He is in pursuit of his dreams or goals, and clothed in a tunic covered in salamanders, representing the element of Fire. The predominant colour in this card is orange, suggesting passion and enthusiasm, qualities this man has in abundance.

The Knights represent the Fire part of the suit and the Wands suit is the sign of Fire, making this Knight the fiery part of Fire. This means that he has all the Fire sign qualities in abundance. These include enthusiasm, eagerness for adventure, a need to pursue goals and often a level of honesty which borders on tactlessness. The Wands Knight can describe a Sagittarian person if accompanied by the Temperance card.

In simple terms this is a card representing moving to another place to live or to work. It is a positive card, one for pursuing goals and rising to challenges. It can represent travel (overseas if accompanied by the Eight of Wands) or travel with work if it appears in a career layout.

Reversed

The Knight of Wands reversed is very impatient, with a very short attention span. He is often only capable of commitment to very short-term goals as he needs immediate rewards for his efforts. When reversed he is essentially immature, preferring to scatter his energy recklessly and to talk about his goals than to reach for them.

Delays for your client in travel or in reaching their goals are shown by the Knight reversed, and sometimes this is due to their having to pace themselves and not scatter their energy in futile pursuits.

For example, Conrad was attempting to complete a novel. To support himself he wrote feature stories for magazines, which paid him on a per word basis. This gave Conrad a reasonable income but it slowed his progress with writing his book. When I read for him, Conrad was writing a feature story for a magazine which was not paying him at all. Therefore, he was devoting his time to writing features which were not supporting him financially and were depleting his energy for writing his novel.

I asked him about his long-term goals.

'I want to complete and publish this novel,' he replied.

'Then how is writing a free story for a magazine that can afford to pay you helping you toward your goal?'

'It isn't,' he stated, and went on diligently to complete his novel.

In short, the Knight of Wands reversed can represent uncertainty about the appropriate action in a given situation, delaying results.

Knight of Cups

In simple terms the Knight of Cups describes a soft-hearted, creative man, who is both romantic and enthusiastic. Like the Page of Cups this card can represent an opportunity being offered to your client.

On the card a man sits in the saddle, holding the horse's reigns with one hand and a cup in the other. His horse moves at a slower pace than that of the Knight of Wands. His tunic is covered in fish, representing the element of Water, and signifying emotions and creativity.

The Knights are the Fire part of the suit and the Knight of Cups belongs to the suit of Water, so he is the fiery part of Water. This means that he has a choice to become the King of Cups (Water) or to become the King of Wands (Fire). This decision may take him years, and he has until he is around thirty years of age to decide which path he should take.

Both paths offer opportunities and restrictions. The Fire path is one of challenges, adventure, achievement, trophies, competition and success measured in what is achieved or conquered. This also makes it a somewhat lonely path, as those who continuously compete with others often experience difficulty allowing those they love to be close to them, as they are subconsciously measuring themselves against everyone.

The Water path is one of creativity, romance, intimacy, shared group activities, inspiration and a need for your client to find their place in a community. It lacks the opportunity for worldly achievement that the Fire path offers but it offers emotional, and perhaps spiritual fulfilment, along with tranquillity.

The Knight of Cups must make the choice between these two paths in order to become a King, and once a path is taken, it is very hard to go back to the other one. I have seen men in their forties surrender the path taken for the one left behind and it has usually cost them everything they have in life. Relationships, family, friendships, career and material possessions have to be surrendered if you want to return to the point of deciding upon a path after you have already chosen one and pursued it for several years.

Reversed

The Knight of Cups reversed can describe the disillusionment which comes from realising that an offer is not what you thought it would be. It can describe a romantic approach to life where your client's hopes and desires cloud their vision of what life is actually offering them. This represents immaturity; the Knight reversed is emotionally still a Page.

The card reversed can describe a man in his twenties who cannot deliver what he claims to, as he is emotionally immature. He dreams of what life will be like when he is in a relationship but he is unaware of the efforts required to make a relationship work in day-to-day living.

The Knight of Cups reversed can reflect your client's inability to choose a path (active or creative) towards their desired goals. The choice between the Fire path of action or the Water path of feelings and creativity may be confusing them at this point. However, commitment to one path is required before they can move towards their goals.

Knight of Swords

KNIGHT of SWORDS .

The Knight of Swords represents an intellectual young man, who seeks to understand the world cerebrally. He has well-developed communication skills, and he likes to ask questions and to state his opinions. If words alone could put the world to right, this man would be in great demand; however, as the Knight of Wands is quick to point out, it is our deeds by which we are eventually judged.

In this card a young man rides furiously, clutching the reigns in one hand and an upright sword in the other. The existence of a strong wind is evidenced by the windblown trees and the clouds streaked across the sky. There are birds on the horse's bridle and butterflies on its saddle, both representing the element of Air (or thought). The butterflies also show the way thought can transform your understanding of life and circumstances.

In simple terms the Knight of Swords represents a young man quick to think and to act, who is well suited to short-term projects and to careers where he can use his communication skills. He has yet to comprehend fully the power of words to heal but also to inflict pain, and this is shown by the way the figure on the card rides with his sword outstretched.

He is restless, as the Knights represent the Fire part of the suit and the Swords suit is Air. This makes him the fiery part of Air. As Air fans Fire, he is the quickest thinking and acting of the knights.

This man has the choice of two paths: those of Fire and Air. If he chooses the Fire path, he will become the King of Wands. This leads to an active, adventurous life, filled with achievement and struggle toward goals. If he chooses the Air path, he will become the King of Swords. This path leads to a rational life, filled with study, precision in thought and in action, and often a career in the professions. By using his mind he keeps his hands clean in the pursuit of an income.

The Knight of Swords can suggest a time to act swiftly to avert disaster or to secure an opportunity, as in effect it depicts a man who is seizing the day.

Reversed

The Knight of Swords reversed represents scattered thought, and action without planning. This man rushes into situations without thinking things through, often resulting in his being cut by his own sword. His words and deeds cause him much pain, which reflection might prevent.

The Knight reversed indicates a man who is more generous in talk than in action, and who does not realise that words alone do not produce results. He is quick to promise, and just as quick to forget his commitments. He can be unpredictable, restless and ever in search of stimulation. His beliefs about life have probably been hastily gathered and not examined too closely.

Peter is an example of how Swords people love words. He was giving a talk to some farmers who were to pay him with two sheep. He liked the idea that 'Talk is sheep'.

KNIGHT of PENTACLES.

Knight of Pentacles

The Knight of Pentacles can represent a young man who is hard working and career-minded. He is prepared to work long hours and study in his own time to advance his career. While the other Knights are out enjoying themselves, this young man is hard at work, building a career and financial security for the future. He usually relaxes in his sixties when he retires from his career, as he can then afford to reward himself for his efforts.

In the image in this card a young man sits on a stationary horse, examining a pentacle in his right hand and the path before him. There is not the sense of urgency evident with the other Knights; this man has an earthy approach to life. He is stationary because he is aware that one step in the wrong direction will require another step back to the right path.

As the Knights represent the Fire part of the element and the Pentacles element is Earth, this Knight represents the fiery part of Earth. This is translated into enthusiasm and passion channelled into practical concerns such as career and long-term plans.

The card symbolises a hard-working young man whose maturity in terms of his worldly concerns is advanced for his years. He is serious, practical, diligent and cautious in the pursuit of new paths. Being somewhat old-fashioned at heart, he seeks a relationship partner who is practical, loyal and hard working, who will assist him in achieving his career plans.

He prefers to work for himself as he detests being told what to do. He is not the most social of the Knights, so he often meets his partners through his work environment. Work, study, planning and saving are what this Knight does best. He is not spontaneous or adventurous, preferring the same holiday destination each year, if he takes holidays at all.

In simple terms this can be a card representing long-term planning, commitment to career goals, and financial discipline. The element of Earth ensures hard work, but also requires a realistic material reward for efforts.

Reversed

The Knight of Pentacles reversed can describe a young man who is lazy and without direction. However, he may be able to commit himself to a career, if only he can find his direction. An example of this was Trent, who couldn't be bothered looking for work but who diligently practised his guitar for several hours every day.

The Knight reversed needs a direction for his Fire energy, but one which appeals to his need for earthly rewards. Sometimes it can describe a man who values material things but is unprepared to work for them, preferring to rely on others instead.

For example, Julian was travelling the world, funded by two credit cards paid for by his father. His father wanted him home to take over the family business, but Julian was avoiding the dismal prospect of working for a living by finding ways to extend his two-year holiday.

The Queens

The Queens in the Tarot can represent women, or aspects of your client (sometimes even when your client is a man) or approaches to life. The Queen of Wands represents a woman who is enthusiastic and forthright, the Queen of Cups one who is sensitive and intuitive, the Queen of Swords one who is talkative and quick thinking, and the Queen of Pentacles one who is practical, stable and moderate.

The aspects of your client represented by the cards are as follows. The Queen of Wands signifies inner strength and courage to face life; the Queen of Cups represents a powerful intuitive and creative connection with the subconscious mind. The Queen of Swords denotes an organised and perceptive approach to life, or when reversed, a tendency to mental self-criticism for perceived failures in the past, while the Queen of Pentacles represents success through a practical approach to planning and through remaining connected to nature, leading to inner balance and harmony.

Three or more Queens in a layout can highlight the presence of powerful women in your client's life. These can include strong, independent women who are in the public eye due to their business or political achievements.

Queen of Wands

In simple terms the Queen of Wands can represent a Leo person (when the Sun or the Strength card appears in the layout) or any passionate, independent woman. She is forthright, courageous and she enjoys a challenge. Therefore, any career which involves achieving demanding goals is likely to suit her. She is a natural leader and organiser, and is capable of motivating a team or a work force toward a target. The Queen of Wands thrives on competition as it spurs her on to greater achievement. This woman needs variation, as routine stifles her.

On the card the Queen of Wands sits on her throne, her wand in one hand and a sunflower in the other. A black cats sits alert at her feet and she is surrounded by lions, both carved in stone beneath her and above her head. The cat at her feet and the cat's head clasp securing her cape represent her intuition and her untamed nature. Even domesticated cats retain a little of their wild origins and this Queen is no exception.

The predominant colours in this card are yellow and orange, suggesting a combination of intellect and passion. The Queen is a passionate woman who can mentally direct her energies toward a useful and creative purpose. The sunflowers in her hand and on her throne represent the joy she brings to others through her positive attitude to life, but beware, for under that joy lurks a strong temper, and when roused to anger she is likely to make her views widely known.

When the Queen of Wands appears as an influence around your client it can describe a woman who is supporting or helping your client to achieve a goal. This Queen also represents a situation where success is achieved through inner strength and your client's courage in acting according to their convictions.

Reversed

The Queen of Wands reversed indicates a faltering confidence and inner strength, and therefore a temporary lack of courage. Your client's nerve in facing life is diminished now, and they are more likely to act out of fear instead of from a position of strength; therefore the decisions they make may not be their best decisions.

Reversed the card can still represent a Leo person, or any enthusiastic and passionate woman, whose energies are presently low due to ill health or exhaustion. Wands people often push themselves too hard and end up collapsing into bed with exhaustion, a cold or some other illness. Life tends to remind them to rest and to pace themselves more carefully.

As an answer to a question the appearance of the Queen reversed can indicate lack of success in a venture, resulting from a lack of energy, or from a lack of inner strength and courage. Perhaps your client is feeling overwhelmed by life at present, and needs to restore their reserves of energy before pursuing their goals.

Queen of Cups

The Queen of Cups is intuitive, emotional and sensitive to the emotions of those around her. She has the capacity to 'read' the energy of a room full of people when entering it, and she often makes her judgements based on what she feels.

In this card a woman is seated on an ornate throne holding an elaborate cup with both her hands. This cup has the figures of two angels on it and a cross at the top of the lid. She sits patiently, but her strong gaze betrays an emotional strength and determination which is often unnoticed at first meeting.

She is suited to careers in counselling, psychology, writing, working with children and any support role. The Queen of Cups doesn't need the limelight, and she is happy to leave centre stage for the Queen of Wands. Instead she needs to know that she makes a difference to the emotional quality of life of those around her.

She can thrive as a personal assistant, but in such a role she is not necessarily as organised as the Queen of Swords. Creative, harmonious surroundings are essential if she is to work to her best standard, as she is sensitive to the energies of her work environment and to those around her.

She is a natural listener, and strangers often feel safe in opening up to her and telling her their troubles. She is also often sought out by children or anyone who needs to be heard and understood, as she is naturally nurturing, tactful and intuitive. She is capable of facing great emotional pain in life, with her strength lying in her emotional depth and patience.

In simple terms the Queen of Cups is a card representing success though the use of creativity and intuition. It can also signify accomplishment through patiently awaiting your opportunities and moving when the time is right.

Reversed

When the Queen of Cups is reversed, unresolved emotional pain can result in her becoming bitter or vengeful. Unresolved issues from her own past colour her vision of the present, making her an unreliable counsellor or confidant, and her attitudes often isolate her from life and from opportunities for healing.

Deanne's marriage of twelve years collapsed when she discovered that her husband had been cheating on her. The betrayal was so painful for Deanne that she drifted into despair and then depression. Five years later she was still distrustful of men, claiming that all men cheat on women; her unresolved grief and anger were preventing new opportunities for love from reaching her.

It was suggested to Deanne that for her husband to lie to her successfully for such a long period of time, it was possible that she had also to lie to herself. This struck a chord with her. It was necessary that Deanne listen to her intuition more closely to know which men are trustworthy. The fact that she could not hear her intuition throughout the twelve years with her husband suggests that she was a Queen of Cups reversed before her marriage collapsed. An upright Queen of Cups is rarely deceived for she is able to read the motives of others intuitively.

The Queen of Cups reversed tends to sulk when she doesn't get her way, and she has a very long memory when it comes to emotional pain. She can quote back to you what you did, said and were wearing when you upset her sixteen years ago as though it were yesterday. Thus, the Queen reversed can suggest that your client needs to forgive someone and let go of the past. This allows can allow new opportunities for emotional fulfilment to present themselves.

Queen of Swords

This Queen of Swords is a quick thinker, organised, perceptive and able to cut through confusion to arrive at the truth, or essence, of a person or a situation. The Queens represent the Water part of the suit, and as the suit of Swords is the element of Air, the Queen of Swords represents the watery part of Air. This means that she is capable of compassion in her judgements, and allows for human nature and unresolved emotional issues when considering people's motivations in acting a certain way.

In this card a woman sits on a throne, with an upright sword in one hand and the other hand outstretched with a tassel hanging from it (a reminder of being tied up in the Eight of Swords); her tunic is covered in clouds. Clear skies above and the clouds appearing below her head suggest that she is clear thinking. Her upright sword also symbolises her clarity of mind, and it clearly shows the double edge or duality of life. The

Queen of Swords represents the watery part of Air, which is a combination of sympathy and rational thought.

The bird above the Queen's head symbolises the mind's ability to soar above day-to-day problems in order to perceive appropriate solutions. Butterflies adorn her crown and a large butterfly is carved into the base of her throne. These represent the capacity of the mind to transform our understanding of life and situations through gaining new perspectives. They also represent the ability to transform yourself through making sense of life by seeing how thoughts lead to actions and actions produce consequences. (I see this as one of the purposes of counselling. Counselling is sometimes the act of assisting clients to untie the knots in which life has tied them.)

The Queen of Swords needs to know the why, what, when, where and who of life, and until she makes sense of her circumstances, she can have trouble sleeping at night. She usually has a good memory, is a natural conversationalist and enjoys social occasions, as she is naturally curious about people. Swords people get the party started with conversation, and they have the ability to talk about subjects that the Cups people wouldn't dare to approach.

An example of this was something my friend Bethany, an experienced conversationalist, once said. We were standing (talking, naturally) together at a party when a man limped into the room. His twisted torso suggested that he had limped since birth. We nodded politely to him, and after a cursory glance at his twisted leg I resolved not to look again. Bethany had no such intention.

'Hi, I'm Beth, and what happened to your leg?' she said, stretching out her hand to him.

'I'm Robert, and I was born with this,' came the friendly reply. They started discussing his leg and Robert mentioned that his hips were lopsided, making walking over uneven surfaces difficult. At this point Bethany disappeared and returned with a tape measure to measure the distance between each of Robert's hips and the floor.

'You're right, you know. The right hip is a good three centimetres higher than the left.' Bethany was genuinely interested and Robert was content to be measured by her. Swords people like to find out what the rest of us secretly want to know but are sometimes embarrassed to ask.

In simple terms, this Queen can indicate success through clarity of thought and planning.

Reversed

The Queen of Swords reversed can be extremely self-critical, reviewing the past and focusing only on those things which did not go according to plan. She still has a desire to understand the why, what, when, where and who of life, but when reversed she can become confused between her thoughts and her feelings.

The Queen reversed often seeks time alone to sort through her thoughts and feelings, in a bid to restore inner peace and mental clarity. This need for time alone is perhaps why some traditional Tarot writers have dubbed her 'the widow'. It is true that she has had more than her share of loss and pain when reversed, but she is capable of returning to the upright position when she makes sense of what life has delivered to her.

The appearance of the Queen reversed can suggest that your client has been released from the restrictions placed upon them in the Eight of Swords, but don't see they are free now. Old memories and pain are triggered by incidental things, making them retreat from life and from what they perceive as dangerous. Those clouds which are now above your client's head blur their vision and their perception of life.

Queen of Pentacles

This card represents a practical woman, whose approach to life is realistic. While the other Queens may dream of the future, this Queen is aware that the future starts right now, and she plans each step carefully, recognising the effort involved.

In this card a woman sits patiently on a throne in a garden, examining a pentacle. The skull of an animal is carved into the throne, along with various fruits and several human figures. A rabbit bounds across the right-hand foreground of the card, reminding us of this woman's connection with animals and nature. She wears a red tunic, suggesting a passionate yet realistic approach to life, and the sky is gold, symbolising good times.

The Queen of Pentacles represents the Water part of the suit and the Pentacles suit is Earth, making her the watery part of Earth. This means that she has emotional depth (Water) and a practical application to realistic goals (Earth). She needs time among nature to restore her energies; time spent among animals usually makes her feel happy.

The Queen of Pentacles is suited to any practical career, including accountancy, banking, financial controlling, growing crops, herbs, fruit and vegetables. She is also suited to working with therapeutic massage (the firm sense of touch being natural to the Pentacles people), real estate, food or general business management.

She is practical, nurturing and methodical, and as a mother she lends an air of stability to her environment through establishing routines and a healthy lifestyle. For example, Alison insists that her five-year-old daughter, Clara, takes a long walk every day.

At first Clara (a Page of Swords) moaned through the whole walk, but soon Alison learned to distract her with stories about particular plants and animals along the way. In time Clara started to look forward to their walks, and the time spent together talking. As this began to happen, Alison increased the distance they walked in order to strengthen her daughter physically and to help discharge some of her restlessness so that she might sleep better at night.

Alison recognises that Clara is not an earthy, practical type of person, but she insists on giving her an opportunity to spend time with nature and to learn to appreciate the outdoors. Therefore, the balance between Clara's mental energy and her physical body is improved through regular exercise.

In simple terms the Queen of Pentacles is a card for success through practical planning and having a realistic approach to the goals at hand, accomplishing them through physical efforts, and having financial discipline and emotional balance.

Reversed

The Queen of Pentacles reversed suggests that your client has lost their connection with nature, and is too focused on career or financial issues. It can sometimes indicate a lack of confidence, someone whose self-worth depends on what she achieves, for example, in her career, and not on who she is as a person.

This Queen may come across as ambitious, overly career-minded and determined to get ahead financially at all costs, but if you delve deeper, you'll usually find someone who is emotionally still a child. She has lost her balance, favouring the earthy (practical) part over her watery (emotional) instincts. She clings to the structure of career to compensate for the chaos within herself or in other parts of her life. She is less likely to be intuitive, creative or compassionate, perhaps due to unresolved emotional issues in her past.

The reversed state may only be temporary, for resolution of the outstanding issues may help to make her the upright Queen again. Some time spent among nature may help your client to gain a wider perspective and recognise the true importance of their career in the greater scheme of things.

The Kings

The Kings in the Tarot represent four mature masculine approaches to life. The King is the earthy part of each suit, so his focus is upon tangible results. This is why when his partner feels sad or upset he wants to do something about it, rather than simply sit with her and allow her to experience what she is feeling.

It is unlikely that a woman would appear as a King in a layout, but it happens occasionally, usually to confirm an astrological sign. The King of Wands is Aries (the accompanying card being the Emperor), the King of Cups is Scorpio (along with the Death card), the King of Swords is Aquarius (along with the Star) and the King of Pentacles is Taurus (the other cards being the Hierophant and the Four of Pentacles).

If you pair each of the suits' Kings and Queens you will notice the following. The King and Queen of Wands stare directly into one another's eyes. Their relationship is intense, straightforward and honest. The King of Cups gazes at the Queen of Cups and she does look at him, but shyly, with her head down. No words are needed as they both know what is unsaid between them. The Queen of Swords stares directly at the King of Swords as though awaiting an answer to a question. The King, in turn, is lost in his own thoughts and attempts at understanding the world. All this suggests that thoughts and ideas preoccupy them. The King of Pentacles looks down at his pentacle, keeping an eye on practical concerns to ensure stability. The Queen of Pentacles does the same, but with less of the air of pride in her achievements shown by the King through his posture.

Examined alone, the Kings look in directions that reveal their natures. The King of Wands looks to his right for the path which is traditionally the path of action. The King of Cups looks to his left, for the emotional and creative path. The King of Swords looks straight ahead to decipher what is real and what is perceived to be real in life, while the King of Pentacles looks downwards to practical concerns in the material world.

KING of WANDS

King of Wands

In simple terms the King of Wands is a card for a forthright man who is suited to any task or career that offers goals and challenges. Routines don't appeal to him; in fact, when routines start to develop, he knows it's time to move on to another challenge. He is not afraid to speak his mind, and so is unsuited to delicate negotiations (he favours the commando-style surprise raid to protracted telephone discussions).

In this card the man seated on the throne stares off into the distance in search of the impending arrival of someone or something to excite and challenge him. He holds a wand in his right hand. His cloak is covered with salamanders and there are lions carved into the back of his seat, suggesting the King's inner strength and confidence in his abilities. His orange robe reveals his passionate, excitable nature, but the fact that he is seated (and not rushing towards his goal, as is the Knight) suggests that he is disciplined in his excitement.

As the element for the Wands suit is Fire, the King of Wands is the earthy part of fire. As a result he is practical and tempers his enthusiasms; he restrains himself so that he does not start projects he has no hope of completing. The elements of Earth and Fire often oppose one another. Where Earth wants to maintain the stability of current circumstances and resist change, Fire prefers to abandon the existing situation in favour of new opportunities and the promise of better circumstances elsewhere.

The King of Wands is suited to a career in sales, teaching, coaching sports teams, acting, singing, professional sports, and most outdoor jobs which give him plenty of freedom to walk or to drive around. If, for example, he has a career in sales and is promoted to a position where he is locked away in an office all day, he is likely to go a bit stir-crazy, as he needs the outdoors and plenty of space. As a manager he has a 'hands-on' style. King of Wands people start new businesses and sell them to the other Kings and Queens.

The King of Wands' appearance in answer to a question can indicate success resulting from self-discipline and controlled enthusiasm. In a health reading the King of Wands can represent headaches or illnesses which affect the head area. Wands people resent anything which impedes their mobility or their ability to pursue their goals, so thoughts of ill-health rarely occur to them until they are actually sick.

Reversed

The King of Wands reversed suggests an immature man, whose need for action betrays a restless spirit and inner discontent. He can be careless with the feelings of others, being essentially tactless, impatient and reckless. Sensitivity and depth of feeling are not qualities found in the King reversed, who can be a bully with a short temper and a shorter attention span.

Randy's desire to teach his nine-year-old son to ski involved strapping boots and skis to his son's feet, and leaving him at the top of a snow-covered mountain as he took off on his own skis down to the lodge, some 2 km away. 'It will toughen him up a bit' was Randy's reasoning. A shivering Page of Cups arrived at the lodge later to find his father drinking a brandy by the fire.

In simple terms this card represents a lack of success due to attempting too many projects at once, or because of a lack of follow-through with plans. In a relationship layout it can suggest an ability to start new relationships that far outweighs the ability to commit to them once they have begun. The King of Wands reversed needs to return to the lesson of the Knight of Wands before he can become an upright King.

King of Cups

KING of CUPS.

The King of Cups represents an emotionally mature man who appreciates a creative life, but who is 'earthy' enough to make a living from his creative pursuit. In simple terms the King of Cups is a card representing creative success through having discipline and a practical approach to creative goals. It can also indicate the presence of a supportive, creative person around your client.

In this card a man sits on a throne resting on a platform surrounded by water. He holds a cup in his right hand and a sceptre in his left. The clasp around his neck contains a fish, symbolic of the element of Water. He is quietly strong-willed, as shown by his strong stare, and he understands the necessity of being clear about your desires before you draw to yourself opportunities you may not want.

As the element of the suit of Cups is Water, the King of Cups is the earthy part of Water. This means that he has a practical approach to creativity and that he is someone who is grounded in reality.

This King is suited to careers in counselling, psychology, psychiatry, music, art, writing or the psychic sciences. He often has an interest in history, genealogy, hypnosis and an attraction to the sea. As this King is a good listener, counselling comes naturally to him. He can read the energy of a room through feelings, and he is quick to sense when those he loves are hurt or in emotional pain. He seeks to be a calming influence in such circumstances.

He is often aware of the shy aspects of his partner's personality, and he tends to them compassionately. If this man is to fulfil his potential a stable love relationship is essential, as he treasures the knowledge that he is loved. He is the 'strong, quiet type' many women are drawn to for his depth and mystery.

Reversed

The King of Cups reversed combines Earth and Water in a negative way. It sometimes represents a bank of earth preventing the natural flow of water. Stagnant water can become toxic, and this King reversed can become embittered unless he learns to resolve his past and allow his emotions to flow naturally again.

He is still a strong, quiet type but darker and more sullen than the upright King. He is liable to bouts of sulking and emotional withdrawal if things don't go his way. He is also vengeful if crossed and his creativity is likely to be channelled into ways of punishing those whom he feels are responsible for his life circumstances. Alternatively he seeks out drugs and alcohol to alleviate the suffering he is sure no one else has ever felt before. He uses his powerful imagination to deceive himself about life, and he cannot see that his burdens and suffering are of his own making. Given the chance he is quite capable of deceiving others into seeing life from his perspective.

Sometimes beneath his apathy and mild depression lurks a powerful anger which, if released, has all the fury of a hurricane. This anger needs an outlet before his creative energies can flow freely again. At best, he simply needs understanding to free his creativity; at worst, he is habitually deceitful, manipulative and constantly seeking power over others in subtle ways.

In simple terms this is a card for a lack of success due to hidden motives and blocked creativity. The person represented by the King of Cups reversed unconsciously sabotages his own attempts at success and will spoil others' attempts also if given a chance. In a health layout this card represents difficulties with the abdomen, bowel and reproductive organs. It can also mean your client suffers from health problems resulting from suppressed emotions.

King of Swords

KING OF SWORDS.

The King of Swords represents the earthy part of Air, making him clear thinking and practical. He is attracted to science and those things which he can prove through using logic. As his mind is sharp he communicates with others easily.

In this card a man sits on a throne and in his right hand holds a sword so that it is pointing upwards. The ring on the Saturn (second) finger of his left hand suggests that he takes his responsibilities seriously and it may also indicate he has unresolved issues with his father. From a palmistry perspective the ring can suggest a father who was absent or very restrictive during their son's formative years. (If you recall, the story of the Swords suit (see *The Tarot Revealed*) dealt with the pain felt by the Page of Swords when she became Queen after the loss of her brother, the Knight. His untimely death may have left behind a son or younger brother who has become the King of Swords.)

The King's blue tunic represents a desire for spiritual understanding, and his purple cloak signifies compassion in the way he uses his mind. His sword is slightly tilted, suggesting that he has not yet the clarity of thought possessed by the Queen, but he is still far ahead of the other Kings in the amount of energy he devotes to learning, reading and mental stimulation. The butterflies on the back of his throne are a reminder that your thinking can transform your life, as your beliefs and attitudes determine what you become. The fact that the clouds are below his head shows his thinking is not 'cloudy', and the birds in the background represent the mind's ability to soar above the problems of the material and emotional worlds.

Career-wise this King is a professional man, who prefers to keep his hands clean in the pursuit of an income. He is suited to the law, medicine, writing (non-fiction), strategic business planning, sales, counselling (modes which favour a change in beliefs rather than a compassionate approach) and business administration. His clarity of thought makes him suitable for any situation where he can plan, and he enjoys puzzles. He likes to play with words, and languages appeal to him.

In simple terms this is a card representing the achievement of success through clear planning and the ability of your client to remain focused on their goal. Asking others for assistance or for advice when pursuing goals can also help your client, as other people may be able to provide what your client seeks or point them towards a source of information that may simplify their path. Swords people tend to know the value of asking others for help and to be aware of the opportunities which arise through communication.

An example of this kind of opportunity arose recently when a client telephoned me to reschedule an appointment and she mentioned that she had transcribed my last Tarot reading for her.

'That was diligent of you,' I said, and she laughed.

'Actually, I played the tape into a microphone linked to my computer and a software package I have did the rest. Out came pages of details and I tidied it up a bit afterward.' I was intrigued.

'I want such a program. I could write a book in a third of the time it takes me usually,' I said, and she gave me the relevant details. Simple conversations often present chances for those who are attentive.

The Internet was designed for Swords people, who sometimes love nothing better than to be able to talk without being interrupted by those receiving the information. Via e-mail, Swords people can keep in touch with twice as many people as they might otherwise see in the course of an average day.

The King of Swords does not need to be in a romantic relationship in the same way the King of Cups does. The Swords King may even be content to have a part-time or a long-distance relationship.

Reversed

The King of Swords reversed can be sharp-tongued and condescending to those who do not share his ability with words or comprehend his wide vocabulary. He may use certain words to confuse or impress those around him.

Sometimes the King reversed is describing a man who is confused and unable to choose between the alternatives life is offering him. He can be reluctant to commit himself to relationships, preferring his freedom instead.

The King of Swords reversed loves a good conversation but it doesn't have to be about anything important or even make sense in the end. He is brimming with ideas which may not amount to very much because he has not yet learned that words do not make deeds.

King of Pentacles

The King of Pentacles is a moderate, conservative man who prefers tradition to innovation, and he can be technology resistant, especially when compared with the King of Wands or the King of Swords. His reliability is attractive to the Queen of Cups and the Queen of Pentacles, but this quality is likely to irritate the Queen of Wands.

In this card the King of Pentacles is clothed in grapes (the fruits of his labours) and sits on a throne from which protrude bulls' heads. He holds a sceptre in his right hand and a pentacle in his left. He sits proudly, aware of his material achievements and ready to measure others by their worldly success. A solid castle stands in the background, and the beast beneath the King's feet has been subdued in his pursuit of material stability and security. This is a man who likes routine, who is not afraid of hard work and who rewards himself well for his efforts.

As the Pentacles element is Earth, the King of Pentacles is the earthy part of Earth, making him practical, realistic and concerned with worldly pursuits. He figures that he wants to be comfortable for his ride through his life, and leaves all the philosophical questions about a possible afterlife to the other Kings.

The King of Pentacles represents the typical man who starts his own business because he doesn't like being told what to do by others. Alternatively, he runs a branch of a business where he is left alone by upper management. He rewards himself with material things, such as a new car, a swimming pool, a holiday home, or some other suitable toy, when he is successful.

He is content to return each year to the same holiday destination, so it makes sense for him to purchase a small holiday home or a time share in a holiday village. His friends, the Kings of Cups, Wands and Swords, are happy to spend the occasional holiday with him but they wouldn't consider returning every year. However, the King of Pentacles' love of routine makes returning to the same place each year a satisfying experience for him.

In simple terms the King of Pentacles is a card representing success through practical application of plans. Through doggedly sticking to their goals and plans, and taking each necessary step to achieve them, your client will succeed, often through sheer persistence rather than through innovation.

Reversed

The King of Pentacles reversed gives the impression of being a practical, financially disciplined man, but it isn't long before those close to him realise that he is in fact impractical and undisciplined with money. His changeability interrupts his path to his goals, meaning he has to start anew.

Although he is still keenly aware of money and material things, he is unable to earn and hold onto them. He searches for a short cut to the good life and this can bring him into conflict with the law from time to time.

The King of Pentacles reversed is often to be found working in a career for which he is entirely unsuitable. When reversed his choice of occupation is frequently designed to please a parent and to prove that he is indeed practical. Yet beneath his veneer of common sense, he can be unhappy and longing to change the direction of his life. However, his lack of the necessary financial discipline often limits him in his attempts to change his career direction towards something more fulfilling for him.

Part Eight

★ 'How Long Will This Take?' ★

(A Final Word)

It may be that our needs are all pretty much the same. People seek enlightenment and the opportunity to probe the deepest parts of their psyche, but they only have forty-five minutes for lunch, so they are confined to a reading of fifteen minutes and even then they have to devour a sandwich as they go. A thorough reading takes an hour and in that time only five or six issues can be examined. Sometimes clients want answers to things they are not prepared to deal with and it is up to you, the reader, to confine them to those things which will benefit them now.

Longer readings allow you to stretch yourself and to improve your technique; short readings usually only teach you the short cuts necessary to glean information rapidly from the layout and to tell it directly to your client. However, short readings have their place. They are suited to clients who have only one or two issues to deal with, and train you to be economical with your choice of words in order to keep the reading within the allotted time.

In building your skills as a reader you can expect to give fifty readings to friends and strangers before feeling confident with the process and the meanings. After many of those first fifty readings you'll return to this book to review a card you feel unsure about, and in this way you slowly master the meanings and the reading process.

By the time you've given 100 readings you'll realise that the examples I've given in this book, particularly in the 'Stranger than Fiction' chapter are all true, as you'll have a few interesting stories to tell others from your own readings. By the time you reach 200 readings you'll have the plots for several novels which may be rejected by those who read them as too imaginative.

A study of the Tarot is a study of the human condition, and we are all searching, even those who appear to be lost or resting. Your task as a reader is to point the way to the path, so that your clients can fulfil their purpose in this life.

When I have painful news to deliver to a client I always ask myself, 'How would I like to receive this?' and I deliver it as though I were about to receive it. In this way, I ensure that I am compassionate in my delivery of information which may ordinarily cause offence or pain.

Sometimes it is inappropriate to say anything. In one Tarot class I was demonstrating how easily I could penetrate the psychic protection of a student, to illustrate how many psychic protection techniques are actually ineffective. I retrieved some simple information from the student and she couldn't relate to it. I felt it was necessary to state a few clear and concise facts which would confirm to her and to the class that I had penetrated her auric energy field, and that I had access to information about her.

What came up clearly was that she was unhappy with her present partner, a man who was aloof and self-absorbed. I then realised that she was looking for love in the wrong place; she was due to have a love relationship with a woman and she'd find fulfilment there. Sensing that she was unaware of her sexuality, it was inappropriate for me to state my findings in front of the class. I told her that I couldn't retrieve anything more and asked for another volunteer to demonstrate the exercise.

However, it is rare that you'll be unable to tell your client what you can see ahead for them, because they will probably be alone with you. If a client appears to be uncomfortable with what you are saying, pause the tape-recorder and offer to continue without recording the section. (Sometimes a client will point silently towards the microphone on the table as a signal that they don't want a question and its answer to be taped.)

Beginners are often daunted by the thought of having to appear to be a competent Tarot reader. Frequently they equate this with being someone who knows all about life, but this is not so. A good reader is one who is focused on the reading at hand, and who is without prejudice in their observations. If you approach the reading accepting that you have no idea what to expect, you may be pleasantly surprised by what the cards reveal to you.

I often say to clients on the telephone when they are booking a session that I have no idea what I'll say to them until I say it, and that ten minutes after that I'll have forgotten what I've told them. In this way I can be free to see what is actually there rather than categorise the client before they sit down for a reading.

Even regular clients can surprise me. One client named Tristan consults me about business issues. He usually comes with twelve questions, despite being told that I can answer up to seven in a one-hour reading, and he would always ask me questions within questions. It was like giving four full readings in one hour. I finally decided not to read for him again after one particular reading, but when he rang for another appointment I had booked him before I realised who he was.

When he sat down I decided to find out his underlying need and to meet it, reasoning that if I did so, Tristan might not feel the need to ask so many questions. I explained the general reading carefully and we talked for a few minutes.

His need became clear to me. Tristan was under great pressure with his business and he needed someone to understand what he was going through. Although his business was successful, Tristan felt that no one around him understood what sacrifices and efforts he regularly made to keep the business going. The more successful he became, the more those around him took for granted that he didn't need to be comforted and nurtured.

After all, he was successful. He was showing me that all of us, even successful people, need to be heard, and loved and nurtured.

I listened to him and he felt heard by me. Then a strange thing happened. This normally aggressive, controlling and exacting man suddenly became a small child, sobbing into the tissues I provided for him. I had found his need: to be allowed to be vulnerable for even five minutes within the demanding life he had made for himself.

He apologised for 'losing control like that' but I was aware that in the preceding five minutes I had probably been of more help to him than in all his previous readings. In essence I had done nothing but to allow Tristan to express what he had stored up within himself. Having met Tristan's deeper needs, we concluded our session five minutes early and he looked completely satisfied. That was the first time in five readings that he left without the need to ask one extra question.

I won't be surprised if Tristan cries in all our future sessions, because those readings may be his only opportunity to release his pent-up emotions. If that is his need, then predictive layouts with the cards are probably unnecessary.

Another example of finding the client's deeper need occurs with my homoeopath, Maeve, an elderly woman I see. During consultations she carefully questions me about what I think I need. Maeve then ignores me, and combines what I've told her with what she feels is right for me. At first I felt upset that she didn't listen to what I wanted, but then I realised that Maeve was listening between my words to my need. Now when I consult Maeve and she asks me what I think I need, I tell her I don't know. She then asks me to tell her how the past months have been for me and I launch into my life story so far. At that point Maeve usually reaches for her bottles and starts to mix me a tincture.

Find your client's need and your reading will be a simple process. However, if you allow yourself to become swept up in what they tell you their needs are, you are likely to become confused and exhausted. The client's real need is often concealed, even to them, but you're the Tarot reader and your task is to find it.

Finding the client's need comes with practice and it requires intuitive development. The simplest way to develop this instinct is to state silently to yourself when your client is shuffling the cards, 'The client's need today is …'. Don't seek an elaborate need, for most needs are simple. The client may need to be loved, to be heard, to be reminded that they have strayed from their path, to be praised for their actions, to be shown compassion, and occasionally to be scolded for their words and actions.

You've read this book because you wanted to learn more about the Tarot, but beneath that surface need, what was your deeper need in reading this book? When you have identified that need, ask yourself these questions: Did this book meet your underlying need? If not, will re-reading particular chapters or practising the techniques outlined help you to meet that underlying need?

All of us have surface needs and underlying needs. Meeting these deeper needs can also sometimes help the surface needs to disappear. The Tarot is a tool for discovering underlying spiritual needs, and it can also highlight the steps to take to meet those needs. The Tarot offers us a glimpse of the hidden, spiritual side of life.

It is a window through which you can glimpse your spiritual purpose. Fulfilling this spiritual purpose can lead you to lasting happiness and fulfilment. As a reader you can help others to glimpse their spiritual purpose, and as more of us find fulfilment, the easier this world will be to live in.

INDEX

Aces, 128
Action Layout, 73
Answer card, 58
Arcana
   Major, 20
   Minor, 124, 127–86

Cards in combination, 77
Career questions, 56
Chariot, the, 31–32
Children, questions
about, 58
Clairvoyance, 12
Clients
   difficult, 207–10
   nervous, 192
   setting boundaries,
      203–06
   story of, 202–03
Consequences Layout, 73
Court cards, 216–17
Cups, suit of, 124
   Ace, 129–30
   Two, 136–37
   Three, 141–42
   Four, 147–48
   Five, 153–54
   Six, 158–59
   Seven, 165–66
   Eight, 171–72
   Nine, 176–77
   Ten, 182–83
   Page, 220
   Knight, 226–27
   Queen, 232–33
   King, 239–40

Death, 40–41
Devil, the, 42–43
Drawing a blank, 13–14

Eights, 169
Emergency readings,
   15–16
Emperor, the, 26–27
Empress, the, 24–25

Family questions, 57
Finance questions, 56
Fives, 151
Fool, the, 21–22

Four approaches to life,
   124–26
Fours, 146
Hanged Man, the, 38–39
Health questions, 57
Hermit, the, 33–34
Hierophant, the, 27–28
High Priestess, the, 23–24
Horoscope Layout, 74–75

Intuitive reading, 9–13

Judgement, 50–51
Justice, 37–38

Kings, 237
Knights, 224

Layouts, 72–77
   cards in combination, 77
   designing your own, 78
   sample, 59–63
Life stranger than fiction,
   195–201
Logical reading, 9–13
Lovers, the, 29–30

Magician, the, 22–23
Major Arcana, 20
Minor Arcana, 124,
   127–86
Moon, 46–47

Nines, 175

One Card Cuts, 66–68
Outcome card, 58

Pages, 218
Pentacles, suit of, 124
   Ace, 132–34
   Two, 138–39
   Three, 144–45
   Four, 150
   Five, 155–56
   Six, 161–62
   Seven, 167–68
   Eight, 174
   Nine, 179–80
   Ten, 185–86
   Page, 222–23

Knight, 228–29
Queen, 235–36
King, 243–44
Personal relationship
questions, 56
Psychic cords, 9

Queens, 230
Questions
   basic, 56–58
   list of, 7
   poorly worded, 6
   yes/no, 58–66

Readings
   basic questions, 56–58
   basic steps, 54
   emergency, 15–16
   for yourself, 16–18
   intuitive reading, 9
   length of, 55, 246–49
   list of questions, 7
   logical reading, 9
   poorly worded
      questions, 6
   process, 54–55
   telephone, 55
Reversed cards, 68–70

Sample layouts, 59–63
Sample readings, 81–122
Sevens, 163
Sixes, 157
Spirituality questions, 57
Star, the, 44–45
Strength, 32–33
Sun, the, 48–49
Swords, suit of, 124
   Ace, 131–32
   Two, 137–38
   Three, 143–44
   Four, 149
   Five, 154–55
   Six, 160–61
   Seven, 166–67
   Eight, 172–73
   Nine, 178–79
   Ten, 184
   Page, 221–22
   Knight, 227–28
   Queen, 233–35

King, 241–42

Tarot
   desire of client for
      particular outcome, 4
   limitations of, 4–9
   paranoia affecting
accuracy of, 5
Tarot reader
   becoming professional,
      188–95
   experienced, 54
   guidelines for, 213–14
   setting boundaries,
      203–06
   specialising, 2–3
   style as, 2
   telling clients what
      they should do, 8
Telephone readings, 55
Temperance, 41–42
Tens, 181
Three Generations
Layout, 76
Three Issues Layout, 79
Threes, 140
Tower, the, 43–44
Travel questions, 57
Twos, 135

Wands, suit of, 124
   Ace, 128–29
   Two, 135–36
   Three, 140–41
   Four, 146–47
   Five, 151–52
   Six, 157–58
   Seven, 163–64
   Eight, 169–70
   Nine, 175–76
   Ten, 181–82
   Page, 218–19
   Knight, 224–25
   Queen, 230–31
   King, 238–39
Wheel of Fortune, 35–36
Workplace, cleansing,
   210–12
World, the, 51–52

Yes/no questions, 58–66